T0362206

DERIVATIVES IN ISLAMIC FINANCE

Edinburgh Guides to Islamic Finance
Series Editor: Rodney Wilson

Edinburgh Guides to Islamic Finance is a series of short guides to key areas in Islamic finance, offering an independent academic perspective and a critical treatment.

Product Development in Islamic Banks
Habib Ahmed

Derivatives in Islamic Finance: Examining the Market Risk Management Framework
Sherif Ayoub

Maqasid *Foundations of Market Economics*
Seif Ibrahim Tag el-Din

Shari'ah *Compliant Private Equity and Islamic Venture Capital*
Fara Madehah Ahmad Farid

Shari'ah *Governance in Islamic Banks*
Zulkifli Hasan

Islamic and Ethical Finance in the United Kingdom
Elaine Housby

Islamic Financial Services in the United Kingdom
Elaine Housby

Risk Management for Islamic Banks
Rania Abdelfattah Salem

Islamic Asset Management
Natalie Schoon

Legal, Regulatory and Governance Issues in Islamic Finance
Rodney Wilson

www.euppublishing.com/series/egif

DERIVATIVES IN ISLAMIC FINANCE

Examining the Market Risk Management Framework

Sherif Ayoub

EDINBURGH
University Press

To my father who taught me that there is no opportunity
without risk.
To my mother who has always been there for risk management.
To my wife without whom the completion of this endeavour
would not be possible.
To my children who are my source of eternal joy.

© Sherif Ayoub, 2014

Edinburgh University Press Ltd
The Tun – Holyrood Road
12 (2f) Jackson's Entry
Edinburgh EH8 8PJ
www.euppublishing.com

Typeset in Minion Pro by
Servis Filmsetting Ltd, Stockport, Cheshire,
and printed and bound in Great Britain by
CPI Group (UK) Ltd, Croydon CR0 4YY

A CIP record for this book is available from the British Library

ISBN 978 0 7486 9569 0 (hardback)
ISBN 978 0 7486 9570 6 (paperback)
ISBN 978 0 7486 9571 3 (webready PDF)
ISBN 978 0 7486 9572 0 (epub)

The right of Sherif Ayoub to be identified as author of this work
has been asserted in accordance with the Copyright, Designs
and Patents Act 1988 and the Copyright and Related Rights
Regulations 2003 (SI No. 2498).

CONTENTS

ABBREVIATIONS

AAOIFI	the Accounting and Auditing Organization for Islamic Financial Institutions
ALM	asset-liability management
CAGR	compound annual growth rate
CFOs	chief financial officers
CLT	the central limit theorem
DCR	Displaced Commercial Risk
Dr	Doctor
e.g.	for example
et al.	and others
etc.	and so on
FRAs	foreign rate agreements
FX	foreign exchange
GCC	Gulf Cooperation Council
GDP	gross domestic product
IASB	International Accounting Standards Board
IDB	Islamic Development Bank Group
IFSB	Islamic Financial Services Board
IIFM	International Islamic Financial Management
INCEIF	International Centre for Education in Islamic Finance
IRS	Internal Revenue Service
ISDA	International Swaps and Derivatives Association
IT	information technology
KLIBOR	Kuala Lumpur Interbank Offered Rate
LIBOR	London Interbank Offered Rate

LTCM	Long-Term Capital Management
MENA	Middle East and North Africa
MYR	Malaysian Ringgit
NPV	net present value
OIC	Organisation of Islamic Cooperation
OTC	over-the-counter
PBUH	peace be upon him
PER	Profit Equalization Reserve
R&D	research and development
SAIBOR	Saudi Arabia Interbank Offered Rate
SAR	Saudi Arabian Riyal
SPV	Special Purpose Vehicle
US	United States
USD	United States Dollar
VaR	Value at Risk

PREFACE

This book is a product of a curiosity that developed as a result of having been witness to the controversy surrounding the topic of derivatives in Islamic finance. This curiosity was elevated as I observed the divergent, and seemingly obstinate, views of some of the notable members of the Islamic finance community who, without any doubt, all harbour a common objective of ensuring that the Islamic finance industry positively contributes to human well-being.

With that, this book, in essence, is a means of responding to the challenge of harnessing the utility in the usage of derivatives, particularly in the domain of market-risk management, all the while addressing the concerns circulating in the Islamic finance discourse that centre on the perception of *Shari'ah* non-compliance. For this, I have strived, as much as practically possible, to include all pertinent viewpoints (found in print and expressed in person) from a wide spectrum of stakeholders in a manner that does not detach these views from the relevant economic theories (as an existing stock of knowledge on how humans behave on economic matters). Obviously, while it is acknowledged that there can never be an expectation for a book to completely dispel controversy, the present endeavour, it is hoped, is a step in that direction.

Apart from the profound gratitude felt for the many members of the Islamic finance community (*Shari'ah* scholars, academics, regulators, professionals, etc.) who have imparted valuable opinions to me, I would like to express here also my deep appreciation to The University of Edinburgh, which served as the centre of this undertaking, particularly Professor Jake Ansell and Dr Essam Ibrahim for their guidance throughout and Professor Rodney Wilson (the University of Durham and the International Centre for Education in Islamic Finance (INCEIF)) and Dr Tina Harrison for their valuable and constructive suggestions. I would also like to thank the Islamic Development Bank Group (IDB) (particularly Dr Abdulaziz Al Hinai) for the support provided to me in the research process. My grateful thanks are also extended to INCEIF (especially Professor Bacha) and the Islamic Financial Services Board (IFSB) for inviting me to undertake research at their facilities.

The views contained in the book are those of the author and are not the views of the Islamic Development Bank Group.

Dr Sherif Ayoub
Jeddah, Saudi Arabia
15 November 2013

CHAPTER 1
INTRODUCTION

The twentieth century has certainly been an interesting period in human history in terms of opportunities and challenges in the economic and financial realms. The advent of globalisation and the continued formation of new structures of the international financial architecture (e.g., the rise and fall of the Bretton Woods system, and the Washington Consensus) along with the concomitant revolution in information technology (IT) have contributed to not only increasing the profit potential for businesses around the world, but also to augmenting the complexity and uncertainty that they have to contend with in the search for that profit.

The past century also saw the (re)introduction of Islamic finance as defined by the economic doctrine of the *Shari'ah* with its three pillars of the prohibition of *Riba* (usury), *Gharar* (excessive uncertainty) and *Maysir* (gambling). For *Riba*, the fundamental basis for its proscription can broadly be related to the elimination of the injustices linked to the financial slavery of individuals by opportunist money lenders who strive to benefit from the sanctity of the repayment of debt obligations in Islam without any of the commensurate risks that exist in the world of commerce. The prohibition of *Gharar* is focused on the increase of certainty within commercial transactions by reducing the information asymmetry as well as the elimination of the malicious devouring of the property of others by dishonesty or deception or by taking advantage of informational ignorance. As for *Maysir*, the objective of Islamic jurisprudence in its prohibition is the promotion of a productive work ethic that increases welfare (both at the individual level and to society) as opposed to concentrating on the unearned gains of gambling with all its associated anti-social behaviour.

Notably, within its relatively short history, modern Islamic finance, which is built on the Islamic theory of *Qiyas* (analogical reasoning) that is centred on linking modern-day financial transactions to the commercial practices of the early Muslim community in the seventh century, has had the challenging task of attempting to provide a sustainable alternative to an advanced 'conventional' financial system that is by no means static in nature in that it continues to evolve to address, and arguably also to introduce, new issues into the global financial markets.

At the heart of the dynamism of conventional finance are theories built mainly on neoclassical economic foundations that, with the assistance of mathematical computing advances, have been significant in shaping the discourse in the domain of risk and return. Specifically, conventional finance has had the unique advantage of a fairly well-developed universe of processes as well as instruments that identify, measure and manage the various risk exposures facing investors (especially entities in the real sector).

In contrast, when one examines the theory and practice of risk management in Islamic finance, it can be discerned that the Islamic finance industry has been in the difficult position of endeavouring to reconcile the risk-management demands by business entities in the global Islamic community with the challenges posed by the seemingly rigid stances taken by some of the *Shari'ah* scholars with respect to the contemporary risk-management framework. Accordingly, in the realm of the management of market risks (particularly interest/profit rate risk, currency risks and commodity risks), these restrictive stances have, in effect, resulted in the proscription in the usage of the majority of hedging instruments, which have derivative-like features, even if they are utilised with a legitimate commercial rationale.

The ensuing problem in undertaking appropriate market-risk management becomes endogenous to an Islamic finance industry that, in its modern form, has grown tremendously from its humble beginnings in the 1950s and 1960s with the mutual banking experiments in Pakistan, Egypt and Malaysia that were followed by institutionalised banking practices in the 1970s in Dubai, Saudi Arabia and Kuwait. More specifically, the Islamic finance industry had grown to an estimated size of US\$ 1.1 trillion by the end of 2012 and in the Middle East and North Africa (MENA) region (including Turkey) the industry has recorded a compound annual growth rate (CAGR) of 20 per cent in the five years ending 2010 vis-à-vis 9 per cent by the leading conventional banks (E&Y 2011). This, it should be pointed out, comes mainly from countries that are endowed with large natural resources and are experiencing high population growth rates in addition to harbouring a desire of seeking to positively interact with an increasingly globalised setting of commercial and financial practices.

Effectively, the aforementioned growth, which can be observed to exist at multiple levels in the Islamic finance industry, inevitably transposes the nature of inherent market risks in Islamic finance from a sedentary role to a position of dominance in the elaboration and implementation of corporate strategies not only for the competitiveness of enterprises seeking to operate within the confines of the economic doctrine of the *Shari'ah*, but also for their survival in the international marketplace. In fact, it has been widely acknowledged by many observers that the Islamic finance industry will not be able to sustainably continue on this growth trajectory, and may even regress, without a proper market-risk management framework that can effectively deal with the complex risks that exist in today's globalised economy.

Subsequent to the foregoing background, it may be stated that the present book is formulated with the objective of advancing knowledge on the topic of derivative hedging instruments within the context of market-risk management in the Islamic finance industry. This objective, in turn, is to be achieved by two means: First, the book will inject economic-centred theories, along with a wider elaboration of the modus operandi of the financial markets, into the Islamic finance discourse on the subject matter. Second, the book will attempt to examine the rationale for the various stances (both in favour and against) on the permissibility of derivative hedging instruments in a manner that not only accounts for the numerous instruments currently existing in the financial markets, but also some of the proposed solutions in the Islamic finance space.

In essence, the aforementioned objective is envisaged to assist in the overcoming of what can arguably be described as an incomplete appreciation by some of the participants in the Islamic finance industry of the economic and financial principles that underlie what is inherently an economic subject matter. This, it will be shown, can be seen by the nature of the current commentary that regularly places paramount importance on the form of the contracts and instruments rather than on the religious substance (that has economic rationales) that regulates its existence.

Consequently, more often than not, the end result observed is a mixture of macro-level (e.g., eliminate all derivative hedging instruments from society) and micro-level (e.g., Arabic-named byzantine transactions) recommendations with little insight as to how these recommendations relate to existing economic theories, introduce new theories that can better explain the economic behaviour of individuals or even how they are meant to be implemented in a dynamic and interconnected globalised setting along with the externalities (both positive and negative) that can result in the course of that implementation.

Thus, the coming chapters will seek to elaborate a multidimensional perspective of the subject matter in the most wide-ranging manner possible that includes an investigation into areas that have hitherto been relatively unexplored in the Islamic finance industry. The aspired outcome, it should be asserted here, is not so much the simple focus on espousing a position on the permissibility of derivative hedging instruments, as it is on seeking to increase the sustainability of the Islamic finance industry by way of ensuring that exposures to market risks are managed in the most effective and efficient manner possible.

With that in mind, the forthcoming discussion is divided into three broad parts comprising eight chapters. The first part contains the introduction and one chapter that can be thought of as the philosophical foundation of the book. Specifically, Chapter 2 delves into the conceptualisation of truth in *Mua'amalat* within Islamic thought, which is deemed to be pertinent in a discussion that relates to religious injunctions that were elaborated by *Shari'ah* scholars with a belief in the injunctions' inherent legitimacy consequent of the perception of a superior proximity to the truth contained in the Islamic scripture (i.e., Quran and *Ahadith*).

The second part, in turn, includes three chapters that concentrate on the aspects in the discourse that are associated with the topics of market-risk management and derivative instruments. In essence, the third chapter of the book commences the substantive discussion with a wide view on the identification and measurement of market risks as well as the strategies (and their rationales) that are used in dealing with them. The fourth chapter attempts to add depth to the discussion by probing the economic aspects of derivative instruments along with the undertaking of instrument-specific analysis, both of which are often overlooked in the descriptive-natured commentary on the subject matter in the Islamic finance literature. As for the fifth chapter, which is a key chapter in the book, it endeavours to examine, in detail, the discourse on derivatives in Islamic finance through the analysis of the juridical, academic and practitioner perspectives, including a scrutiny of the design of contemporary derivatives in the Islamic finance industry.

The third part of the book, for its part, seeks to add new facets to the consideration of market-risk management and derivatives that were, despite their relative neglect in the literature on the subject matter, deemed to be important to add further contextualisation to understanding. This includes the sixth chapter that centres on the unease of *Shari'ah* scholars in condoning the permissibility of financial instruments that have monetary benchmarks, such as interest/profit rate and foreign exchange, as underlying variables. The unease, in turn, can be discerned to have resulted in a systemic avoidance of an effective debate on the recognition of these contracts (or even their 'Islamic' equivalents) on the financial statements of the entities that use them in the Islamic finance industry. The seventh chapter, as the final substantive chapter of the book that is followed by the conclusion chapter, concerns the constant perception of a static association between the prohibition of *Maysir* (gambling) and derivative instruments, which was a recurring theme in the existing discourse on derivative instruments in Islamic finance.

2.0 Introduction

The subject matter of the book, being focused on derivative hedging instruments for market-risk management in Islamic finance, naturally involves the amalgamation of religious and economic concepts. In fact, within the Islamic finance industry there is perhaps greater credence given to the religious concepts as a means of ensuring that the dealings between individuals (i.e., *Mua'amalat*) are undertaken in a manner that follows the essence of Islamic jurisprudence with its emphasis on wealth creation, fairness and human well-being.

The above can be clearly observed in that, as opposed to the conventional finance industry, the Islamic finance industry is regulated by myriad non-governmental type institutions that are defined by their religious authority (e.g., Fiqh Academies, the Accounting and Auditing Organization for Islamic Financial Institutions (AAOIFI), the Islamic Financial Services Board (IFSB) and the International Islamic Financial Management (IIFM)). This institutional regulation is complemented by the powerful opinions and rulings of Islamic scholars and commentators on matters relating to Islamic finance that, in turn, affects how the stakeholders in the Islamic finance industry (from governments to corporations to individuals) view and act on the choices that are before them in the economic realm.

In light of the foregoing, it may be valuable, prior to delving into the technical nature of the discussion on the usage of derivatives in the Islamic finance industry, to examine how truth is formed in *Mua'amalat* and what that means for the attainment of the noble objectives of Islamic jurisprudence. The importance of this examination will become apparent in the coming chapters wherein it may be discerned that particular religious conjectures and interpretations in the sphere of Islamic finance are deemed by some to be certain in their validity and proximity to the truth as they pertain to divine will. In effect, the above observation inherently requires one to develop a theoretical and conceptual basis upon which a more thorough assessment can be undertaken of the religious rulings and commentary that have shaped (and that continue to shape) the Islamic finance industry.

2.1 The path to the truth: the role of *Maslaha, Qiyas* and *Igma'a*

Truth, however it is constructed, does have particular ontological assumptions about the nature of reality as well as some theoretical perspectives that shape logic in the construction of that reality. With that, one can observe that, in Islam, ontology is mainly realist in nature in that it views reality as existing independently of our senses, ideation and volition. In other words, God, the divine guidance manifested by the scripture, among other fundamental themes in Islam, exists outside of the human mind despite the fact that they are central objectives of human intellectual comprehension of universal existence.

Within the context of *Mua'amalat* in Islam, the theories of *Maslaha* (public interest), *Qiyas* (analogical reasoning) and *Igma'a* (consensus) contribute to the process of truth formation in that they seek to produce a logical unity in Islamic thought with the scripture at its base. More specifically, Ibn Khaldun details four sources of legal evidence in Islam in that he states:

> The basic sources of legal evidence [in Islam] are the Qur'an and, then, the traditions [*Ahadith/Sunnah*] which clarify the Qur'an. Then, general consensus [*Igma'a*] took its place next to the Qur'an and the traditions (Sunnah). Now many of the things that happened after the Prophet are not included in the established texts. Therefore, they compared and combined them with the established evidence that is found in the texts, (and drew their conclusions from analogy [*Qiyas*]) according to certain rules that governed their combinations. This assured the soundness of their comparison of two similar (cases), so that it could be assumed that one and the same divine law covered both cases. This became (another kind of) legal evidence, because the early (Muslims) all agreed upon it. This is analogy, the fourth kind of evidence. (Ibn Khaldun *et al.* 1969 [1377]: 347)

The foundation, or more appropriately the rationale, for the third and fourth sources of legal evidence in Islam, namely *Igma'a* and *Qiyas*, is the theory of *Maslaha*. *Maslaha* translates literally into interest (or benefit); however, its usage in Islam tends to be generally associated with the many rather than the few (or individual) in how it deals with religious directives. Thus, *Maslaha* can be thought of as the ethical end of increasing the piety of Muslims in addition to the well-being of humankind (i.e., public interest) by legitimising rulings based on the concepts of *Igma'a* and

Qiyas, which, in turn, depend on either specific references in the scripture and/or *Maqasid Al Shari'ah* (i.e., objectives of Islamic law). The opposite of *Maslaha*, in contrast, is *Mafsada* (i.e., public harm). Therefore, according to the theory of *Maslaha*, Islamic law should seek to increase *Maslaha* and/or reduce any *Mafsada*.

As a background, the development of the theory of *Maslaha* effectively commenced in the eleventh century through the writings of the Shafi'i jurists Al-Ghazali and Al-Razi; it was later developed by Al-Maliki jurists Al-Qarafi and Al-Shatibi as well as the Hanbali jurist Al-Tufi (Opwis 2007). In effect, since its establishment, *Maslaha*, as a theory of utility (or reduction of hardship), has been used to extend and adapt the *Shari'ah* to not only matters that are derivations of the rulings that existed at the time of the Prophet (peace be upon him (PBUH)) (e.g., inheritance and guardianship), but also to the changing circumstances and specific issues facing Muslims in different times and geographies.

Needless to say, the challenge of *Maslaha*, and the source of hesitancy of jurists in the history of Islamic thought of elaborating it, is that it may be a source of opening the gates of falsity, doubt and illegitimacy in Islam consequent of the prospective insertion of subjectivity and arbitrariness into the formulation of Islamic law. This hesitancy can be made more apparent in the distinction of the extension vis-à-vis the adaptation of *Shari'ah* in that while the extension, even if speculative, of the *Shari'ah* can be construed as an extension of the truth, the adaptation can be particularly problematic because it may imply that what was long held as true may be, in fact, partly true.

For example, within the realm of Islamic finance, the objective of the prohibition of *Riba* (usury) is arguably focused on limiting the financial slavery of individuals by opportunist money lenders, but the restrictions placed on some contemporary practices such as central banking, asset pricing and risk management (including insurance) may only be true in part and may require a broader conceptualisation of the truth in that particular subject matter (i.e., it is not the colour of the wine that makes it prohibited in Islam, but rather it is the intoxicating effect of wine).

With that transhistorical challenge in mind, Muslim thinkers have worked to devise a framework through *Qiyas* and *Igma'a* that controlled the scope of the use of *Maslaha* as well as having worked to develop a set of procedural criteria that seek to objectively elaborate the truth as it pertains to divine will (see below). In terms of the scope for *Maslaha*, Al-Ghazali in his *Al-Mustafa Min Ilm Al-Usul* (1993a) limited the use of *Maslaha* to five essential elements (i.e., *Al-Durariyat Al-Khamsa*) for the well-being of Muslims; these are: religion, life, intellect, offspring and wealth. Although, Al-Ghazali, perhaps in a search for greater assurance, was also specific in that he stated that *Maslaha* is limited to areas that are known with certainty (*Qati'i*) and that are universal (*Kulli*) in nature. Consequently, for him, *Maslaha* is a way to extend (not adapt) the *Shari'ah* based on the truth contained within the religious scripture as commonly understood and practised.

Other prominent Muslim thinkers sought to increase the scope of *Maslaha*, as elucidated by Al-Ghazali, in an effort to expand the sphere of truth-seeking in Islam. Notably, Al-Razi argued that the *Shari'ah* should also seek truth in the domain of high probability (i.e., considerable certainty) rather than be bounded by the requirement of absolute certainty, which may never be achieved. Moreover, Al-Razi felt that the application of *Maslaha* to the five essential elements, while important, is unnecessarily restrictive; accordingly, he proposed the inclusion of the concepts of need (*Haja*) and improvement (*Tahsin*) in the sphere of *Maslaha*.

Al-Shatibi, for his part, complements the thinking of Al-Razi in that his writings demonstrate that absolute certainty is characteristic of only the source of *Shari'ah* (i.e., God). In particular, he argues that while the Quran and the *Ahadith* were certain in their validity, some areas of understanding can be considered probable and required modification of *practice* depending on the place, time and person. However, Al-Shatibi was clear that *Maslaha* does not pertain to the issues of *Ibadah* (worship), acts that happened or could have happened during the time of the Prophet (PBUH) and the continuous practice of the early Islamic community.

Notwithstanding the above conceptualisation of *Maslaha*, as mentioned earlier, the use of *Maslaha* in truth formation was conceived to be controlled through the framework of *Qiyas* and *Igma'a*. For *Qiyas*, the concept of *Maslaha* essentially operates through the conduit of intellect in perceiving the origin (*Asl*) of the *Shari'ah* in the scripture, while reason works to identify the effective causes of things (*'Illah*) and attempts to link them to a particular issue (*Far'*) in order to pronounce a ruling (*Hukm*) that can be deemed as the bearer of truth. Throughout the process, the objectives of the religion (*Maqasid Al Shari'ah*) are normatively elaborated and communicated in a manner that is in harmony with the scripture and agreed to in a process of *Igma'a* (consensus).

That being said, it is perhaps necessary to state that *Maslaha* should not be perceived to be exclusively limited to the domain of *Qiyas*, as is often done, for example, in the Islamic finance industry. This is because the situations that existed during the time of the Prophet (PBUH) were not all-inclusive and infinite in that they can be expected to provide guidance for analogical reasoning through time and space. Put differently, *Maslaha* ought to depend on *Qiyas* where appropriate but should not be shackled by the forcing of analogical reasoning in every matter that concerns *Mua'amalat* in the Muslim world.

In effect, even with the recognition that the highly formalised and intricate set of rules of the *Qiyas* process can and do result in the limitation of falsity within the religious pronouncements (*Fatwas*) by the Islamic jurists, one has to also acknowledge the fact that this modality of discerning the truth can only be described as merely an effort to add substantive rationality to a process that is inherently speculative and probable in relation to the will of God. That is to say, the rules of *Qiyas*, even though important from a procedural sense, much like seemingly objective scientific processes, cannot be perceived as an independent grantor of truth as such simply because they are human instruments of reason rather than absolute, universal and infinite Godly instructions.

The theory of *Igma'a*, for its part, serves an important role in the development of Islamic jurisprudence in that it confirms the conjectures developed through *Ijtihad* by jurists (whether by *Qiyas* or interpretation (see the next section)) as truth and that thus require adherence in belief and practice. The basis of this theory, and the perception surrounding its existence, is perhaps the fact that it is the theory that is most referred to among those aforementioned in the Quran (Quran 3:103, 4:115 and 18:29) and the *Ahadith*. Further, it is arguably among the most commonly referenced theories in the Islamic religion in matters that relate to the truth contained within divine revelations.

Specifically, even though *Igma'a* does not partake in divine revelations, as such, it is given a special status within Islam consequent of the confidence of God in the faith of the Muslim community (*Ummah*) and their ardour in upholding the integrity of the *Shari'ah* through unity in thought and practice. In fact, Al-Ghazali believed so strongly in *Igma'a* that he maintained that a united Muslim community is as close as one could get to being infallible and immune from error.

That being said, it may be stated here that the way to achieve the *Igma'a*, and truth by virtue of its theory, is, understandably, a contentious matter, as it transcends the world of idealism to the realm of practical application. First, the actual participants of consensus have to be defined. For this, it became accepted that the process of truth-seeking within Islam should be reserved for those with sufficient intellect and reason (*Ula Al-Albab*) to be able to appreciate the scripture and the objectives of the Islamic law.

While the rationale for such interpretation of *Ula Al-Albab* is theoretically sound, it should also be acknowledged that the lack of wider participation in the forming of consensus does limit the scope of the truth of the Islamic jurisprudence. In essence, the learned jurists that partake in the *Igma'a* are limited in their knowledge to what they perceive by their senses as well as their state of intellect as opposed to the universal discernment by the populace – even if they harbour a lower level of sophistication.

Second, the term '*Igma'a*' itself needs to be defined in order for the theory of consensus to operate properly as a conduit to the truth contained in divine revelations. For while the term in the Arabic language may be translated to consensus in a unanimous fashion, its adoption by some jurists in this manner does, in effect, condemn this vital theory in Islam as inconsequential. This is because not only is the notion of unanimity in an absolute sense not supported in the scripture (Quran 11:118), but also even as an aspiration, although ideal, it may never be attained. This is because the interpretation and understanding of the divine revelations through human perceptions are not static across all temporal and spatial conditions and will always be subject, by virtue of human intellect and reason, to error and falsity.

Thus, for all intents and purposes, consensus, within the theory of *Igma'a*, can very well be considered in the broad (e.g., two-thirds, three-quarters or four-fifths) rather than in a unanimity (100 per cent) sense at any given time simply because *Maslaha* itself, and our interpretation and understanding of the scripture, changes over time. The strength of the truth in this framework is a product of the degree of consensus through discourse that is undertaken with respect to particular topics mainly by the Islamic jurists, as *Ula Al-Albab*, but also by the members of the various Muslim populaces.

Once more, the last point regarding the inclusivity of the discourse cannot be over-emphasised, even if one acknowledges that the consensus generation is, and has been for centuries, being exclusively held within the realm of the religious scholarly community. In essence, it cannot be expected that the Islamic jurists be cognisant of the myriad multivariate complexities, along with the various interactions, that surround *all* topics that deal with the Muslim faith whose truth is viewed by Muslims more as a way of life than as simply a collective set of religious directives. For that, the inclusion of the various epistemic communities (economists, lawyers, social scientists, natural scientists, etc.) in the discourse as *active* participants in a dynamic process that may include differences in particular scientific conjectures should provide invaluable insight that ensures a greater correspondence to the truth both in an objective sense as well as in relation to *Maslaha*.

Thus, it can be stated in summary that, within Islamic thought, truth is always striving to correspond to the true words of God, as revealed in the scripture and the spirit of his will upon humankind, which will ultimately lead to salvation and bliss. The theories of *Maslaha* (as an intermediary objective), *Qiyas* (as a tool) and *Igma'a* (as a validator through discourse) can, and should, extend and adapt the law as instruments of truth. However, it should be also realised that these theories, as with any other theory, are merely instruments that assist in understanding. They are a means of acquiring proximity to the truth but are not endowers of complete and certain truth, as such.

With that overarching realisation, it should be notable that the interpretation and understanding by Muslims of their religion, particularly in matters of *Mua'amalat*, is never complete or static in time and space; they are always evolving, moving to an ever higher degree of discernment of the truth. This is where the discussion enters into the realm of the theoretical perspectives that underlie the path to the truth, which will be discussed next.

2.2 Truth-seeking in the scripture: the reality imposed by critical rationalism and hermeneutics

The previous section concentrated on *Qiyas*, *Igma'a* and *Maslaha*, which were shown to serve as legal mechanisms that complement the primary sources of juridical evidence in Islam, namely the Quran and the *Ahadith*. In this section, the discussion focuses on those primary sources in order to emphasise the intricacy that entangles their proper interpretation and understanding. The importance of this endeavour will become evident in the coming chapters wherein it can be observed that the content of a not insignificant amount of commentary and number of opinions circulating in the Islamic finance space with linkages to the primary sources of juridical evidence could arguably be shown to be only partially true, or even false.

That being said, the above contention can only become recognised if one takes a few steps back and appreciates the fact that their comprehension of the Quran and the *Ahadith*, particularly in matters relating to Islamic finance, may not be perfect and may consequently require an emphasis on a scientific process that revolves around more thorough research, a deeper analysis and a wider knowledge base (including law and economics).

We start with the assertion that the examination of contemporary economic issues (i.e., *Mua'amalat*, not *Ibadah*) within the context of Islamic thought straddles many theoretical perspectives, which can be conceptualised as a process of logic in the construction of reality. In particular, critical rationalism (also known as post-positivism), as developed by Karl Popper in the 1930s, and hermeneutics (interpretivism and historical hermeneutics) are considered as important links to the ontological assumption of realism in Islam.

As a background, positivism advances the position that only what can be garnered through objective observation and analysis through the senses can be viewed as real and as worthy of the attention of science. Critical rationalism, for its part, while sharing positivism's ontological assumption of realism does not believe that experimentation and senses lead to outright undisputable knowledge of reality. This is because critical rationalism does not distinguish between observational data and theoretical statements since all observations are considered to be theory-dependent.

More specifically to critical rationalism, in his *Conjectures and Refutations: The Growth of Scientific Knowledge* (1969), Popper cites a belief that scientists generate new knowledge not through observation and experimentation alone, but rather by way of engaging in a continual process of conjecture and falsification. Essentially, there is an emphasis on a logical and critical scientific process that seeks to continuously generate and falsify theories in a bid to move ever closer to truth, which will, theoretically, never be achieved. In effect, Popper, as evidenced by his earlier writings, believes that 'every scientific statement must remain *tentative for ever [sic]*' (Popper 1959: 280; emphasis in original) until it is refuted.

Popper then concludes by saying that 'science never pursues the illusory aim of making its answers final, or even probable. Its advance is, rather, towards the infinite yet attainable aim of ever discovering new, deeper, and more general problems, and of subjecting its ever tentative answers to ever renewed and ever more rigorous tests' (281). However, instead of rendering science as an irrelevant, self-indulging process, he maintains that striving for knowledge and searching for the truth are the strongest motives for scientific discovery.

Notwithstanding the above, there is one facet in Popper's writings that is especially relevant to us here. This facet is his insertion of the concept of belief into the realm of critical rationalism, which may be erroneously viewed by some as uncharacteristic of matters of science. In particular, he advances the position that scientific motives are guided by *unscientific* faith in the truth. In particular, he states that 'only in our subjective experiences of conviction, in our subjective faith, can we be "absolutely certain"' (280).

The views of critical rationalism, especially the point on belief introduced by Popper, were predated, in a sense, by the concept of 'necessary truths' as elaborated by Imam Al-Ghazali in the eleventh century. Specifically, during his quest for *certain knowledge*, Imam Al-Ghazali, never himself a partisan of philosophical thought as evidenced by his book (translated by Mamura) *The Incoherence of the Philosophers* ([n.d.] 1997), became acutely aware (to the point of a two-month physical and mental illness) that the human mind cannot entertain the possibility of infallible and error-free knowledge. Eventually, the relief for him was his faith that the necessary truths in the universe do not depend upon strict and infinitely enduring proof, but rather the truths in the universe rest upon the mercy of God.

Thus, critical rationalism can be related to Islamic thought in that it not only introduces a faith element to the scientific process, which the field of religious studies (especially the observation and analysis of the scripture) is considered to be a beneficiary of, but also relates to the theories of *Igma'a* (consensus) and *Qiyas* (analogical reasoning) in Islam, which together provide a foundation for the infinite search for truth.

In fact, the Quran explicitly expresses the reality that human knowledge is finite and incomplete (Quran 102:3–5), and the inclusion of this divine message within the latter verses of the Quran may indicate that humans should endlessly continue to strive for true knowledge and should not assume that their knowledge of Islam is omnipotent. For, if this were the case, Islamic research institutions (e.g., Al-Azhar) would cease to exist since their role would be no longer needed consequent of the human attainment of all-inclusive knowledge of the truth.

The second theoretical perspective of relevance in the conceptualisation of truth within Islam is hermeneutics with its interpretivism and historical branches. The term 'hermeneutics' itself came into modern use in the seventeenth century and is considered the science of biblical interpretation. Essentially, interpretivism hermeneutics views texts as means for transmitting meaning, beliefs and values from one time to another. It, therefore, seeks to not only be concerned with searching for meaning in religious texts (as in the case of religious hermeneutics) but seeks to partake in an expanded role of enquiry of how texts can and should be applied.

With that, Ricoeur (1973), while adhering to Dilthey's differentiation between interpretation (*Auslegung*) and understanding/comprehension (*Verstehen*), states that hermeneutics concerns the rules required for the interpretation of written documents. The indicated difference between interpretation and understanding is quite important in the hermeneutical process according to this branch of thought. For while these two concepts can be considered to be two sides to the same coin, they are quite distinct on many levels, not the least of which is language.

Notwithstanding the above, Ricoeur appears to have been cognisant of the challenges facing this version of interpretational hermeneutics that is based primarily on words and linguistics for understanding in that he also cautions the readers by stating the proposition that any text is not a mere sequence of sentences that are all equal and separately understandable. In effect, he advises that there needs to be a certain element of judgement in recognising the circularity of understanding from construing the whole based on the parts (i.e., words and sentences) and comprehending the parts based on the character of the whole.

Furthermore, it is perhaps necessary to note that the meaning elucidated by a word in relation to an object can be interpreted, and therefore, understood on different, and possibly contradictory, levels depending on the prevailing perceptions of the subject matter and the distinct theoretical positions of the interpreter. These theoretical positions, which centre on words as a fundamental criteria for understanding the truth, in turn could be perceived as emanating from the ancient debate between 'conventionalism' and 'naturalism', as illuminated in Plato's *Cratylus*. Effectively, the contradictions between these views have made the relationships between word and meaning, subject and object, truth and falsity in the context of linguistics, which is central to all religions, subjective and quite complex.

More specifically, linguistic conventionalism advances the position that the association between word and object is determined by a consensus within a speech-community that determines the appropriate convention that applies to a particular word. In contrast, naturalism believes that there is a natural bond between an object and its name that is independent of convention and, therefore, cannot be arbitrarily changed.

Needless to say, there are limits and challenges that face each theory when it is taken individually. To start with, a language, as a formalised system of communication that transcends time and space, even with its innovative components, cannot arbitrarily change the association between word and object simply by convention. Conversely, a language system, as a precursor and a product of discourse, does, for myriad reasons, evolve under different temporal and spatial conditions, which defies the idea of a word belonging statically and naturally to the object to which it is connected.

The key to overcoming the challenges faced by Ricoeur of placing words and linguistics at the heart of understanding and truth, according to Gadamer, in his seminal work, *Truth and Method*, is the acknowledgement that 'no truth can be attained in language' (Gadamer 1989: 407). Thus, while there is no such thing as knowledge without language, the object, particularly in the realm of religious scriptures, does not necessarily acquire the distinction of being true as the result of linguistics. Rather, on the contrary, the adequacy of the word, within language, is a function of the multifarious epistemology that is independent of the object that it attempts to embody as it confers a finite set of meanings to an infinite range of possibilities.

In theology, the case of the divine word in the religious scripture, as communicated by God, is a case in point, as it introduces a special component of complication to linguistics within the sphere of religion. For, as asserted by Gadamer: 'If the whole of the divine mind is expressed in the divine word, then the processual element in this word signifies something for which we basically have no analogy. Insofar as in knowing itself, the divine mind likewise knows all beings, the word of God is the word of the Spirit that knows and creates everything in one intuition' (Gadamer 1989: 423). In sum, the divine word is the truth (Quran 4:122).

Therefore, there is an element of incompleteness to *human* words within the realm of theology that affects understanding when one examines subjects that are related to religion. This is because human words (whether in Hebrew, Aramaic, Greek or Arabic) are not only finite verbally, but also are not as perfect (or as true) as the words of God in the mind of the Divine. Consequently, humans, unlike God, are not only incapable of expressing their minds completely with one word (i.e., we require multiple words as linguistic intermediaries to knowledge), but also, traditionally, human minds exhibit temporal and contextual finitude that limits the universality of language.

Here one may ask: Why is the above important to the discussion at hand, which focuses on derivatives in Islamic finance? Well, it could, based on the foregoing, be conceivable that the definitions and meanings given to the myriad concepts in Islamic jurisprudence (e.g., *Riba*, *Gharar*, *Maysir* and *Sarf*) that are used by the partisans of particular conjectures (both for and against derivatives, for example) are susceptible to re-interpretation and re-examination.

Notwithstanding the above, the views of Gadamer are quite interesting, particularly in the field of religious studies, in that they espouse an opinion that it is not so much the mastery of language, with all its rules, as suggested by Ricoeur, that is important in hermeneutics (especially in relation to deciphering religious scripture) as much as it is the primacy of conceptual articulation, through the medium of language, of the subject itself.

In essence, conceptual articulation (especially in matters of religion) *through discourse* of an objective reality is where the truth resides, not in the individual words, and not even in all the stock of words of a particular language, no matter how perfect it may be perceived to be. This was well verbalised by Gadamer in that he stated: '[I]t is not the word (anoma) but the logos [i.e., discourse] that is the bearer of truth. From this, it necessarily follows that being expressed, and thus being bound to language, is quite secondary to the system of relations within which the logos articulates and interprets' (Gadamer 1989: 412).

Here one notes that the case of written text, as a form of discourse, is particularly important, especially in religious subject matter that has a large historical orientation. In effect, instead of having religious texts addressed to only one reader (that a religious text does at any one moment in time), the written texts are addressed to an audience that the writing itself creates with an almost universal range. The counterpart of the author of the text is, essentially, anyone who knows how to read (or can listen to someone who reads).

In addition, there is also a unique sense of duality in any particular text. This duality starts at the basic character of texts themselves in that, on the one hand, texts, as mentioned by Droysen, are 'enduringly fixed expressions of life' (Droysen cited in Droysen and Hübner 1937: 63) that provide a window to the past; yet on the other hand, as noted by Ricoeur (1973), texts are an ensemble of references to the world, past and present, which light up our own situation.

The aforementioned duality does have implications for meaning and understanding, which were perhaps best recognised by Gadamer (1989). On the positive end, as opposed to speech, the meaning of what is written exists purely for itself in the abstract ideality of language in a manner that is identifiable and repeatable. However, the paramount weakness of texts, which was demonstrated by Plato, is that the author can no longer come to the aid of the written word if it falls victim to misunderstanding, either intentional or unintentional (Plato Seventh Letter). It is, therefore, discourse that is based on intellect and reason as well as faith that can ultimately lead to the truth.

In other words, it is a matter of judgement by the reader, through reason and faith, which serves to bridge the gap between the spirit of the original words and their contemporary interpretation, through discourse, within the context of the subject matter. This is perhaps why Al-Ghazali felt so strongly in favour of *Igma'a*. However, as with the critical rationalism theoretical perspective, one should acknowledge that this gap can never be completely closed consequent of a number of reasons, not the least of which is the fact that every interpretation has to adapt itself to the particular language structure and hermeneutical situation.

With that, it is important to recognise that the dependence of the interpretation on the language structure and the hermeneutical situation does not change the character of the text itself. This can be evident in that the form of text, however ancient, is continuously contemporaneous consequent of a unique co-existence of past and present whereby a genuine opportunity to change and widen the horizon presents itself and provides a real possibility to enrich the world by a new and deeper dimension of understanding (Gadamer 1989: 391).

The understanding is not arrived at solely by reasoning one's way back to the past, but also by having a present involvement, in a manner that is common to present life, of what is being communicated through the discourse of the text. Further, as noted by Gadamer (1989), the understanding is augmented with the realisation that even though we may have more than one interpretation, it is *the same text* that is presenting itself in each one of those interpretations even if the text is being oriented by the reader's own linguistic orientation of the world.

Essentially, the multiple interpretations of the text are the result of the text forcing us to make interpretive conjectures as a result of the language structure and hermeneutical situation, which can be tested, criticised and falsified, and that in turn lead to the true meaning of the text attempting to assert itself. Here one returns to Ricoeur (1973) who teaches us that within the sphere of interpretation, the conjectures and falsifications can be thought of as products of the logic of qualitative probability that, consequent of the inherent subjective uncertainty that rests on faith, lead to *validation* rather than the empirical *verification* of scientific laws.

Thus, an interpretation must not only be probable, but it must be more probable than another interpretation in light of the language system that recognises what is perceived of the past and known of the present as well as that absorbs the signs of God that illuminate faith (Quran 2:118). In effect, it is the distinction between validation and verification that is valuable in that regard because it allows the interpreter to move between the limits of dogmatism and scepticism and all the probable interpretations in-between to seek an agreement, even if this agreement is based on the most probable interpretation.

Historical hermeneutics, for its part, as the second branch of hermeneutics of relevance to the elaboration of truth in *Mua'amalat* within Islam, was predominantly elucidated by Gadamer as being not so much a subjective act than a complex process of transmission in which the past (the strange) and the present (the familiar) are being constantly mediated. To illustrate, in the case of *Shari'ah*, one can observe that Muslims today try to understand the Quran and the *Ahadith* through a constant mediation between three forces: first, the Quran and the *Ahadith* as they are written during the time of the Prophet (PBUH); second, as they are interpreted (and re-interpreted) through time, especially during the time of the Imams of the four main 'Madhahibs' or 'Ways/Schools' in Islam (i.e., *Maliki*, *Shafi'i*, *Hanbali* and *Hanafi*); and, third, as they can be understood in modern times.

Historical hermeneutics, therefore, complements the interpretivism branch of hermeneutics, with its focus on the subjectiveness of linguistics in the process of truth formation, in that it seeks to actively include the historical consciousness perspective, with all its prejudices and preconceptions, at the fore of understanding. In addition, historical hermeneutics seeks also to actively demonstrate the powerful influence of the reality and efficacy of history within the perception of truth itself.

The last point mentioned above about history is a crucial concept to consider in the evaluation of *Shari'ah* directives in relation to some contemporary issues. The concept, essentially, proposes the need to appreciate the unrecognised and unregulated force of historical consciousness that affects our understanding of text (in this case, religious text), especially when historical objectivism is *assumed* to operate in an elevated position within the process of critical scientific enquiry. In effect, while truth and reality are objective, as in the realist ontology behind Islamic thought, our understanding, consequent of temporal distance, may not be endowed with the same degree of objectivity, causing an ultimate deformation in knowledge.

The solution to the impasse of mediating the past (tradition through historically effected consciousness) with the present, in Gadamer's (1989) view, is to bring together the horizon of the past and the horizon of the present in a merged horizon whereby the concepts of the historical past are regained in a wide-ranging way that includes a wider comprehension of them. One may venture to assume that within Islamic thought, *Qiyas* (analogical reasoning) and *Igma'a* (consensus) are tools for that purpose.

In spite of its negatives, temporal distance does, however, have important positive effects on our understanding of an object because it allows the true meaning of an object to emerge fully. According to Gadamer:

> The discovery of the true meaning of a text or a work of art is never finished; it is in fact an infinite process. Not only are fresh sources of error constantly excluded, so that all kinds of things are filtered out that obscure the true meaning; but new sources of understanding are continually emerging that reveal unsuspected elements of meaning. The temporal distance that performs the filtering process is not fixed, but is itself undergoing constant movement and extension. And along with the negative side of the filtering process brought about by temporal distance there is also the positive side, namely the value it has for understanding. (Gadamer 1989: 298)

The aforementioned view on the positive effects of the temporal distance can be related to critical rationalism and its viewpoint on the elaboration of the truth. This is because historical hermeneutics serves in the role of the link of the finitude of the historical experience with the contemporary environment in the wider process of scientific enquiry that deals with propositions, interpretations and refutations that are central to the search for truth and the acknowledgement of reality.

At the heart of the role of historical hermeneutics is ceaseless research with all of its qualitative infiniteness. For, in contrast to research in the natural sciences, where the *tentative* results and understanding are more apparent to the senses through experimentation, the results of research into historical subject matter (i.e., understanding the past), even though a science according to Dilthey (1989), can never come into view.

Thus, within the domain of history, as in linguistics, it can be construed that truth resides in the realm of validation through probability by way of the use of seemingly unlimited research and scientific analysis (hence we need Islamic research institutions and the Islamic academic discipline after all) that rest on elements of intellect, reason and faith rather than through a verification of an undisputed version of comprehension based on history that confirms or negates the basis of a certain event, practice and/or directive.

2.3 Conclusion

The discussion into the formation of truth in *Mua'amalat* has thus far touched upon many legal and religious concepts concerned with truth-seeking along with the various relevant theoretical perspectives that relate to the analysis and understanding of the scripture. In particular, it was argued that the nature of scientific examination, especially in the sphere of religious studies, requires a firm belief that truth exists independently from our senses. This belief should be coupled with the recognition that the cognitive challenges posed by the nature of religion, namely temporal, linguistic and contextual detachments, require the use of a critical scientific process to attempt to get closer to the truth and reality of all that is associated with divine guidance.

In effect, one can never know, unequivocally, no matter how learned they may be, the causes and objectives, as in the mind of the Divine, of a particular religious directive let alone completely transcend the linguistic difficulties and the historically affected consciousness in formulating proper understanding of the scripture, especially as they pertain to new and changed circumstances.

This shortcoming can be even more pronounced with the fact that the majority of religious directives in Islam are based on the *Ahadith*, which can be contextual and subject to varying degrees of strength (e.g., solitary *hadith* and one without consensus as proof), rather than the majority of religious directives in Islam being based on the universal and substantive directives from the Quran itself. And even as one considers the Quran, the apparent incapacity of Muslim scholars to overcome falsity in properly interpreting and understanding the word '*Dahaha*' in the Quran (Quran 79:30) (i.e., the earlier conceptualisation of a flat Earth) more than a millennia ago should all but serve as a humbling reminder of our own intellectual and logical shortcomings in this most specific of scriptures.

As one prepares to embark on the substantive components of the economic-centred discussion in the coming chapters, the above is important insofar as it was deemed illogical to debate the technicalities surrounding the usage of derivative instruments in Islamic finance in the absence of the acknowledgement that seeking the truth within *Mua'amalat* does depend on a certain sense of freedom from religious dogmatism. This should be coupled with a renewed confidence in the fact that intellect and reason alongside faith shall lead to the proper adherence to the will of God that ultimately seeks salvation and bliss for humankind.

CHAPTER 3

MARKET RISKS AND THEIR MANAGEMENT

3.0 Introduction

The previous chapter on the philosophy of truth forma-tion in Islamic thought presented detailed argumentation that delineated a position that one must be humble with their epistemological stances that emerge throughout the interpretation of the religious scripture (in this case, Islamic scripture). This, it has been shown, is consequent of the many difficulties that exist in developing a proper under-standing of the objective truth (that does exist), not the least of which are linguistic, circumstantial and temporal chal-lenges. In fact, with particular reference to Islam, it can be contended that the advocated humility in interpreting the religious scripture is inherent in Islamic thought with its conjecture-related Islamic theories of *Igma'a* (consensus), *Qiyas* (analogical reasoning) and *Maslaha* (public interest).

The commencement of the examination of the topic of market-risk management and derivatives in Islamic finance will begin in this chapter and will continue in the coming ones. Specifically, this chapter will delve into the types of market risks faced by contemporary real-sector entities (and the financial institutions that support their operations), the modern risk-management framework and the rationale behind the concept of hedging. Throughout the chapter, particular emphasis will be given to the conceptualisation of risk and risk-management practices from the prevalent economic and Islamic juridical viewpoints (particularly the theory of *Maslaha*).

With that, it should be stated that there are three reasons why this examination is important: First, it seeks to contribute to the development of a broader understanding in Islamic finance circles on what is inherently an economic subject matter, which should, in turn, instigate an enlargement of the existing dialogue that is almost entirely centred in the legal sphere with a particular focus on contractual forms. Second, it strives to address the view by some commentators that participants in the Islamic finance industry should accede to the belief that Islam forces the acceptance of all the risks in economic ventures in order to get full rewards with little regard to the potential of relinquishing some rewards as a result of avoiding the assumption of some risks. Third, it attempts to demonstrate that any gaps that may currently exist in the implementation of sound risk-management policies is not consequent of the nature of how Islamic jurisprudence views risk management, but rather concerns how some decide to interpret divine guidance.

3.1 Risk and its management

Risk and its rationalisation has been an integral part of human intellectual formation regarding the essence and prospect of existence on Earth. In his seminal book on risk, Bernstein proclaimed that risk 'touches the most profound aspects of psychology,[1] mathematics, statistics, and history' (Bernstein 1996: ix). Thus, in order to appreciate risk and its deep influence on human behaviour, one would have to understand precisely the multifarious conceptualisation of risk and how it is perceived by those who face it.

One can start with the assertion that the substance of risk is the uncertainty about an exposure that is related to the nature, occurrence and extent of events that affect human beings in a future time period. Notably, while it is acknowledged that risk is usually defined as a probability of loss and that exposure is typically thought of as the possibility of loss, the discussion in this and the coming chapters will use those two terms interchangeably.

In Islam, the presence of uncertainty is fundamental to human existence, as evidenced by the divine words in the Quran stating: 'Indeed, Allah [alone] has knowledge of the Hour and sends down the rains and knows what is in the wombs. And no soul perceives what it will earn tomorrow, and no soul perceives in what land it will die. Indeed, Allah is Knowing and Acquainted' (Quran 31:34). In fact, for Muslims, the dependence on God for their daily personal and commercial affairs is so profound that it may be ostensible more often than not that any reference to the future is invariably associated with the term '*Inshallah*' (God willing) to demonstrate *Tawakul* (reliance on God).

The importance of *Tawakul* itself in Islam is quite apparent with the multiple references to and concerning the concept in the Quran and in the *Ahadith*. However, with that in mind, there is also ample evidence in Islamic thought to support the distinction between lethargic passivity in the face of uncertainty regarding the future and the protection of wealth as part of the five essential elements (i.e., *Al-Durariyat Al-Khamsa*) as advocated by Al-Ghazali. Specifically, in Islam, it is pronounced that, in commercial settings, one should undertake the means that are necessary in order to protect their wealth from the various risks that may negatively affect it.

For this, *Shari'ah* scholars have widely recognised, and have indeed promoted, the proposition that human welfare, in addition to being dependent on a faith in God in enabling the appropriate outcome, is a product of a constructive work ethic, which includes proactive risk management, as part of the Islamic doctrine of *Al-Akhdh Bel-Asbab* (i.e., pursuing the legitimate means to reach desired ends). Moreover, Islamic jurisprudence has advocated a risk–return economic rationality with the institutionalisation of the axiom *Alghonom Bialghorom* ('The gain is with the loss') that, it has been contended, dictates the importance of the inseparability of risk and return for sustainable wealth generation (Al-Suwailem 2006; Khan and Ahmed 2001). In particular, it has been established in Islamic jurisprudence that any return without the assumption of risk is an illegitimate return (Al-Shubaili 2012: 40).

Moving beyond Islamic thought, modern economic theory is particularly cognisant of the importance of risk and its management for economic progress. Marshall, in his *Principles of Economics*, stated that 'when a trader or a manufacturer buys anything to be used in production, or be sold again, his demand is based on his anticipations of the profits which he can derive from it. These profits depend at any time on speculative risks and other causes' (Marshall 1910: 92). Knight's (1921) ground-breaking work *Risk, Uncertainty and Profit* is dedicated to the exploration of the subject matter as given in the title. Nobel laureate Kenneth Arrow, for his part, affirmed the significance of risk in that he stated that modern-day institutions are shaped by its existence, which within itself is a result of the search for profit (Arrow 1951: 408).

With that overview into the conceptualisation of risk and risk management in Islamic jurisprudence and economic thought, one could proceed to the specifics that surround its management, which can be thought of as depending largely on three core elements: identification, measurement and strategy.

3.2 Risk identification

Identification, as the first element of risk management, concerns the formulation of the types of risks facing a particular organisation, which can be classified as either core risks or non-core risks. Specifically, Culp clarifies that classification by stating that:

> The core risks facing a firm may be defined as those risks that the firm is in business to bear and manage so that it can earn excess economic profits. Noncore risks, by contrast, are risks to which a firm's primary business exposes it but that the firm does not necessarily need to retain in order to engage in its primary business line. The firm may well be exposed to noncore risks, but it may not wish to remain exposed to those risks. Core risks, by contrast, are those risks the firm is literally in business not to get rid of – at least not all of them. The distinction between core and noncore risk is entirely subjective and varies firm by firm. What is core risk for one firm may not be for another one, even when the companies are in the same sector and industry. The classification of a risk as core by any given firm, moreover, depends not just on the quality of information the firm actually has, but also on the firm's perceived comparative advantage in digesting that information. (Culp 2004: 27)

The classification of risks into core risks that are related to the main production/service, or simply the raison d'être, of an enterprise and others as non-core is important because it is often contested, explicitly or implicitly, by some *Shari'ah* scholars and commentators in the discourse on the topic of risk management in general and derivatives in particular, that the inseparability of risk and return signifies that those who are not willing to accept *all* risks (core and non-core) in the business world are not worthy of any profits generated.

Thus, in the realm of Islamic finance, Culp's differentiation between core and non-core risk, and the earlier stated general conceptualisation of risk, can be thought of as going perhaps one step beyond the often-made assertions that no economic growth can take place without taking risks. In essence, in accepting that risk is both a precursor to and a product of economic progress, it could be logically argued that one can distinguish between the risks that are endogenous, and to a certain extent controllable, to the enterprise, in that they arise from the uncertainty of future income consequent of changing consumer tastes and market competition as well as the effectiveness and efficiency of profit/cost centres, and those uncontrollable exogenous risks that are purely within the realm of the randomness of the financial markets. Furthermore, within the context of the distinction in the nature of risk, it is also crucial to take note of Culp's observation regarding the subjectivity in the classification of the risks existing in the global marketplace to the various enterprises that are exposed to them.

To illustrate, an airline is in the business of transporting people from one destination to another. It has to consider its route network, airline fleet, quality of customer service, competition, partnerships/code shares and cost structure, among many other core business variables that fall largely under its control. The volatility in the costs of fuel and the volatility to the exchange rates, which are mostly independent of its decision capability, can exert enormous pressures on profitability and in some cases may result in swift bankruptcies no matter how well it manages its core risks (e.g., the UK's Laker Airways in the early part of the 1980s).

Similarly, the existence of a bank, be it a conventional one or an Islamic one, is arguably a result of its focus on managing the risks associated with the extension of financing in order to ensure for its depositors the soundness of its capital base. In undertaking that function, it is exposed to multiple mismatches between its assets and liabilities consequent of the different preferences (tenor, fixed/floating, currency, etc.) of depositors and borrowers.[2] In the management of these mismatches, the exogenous market risks have been shown to have a severe influence on banking institutions and if systemic can threaten an entire banking system (e.g., the savings and loans' crisis in the United States in the early 1980s) even if proper due diligence (investigation to acquire information for deliberation) on the borrowers and their financing needs is undertaken.

Therefore, consequent of the significance of the market risks, as non-core risk exposures, on the financial health of companies in the real sector (and on the banking institutions that facilitate their existence), the remainder of the book will concentrate chiefly on the market risks. With that focus in mind, it may be appropriate to start with the elaboration of the concept of market risk.

Market risk can be thought of as being the potential loss arising from unexpected changes in market prices (e.g., commodities and equities) and market rates (e.g., interest and foreign exchange rates).[3] With that definition, it is perhaps important to provide some detail regarding the exogenous market risks that businesses, in hedging contexts, are endeavouring to pre-emptively avoid.[4] The first market risk to be examined is interest-rate risk, which can be defined as: 'interest rate mismatches in both the volume and maturity of interest-sensitive assets, liabilities, and off-balance sheet items' (Heffernan 1996: 167).

This particular type of market risk has gained prominence

in the period after the fall of the stable, yet economically unsustainable, Bretton Woods monetary system in the 1970s consequent of the increased intensity of the divergent inflation pressures and the subsequent alterations in the monetary policies of central banks in order to contain it. Apart from inflation and monetary policies, the interest-rate movements are also influenced by the general economic conditions, foreign exchange market activity, foreign investor demand for debt securities, levels of outstanding sovereign debt and financial and political stability.

Notably, while interest-rate risk affects all institutions, it affects banking institutions the most consequent of the nature of their assets (loans, investments, etc.) and liabilities (deposits). Specifically, banks are influenced by interest rates' (e.g., Treasury rates and the London Interbank Offered Rate (LIBOR)) changes by virtue of their exposure to variations in the pricing and valuation of their financial assets and liabilities, the consequences of their extension of financing and their measurement of performance relative to a commonly understood benchmark. Interestingly, the influence of interest rates is equally powerful to the Islamic finance industry in that not an insignificant portion of the assets on the balance sheets of Islamic banks are recorded on a mark-to-market basis that is derived from the usage of net present value (NPV) and the interest-rate yield curve.

All of these factors, in turn, influence the earnings and the economic value of banking institutions as well as the overall health of the real economy insofar as that a major source of financing to companies in the real sector comes from banks. That is to say, the importance of interest-rate risk on the real economy is partly a factor of the reduction in the lending capacity by banking institutions to deserving borrowers consequent of concern with the management of the exposure to this type of market risk that has become more volatile in recent decades.

Islamic banks, despite the prohibition on *Riba* (usury) on their financing operations, have not been immune to the influence of interest rates (aka 'mark-up rates' or 'benchmark rates'). In fact, there are numerous notable writers who have demonstrated that the Islamic finance industry is affected by interest-rate volatility and will undoubtedly be affected to a greater extent in the future as the industry expands in terms of product range and geographical reach.

To illustrate, a study by Khan and Ahmed (2001) demonstrated that rate of return risk (i.e., interest-rate risk) is the most critical risk facing Islamic financial institutions – a finding that was confirmed in subsequent empirical examinations by Bacha (2004a) and Kasri and Kassim (2009) on the subject matter in the banking industry. In fact, the Accounting and Auditing Organization for Islamic Financial Institutions (AAOIFI) *Shari'ah* Standard No. 27 (AAOIFI 2010), which accepts the usage of LIBOR as a benchmarking index, along with discourse on the topic in the Islamic economic literature (Chapra and Khan 2000: 54; Khan and Ahmed 2001: 145) is but a simple recognition of that reality.

Indeed, characterising Islamic banks as being more interest-rate sensitive than their conventional counterparts may not be an inaccurate statement and has been increasingly supported in the Islamic finance literature (Bacha 2004a; How *et al.*, 2005; Rosly 1999). This is because the majority of the assets of Islamic banks are fixed-rate in nature, such as the *Murabaha* (instalment sale) and *Istisna'a* (commission to manufacture) modes of financing, and extend traditionally to tenors that are on the longer-end of the maturity scale in order to suit borrowers in the real sector. Moreover, the inability of Islamic banks to impose pre-payment penalties in periods of lower interest rates, despite being a competitive trait of fairer banking practices, further exacerbates their interest-rate risk-management challenges.

On the other hand, the liabilities of Islamic banking institutions are mostly shorter-term 'investment accounts' (e.g., deposits) that must provide competitive, mostly variable, rates that are market sensitive in order to meet the expectations of their investment account holders or face what is called in the industry Displaced Commercial Risk (DCR). This particular type of risk is essentially the danger that the Islamic bank will have to forego profit in order to ensure the payment of a competitive rate of return on its liabilities, mainly through a Profit Equalization Reserve (PER).

In stressing the challenges posed by this liability structure, Moody's Global Corporate Finance (2010) has cautioned that DCR should be properly considered by the Islamic banking industry since in the event that the payments to the investment account holders do not meet their expectations there is always the prospect of the withdrawal of investments that has the rather serious potential of affecting the bank's liquidity position and ultimately its solvency.

Thus, it appears that the arguments by some writers advocating the position that the lack of pre-agreed return on deposits in Islamic finance reduces exposure to interest-rate risk may not be completely exact (Greuning and Iqbal 2008: 159). On the contrary, it may be estimated that the ambiguity imposed by the structure of the payoff to the investment accounts along with the presence of the DCR (and a finite PER) can cause a vague perception of the nature of risk–return trade off by the investment account holders. This, in turn, could result in overly optimistic expectations that if unmet can result in an increase in the DCR and, in extreme circumstances, ultimately lead to bank failures.[5]

Notwithstanding the aforementioned viewpoints, it should be stated that the mostly juristic theoretical aspirations of having the Islamic banking assets in illiquid private equity-like, or even liquid mutual funds, *Musharaka* (profit-sharing agreement) in addition to agency-type *Wakala* and *Mudharaba* financing arrangements along with units of these 'investments' given to investors/depositors on the liability side in a bid to eliminate interest rates and their exposures from society (see Khan and Mirakhor 1994) are not realistic within the framework of current economic theories and do not propose new theories as such.

This is simply because these ambitions do not appear to factor in the economic foundations of the market segmentation theory, which are based on the liquidity and risk/return preferences of capital providers (i.e., depositors/investors). The challenges posed by the presence of asymmetry of information, monitoring costs and the principal-agent problems, especially in cross-border investments, only serve to further exacerbate the potential for the attainment of these aspirations.

The second type of market risk to be discussed is the foreign exchange risk that, one should note, did not exist under the relatively fixed bi-metallic monetary (gold and silver) system in seventh-century Arabia. Particularly, foreign exchange risk in recent years has developed into a full-fledged hazard with the breakdown of the quasi-fixed exchange rate system under the Bretton Woods agreements in 1971 that ushered in the floating exchange rate regime and all associated uncertainties.

In the real economic sectors, this threat is especially apparent in the modern era of globalisation in which inputs, including labour for the service sector, are increasingly being sourced from international suppliers in an ever-dynamic process of searching for improved quality and economies of scale. Consequently, the inputs are then manufactured and then sold through an international sales network to customers around the world.

To refer back to the core competency of enterprises outlined earlier, a particular company with sufficient foresight has a relatively high degree of control over its domain (suppliers, employees, production, research and development (R&D), innovation, etc.) through the whole process of production through to sales. However, what it does not control is the expected covariance between its home currency and those multiple currencies that it must be exposed to in the discharge of that core competency. Along the same lines, in the investment sphere, the exchange rate risk can prove to be an obstacle to cross-border investments in that it can inhibit investments by regions with surplus funds (e.g., the Gulf Cooperation Council (the GCC)) to fund deficient regions (e.g., emerging markets) that may host superior investment potential.

Having discussed the effects of foreign exchange rate volatility and prior to moving to a discussion of commodity price risk, it is perhaps valuable to shed some light on the specifics that determine the foreign exchange rates in the financial markets, which should add further credence to the argument that this type of risk is non-core in nature and ought not, therefore, be forced upon companies operating in the real sector (in some sort of bid to comply with the rules of the *Shari'ah*) unless they choose to do so based on detailed analysis as part of their risk-management framework.

Foreign exchange rates are determined by the various levels of supply and demand in the financial markets for currencies. The supply and demand of currencies, in turn, are a function of the interest-rate differentials between countries net of expected inflation, balance of payments as determined by international capital and trade flows, macro-economic fundamentals (e.g., gross domestic product (GDP) growth rates), investor sentiment, financial and political stability, monetary policies of the central bank and debt levels. In effect, the foreign exchange rate at any given time is the equilibrium of the supply-and-demand forces as established by way of the analysis of the various economic and financial indicators outlined above by participants in the foreign exchange markets.

Commodity price risk, the final market risk to be examined, is of particular significance to an Islamic faith that places the creation of wealth as the result of the production of goods, including many commodities, in high regard. Apart from the religious admiration, the importance of commodities, and their associated risks, in the economic and financial affairs of Muslims is quite enormous. This is because: first, the member-countries of the Organisation of Islamic Cooperation (OIC) provide a sizeable amount of global commodities trade (petroleum, natural gas, wheat, palm oil, cereals, cocoa, etc.); and, second, as will be discussed in Chapter 5, the current paradigm of Islamic finance is focused on the structuring of financial transactions around tradable commodities, even if unrelated to the original transaction.

Notwithstanding the above, in terms of pricing behaviour, in a manner similar to foreign exchange rate determination, the prices of commodities are also derived from the equilibrium between the forces of global supply and demand. However, commodities markets are unique in that they factor in expectations regarding, for example, the effects of seasonal variations, weather and crop failures, labour disputes, expected levels of inflation and interest rates, general economic conditions, political stability and the availability of substitutes in the derivation of the equilibrium price.

3.3 Risk measurement

Having discussed the identification of market risk factors, the next step in the risk-management process is risk measurement, which includes a set of techniques to evaluate the exposure of an entity to market risks by way of sophisticated mathematical and computational tools. Specifically, market-risk measurement, as a practice, is usually defined as the determination of the volatility of a particular variable, as quantified by the standard deviation of historic outcomes over a standardised period of time.

However, volatility, although an informative figure regarding the relative riskiness of a market variable, is meaningless to companies and banking institutions unless it is linked to an indicator that appropriately measures the consequence. The indicators that serve that purpose range from specific risk measures that range from gap and duration analysis (and the combination of both as in the duration-gap analysis) to a wider all-inclusive risk measurement framework such as Value at Risk (VaR).

Gap analysis is a well-known balance-sheet management technique for institutions that are interest-rate sensitive; the sensitivity, in turn, depends on the structure of the assets and liabilities. More specifically, an entity, typically a banking institution, can be liability-sensitive in that its interest-sensitive liabilities are affected to a greater degree consequent of lesser maturities and re-pricing in a given period than their assets, or asset-sensitive in which the opposite is true. The 'gap' is the difference, or mismatch, between interest-sensitive assets and liabilities for a given time frame. For this, the assets and liabilities are categorised into buckets according to their maturity (if fixed rate) or time remaining to their next re-pricing (if floating rate), which are then used to assess the interest-rate sensitivity of earnings to changes in interest rates in the financial markets.

Duration analysis, on the other hand, measures the influence of the variations in the interest rates on the economic values of balance-sheet items, as opposed to looking at earnings alone. It is also different from gap analysis in that it allows for the possibility that the average life (i.e., duration) of an asset or a liability, consequent of repayments and/or pre-payments, differs from its stated maturities.

In time, it was recognised that there is a need to account for both types of measures of interest-rate risk that are included in the gap analysis and the duration analysis, which resulted in their amalgamation into a combined measure named the duration-gap analysis. This interest-rate risk measure essentially includes the time and value weighted duration of the assets and liabilities by way of factoring-in all of the cash inflows and outflows that relate to net worth, which is the ultimate absorber of shocks caused by adverse movements in interest rates.

The utility of the duration-gap analysis is derived from the prospect that an institution can choose to not speculate on the expectations of interest rates' levels by using the analysis provided in this risk measure to 'immunise' their balance sheet to obtain a fixed yield for a certain period of time because the duration of both sides of the balance sheet are matched (i.e., a duration-gap of zero). With that, it should be noted that the balance-sheet immunisation in this context, although useful in partly mitigating interest-rate risk, is not a perfect tool for three main reasons.

First, the duration-gap analysis only focuses on interest-rate risk and does not consider the other risks that can affect the balance sheet of an institution. Second, the analysis provided by the duration-gap analysis is simplistic in that it does not consider the convexity of the relationship between the interest rates and economic values (i.e., the duration is not static in that it changes as the yields change). Third, the duration-gap analysis assumes that changes to the yield curve will be by the same amount across the maturity spectrum (i.e., parallel shifts), which is not always the case because short-term rates exhibit more volatility than, and are thus not perfectly correlated with, long-term interest rates. In fact, in some limited circumstances, the short- and long-term rates have been shown to move in opposite directions from each other.

It is in the recognition of the challenges of the proper measurement of market risks that present themselves in the duration-gap analysis that an arguably superior measure of market risk emerged, namely Value at Risk (VaR). VaR is a measure of the minimum loss that is expected over a period of time under a given probability. For example, a VaR of US$ 1 million for one day at 5 per cent probability (i.e., 95 per cent confidence interval) means that the institution can expect to lose US$ 1 million in one day about 5 per cent of the time. Notably, the potential losses examined in the VaR analysis are broader than those studied under the duration-gap analysis in that those losses include not only losses related to interest-rate risk, but also those that relate to, among others, foreign exchange and commodity price risks.

As for the choice of the variables that underlie the VaR analysis (i.e., amount of the minimum loss, confidence interval, and time span), it is dependent on the nature and the level of risk-aversion limits desired by a particular business. For instance, a US$ 1 million exposure can be considered substantial for a medium-sized enterprise and such an enterprise may therefore require a higher confidence interval of, say, 97.5 or 99 per cent. Similarly, the time span of a banking institution whose assets may be recorded on a mark-to-market basis, consequent of monetary regulations and accounting rules, will likely have a shorter time frame for the VaR analysis than a traditional production or service company.

That said, it should also be stated that the accurateness of VaR and its flexible nature does come at a cost, namely the complicated calculations involved in order to produce meaningful results that rest on a large list of assumptions. Specifically, in addition to the traditional statistical assumptions, the VaR considers the following risk components of market risk: absolute price or rate change (*delta*), convexity (*gamma*), volatility (*vega*), time decay (*theta*), basis or correlation, and the discount rate (*rho*) along with multiple approaches to estimation.

Additionally, there has been some evidence that the VaR calculation requires some adjustment in order to account for the statistical fat tails wherein there may be more chance of extremely high losses than a normal distribution would imply. However, despite the many criticisms directed at the VaR's many assumptions and the complexity of calculation, it has been used extensively in the risk-management domain by risk managers, regulators and traders in financial and non-financial firms consequent of its comprehensive nature.

3.4 Risk strategy

The third, and final, element of an organisation's risk-management framework is the risk strategy. It has been previously contended that market risks are inevitable in today's globalised marketplace; thus, after having properly identified and measured the relevant market risks, an organisation should endeavour to devise a detailed strategy to be able to deal with them. These strategies, as noted by Culp

(2004), traditionally involve: retention, reduction, consolidation and risk transfer (with specialisation as a focus).

In the retention risk-management strategy, an enterprise perceives the potential for adverse outcomes but decides to not undertake any actions to mitigate these risks. This could be because its management and shareholders feel that these risks are a necessary component of the business of the enterprise and should, therefore, be borne in order to attain maximum profits. Accordingly, the pursuit of the retention strategy, and its ultimate success, depends on the judgement by management in running the day-to-day operations of the company and on what Hardy calls the 'accumulation of reserves to provide for meeting the risks' (Hardy 1999 [1923]: 11). The reserves can be accumulated as part of withholding free cash flows into a reserve account, investing additional funds by current shareholders or by issuing new securities to the market (who may or may not choose to partake in the offering).

In meeting the core risks of a business that are central to its function and relatively under its control (e.g., production, suppliers, sales and marketing, and response to consumer tastes), the risk-retention strategy is not only understandable but also forms a necessary precondition to the generation of profits. In contrast, market risks are a different matter since, as stated previously, they are exogenous to the operations of any particular enterprise and are therefore not within the control of its management. Effectively, as demonstrated by modern finance theories, any attempt to formulate expectations regarding the future movement of market rates or prices is quite simply within the realm of speculation.

The acknowledgement of that reality has significant implications for businesses operating in the real sector in terms of the viability of the retention method in the management of their exposures to market risks. For it could be possible that the market risks identified and measured previously have loss provisions that extend beyond the designated confidence interval in the statistical analysis used and consequently venture into a territory in which neither the accumulated reserves nor additional financing (if it ever arrives) can be of assistance. The aforementioned fat tails in the VaR analysis have been shown to exacerbate that predicament.

Interestingly, the appearance of the term 'speculation' in this circumstance, although appropriate, carries with it a unique sense of irony to the Islamic finance industry that actively seeks to avoid practices that can resemble *Maysir* (gambling). In essence, it could be argued that the acceptance of the non-core market risks as a consequence of the core operations of the institutions that are seeking to comply with the economic doctrine of the *Shari'ah* should not also prelude a decision to mitigate them as a way to avoid speculating on the movements of market prices.

The second risk-management strategy available to institutions is risk reduction whereby an organisation, after having identified and measured the relevant risk exposures, decides that it would rather not be subjected to these risks, in whole or in part, and as a result proceeds to alter its operational and financial policies accordingly. One of the main schemes used in this particular type of strategy is the 'natural hedging', or internal hedging, concept, which is advocated by some in the Islamic finance industry as a form of *Shari'ah*-acceptable risk-management methodology (Al-Rubaia 1992; Al-Suwailem 2006: 114–15; Al-Suwailem 2012: 9; Bacha, 2004b).

Essentially, this form of hedging, as described by Gastineau *et al.*, entails:

Asset liability selection – for instance, managing credit risk by setting exposure limits with specific customers and managing foreign exchange (FX) risk by raising funds in currencies for which the enterprise has net operating revenues. Another example of internal hedging is interest rate immunization, whereby the risk characteristics (i.e., the duration statistic) of assets and liabilities are intentionally matched. The underlying risk could be operational, rather than strictly financial. For instance, a firm could choose to diversify across production technologies or energy sources. The key feature is that internal hedging happens naturally in the course of making routine investment and financing decisions and often appears without comment in the financial statements. (Gastineau et al. 2001: 4)

It needs to be emphasised here, however, that the risk-reduction strategy, within the realm of market-risk management, is difficult to implement for both banking institutions and real-sector companies. More specifically, for banking institutions, despite having a greater level of flexibility with respect to balance-sheet management, there are substantial limitations imposed by the competitive pressures in the banking industry and the liquidity of the assets in their portfolios. In effect, more intense competitive pressures and lower asset liquidity levels demonstrate a reduced ability to engage in natural hedging. With that characterisation, Islamic banking institutions, consequent of their portfolios consisting mainly of illiquid assets (particularly *Murabaha* financing) and strong competition emanating from both conventional and other Islamic banks, should not be expected to garner much success in marketing financial products to their depositors, investors or borrowers if their preferences do not match those in the banks' risk-reduction strategy.

For companies in the real sector, on the other hand, it is acknowledged that a particular company, in order to reduce risks, could technically decide to change its cost (e.g., choice of suppliers and materials), production (e.g., locations and vertical integration) and sales strategy (e.g., target regions) in addition to altering its financing structure (e.g., fixed versus floating, and multicurrency share capital) in order to meet the desired market-risk exposure. In time, however, it will become apparent that although these measures can, and do, alleviate some of the exposures to market risks being faced by the company, they do have their costs.

For example, the cost of the operational and financial alterations may become evident in that they could provide for inputs that are not ideal in terms of quality, actual net expense and/or convenience. As for the focus on market-risk-friendly regions, as envisioned by some of the partisans of the risk-reduction strategy, this policy may have negative effects in terms of sales, which in turn can impair the ability of businesses to achieve economies of scale. Indeed, companies look for exports in today's globalised world as a necessity for survival rather than as being a bonus of increased profits. Finally, it is apparent in the financial markets that a firm's financing structure is not entirely decided by its management; the preferences by its shareholders and creditors play an integral part in shaping the ultimate financial policy.

Thus, for all intents and purposes, the risk-reduction strategy, although useful to some extent, cannot serve as the sole risk-management strategy for an organisation seeking to be competitive in the global marketplace. This observation is made even more apparent by the dynamic, complex and uncertain character of the business and financial worlds where it is quite difficult to anticipate the exogenous factors that affect an organisation's cash flows.

With that realisation, the next two risk-management strategies – consolidation and transfer – become funda-mental complements to effective and efficient market-risk management, especially when viewed from a portfolio perspective (i.e., not transactional-oriented risk manage-ment as is often advocated in Islamic finance), within an enterprise-wide risk-management framework.

The rationale behind the consolidation risk-management strategy is two-fold: combination and diversification. For combination, Knight and Hardy were among the first eco-nomic thinkers who articulated the proposition that risk and uncertainty can be better managed by the improvement of predictions arising from the combinations of events (Hardy 1999 [1923]; Knight 1921). Essentially, firms have more con-fidence about their ability to manage a group of risks than they have confidence in their ability to manage individual risk components. Specifically, Hardy asserts:

> A single event defies prediction, but the mass remains always practically the same or varies in ways in which we can predict. It is obvious that any device by which we can base our business decisions on the average which we can predict, instead of on the single event, which is uncertain, means the elimination of the risk. The larger the number of cases observed the less is the deviation of the results from those which a priori were most probable. (Hardy 1999 [1923]: 21–2)

Although many contemporary economists would rightly argue against Hardy's statement regarding the prospect of the 'elimination of the risk' as a result of combination, the concept, nevertheless, is useful in the context of market-risk management in light of the statistical scientific advance-ments in the modern era. Specifically, in statistics, the cen-tral limit theorem (CLT) states that the distribution of the average risk of a large group of independent and identically distributed random variables is approximately normally distributed, regardless of the shapes and properties of the individual risk distributions.[6] Thus, the combination of market risks, while not reducing the maximum loss that an organisation faces, should, nevertheless, increase its capacity to manage the consolidated exposure by improving the ability to measure and predict losses.

The second rationale behind the consolidation risk-management strategy is diversification. The benefits of diversification were first quantified in Markowitz's pioneering work on portfolio theory, where he demonstrated that if the volatility of the various financial positions in a portfolio is not perfectly correlated, the total risk will be less than the average volatility of its individual holdings (Markowitz 1952, 1959). Accordingly, after identifying and measuring its market risk exposures in an enterprise-wide portfolio context (i.e., not at the transactional-level), an institution will be pleased to discover that because of less than perfect correlation in their market-risk exposures statistics and modern finance theory have eliminated some of their risks for free. Notably, as opposed to the pure risk-reduction strategy, diversification within the consolidation framework does not require active alterations in the way an institution does business (financially and/or operationally).

Risk transfer, as the last risk-management strategy examined, can be defined as 'the explicit process by which the adverse impacts of a risk are shifted from the shareholders of one firm to either one or more individuals or to the shareholders of one or more firms' (Culp 2004: 59). The economic rationale behind risk transfer centres on the increase in the efficiency of the allocation of resources across agents in an economy (Arrow 1964; Debreu 1959). However, while these agents may exchange the risk exposures with one another as hedgers, the probability of finding a counterpart for a specific market-risk exposure (and the cost of the associated search) makes it an unlikely scenario. Further, it has been reported by Teweles *et al.* (1999) that hedgers can exhibit similarity in behaviour in that there are situations where the hedging community wants to buy or sell an underlying asset at about the same time.

This structural difficulty in the hedging sphere has led to the introduction of financial intermediation as a facilitator for hedging transactions among economic agents. In essence, the financial intermediary, for a contractual spread, becomes the counterpart to every tailored market-risk exposure of hedgers. In undertaking its role, the financial intermediary, in turn, utilises the aforementioned benefits of combination (i.e., better statistical inferences in addition to the reduction in information costs consequent of economies of scale in gathering market intelligence and its analysis) and diversification (mismatches in the currency, tenor, fixed/floating, commodity, etc. as well as the spread of the counterparty risks), and then makes a decision as to whether it wants to remain exposed to the residual market risks or offload them to other financial intermediaries.

At the heart of the risk-transfer process are techniques that involve derivative hedging instruments, which entail the acquisition of a financial instrument that reduces the variability of a firm's cash flows by generating a positive payoff in the same states of nature that a market-risk exposure imposes a negative payoff on the firm's normal business operations. Specifically, subsequent to entering into a derivative hedging transaction, markets forces should ensure that the economic factors that contribute to the worsening of the balance-sheet position of a hedger are largely offset by the rise in the value of the derivative instrument.

The cost of this practice (if forward-based instruments

are used (see the next chapter)), in addition to the fees paid for the financial instrument, is sacrificing any potential gain that could have occurred in an unhedged scenario. However, many institutions are willing to accept that cost in return for avoiding the uncertainty (timing, magnitude, etc.) of the exposure to losses that can appear, with profound consequences, in the uncontrollable movements of rates and prices in the financial markets.

With that understanding, it can be argued that the axiom of *Alghonom Bialghorom* mentioned earlier is especially relevant in this context. In essence, *in a true hedging transaction*, the cost of the protection from a market-risk exposure is the lost benefits that could have accrued if the exposure was unhedged. Conversely, if the institution had chosen to speculate and keep the market-risk exposures unhedged, then the losses (gains) garnered are a function of the gains (losses) that *could have* accrued had the market rates and/ or prices moved in a favourable (unfavourable) manner. In other words, the risk and return are indeed inseparable, as advocated in the Islamic finance literature; its level, however, is a matter of how risk-averse the enterprise is.

Here I should state that the acceptance of the proposition that the *Alghonom Bialghorom* axiom is a relative concept rather than being absolute in nature is of paramount importance to the progressive evolution of market-risk management in Islamic finance. For it may be apparent subsequent to the foregoing illustration that the axiom indicates that the degree of gain (*Alghonom*) is a function of the degree of potential losses (*Alghorom*).

Effectively, it is difficult to support the economic argument, as articulated by Hassan (and other commentators), that the 'required' application of the *Alghonom Bialghorom* axiom entails that an entrepreneur needs to accept *all* of the risks associated with the undertaking of their operations (core and non-core) in order to legitimise their returns (Hassan 2012: 25), especially when viewed in the context of modern-day financial markets. In fact, the likely outcome of that viewpoint is lower investment and overall economic underdevelopment, which is the case in many Muslim countries.

Besides the issue of the relativity of risk and return, one of the main challenges facing the risk-transfer strategy in the Islamic finance industry is the unease in the acceptability of the concept of risk transfer itself by some *Shari'ah* scholars. This unease, in turn, can be ascribed to two inter-related issues. The first issue is the concern regarding the introduction of *Maysir* (gambling) into the industry under the guise of hedging whereby instead of risk transfer there are the very real ingredients of adding risks to the financial system.[7] The second is related to the role of the financial intermediary for its risk-transfer services, which are deemed as improperly taking advantage of people's needs.[8]

Realising the importance of risk transfer, there have been propositions circulating in the Islamic finance literature to alleviate these concerns. These centre on: first, altering the hedging contracts in a manner that promotes more risk sharing among the participants in the real sector (suppliers, producers, financiers, etc.) (Askari *et al.* 2012); and/or, second, introducing 'Islamic' derivative hedging instruments, which assume either a fee-less arrangement (at least explicitly) by financial intermediaries or some sort of a cooperative system for risk sharing among external parties.

While the issue of *Maysir* and the role of the financial intermediary (and their fees) will be discussed at length in Chapter 7, it is perhaps necessary to address the propositions circulating around the concept of risk sharing in the Islamic finance industry. To begin with, and at a basic theoretical level, it should be noted that risk sharing *is a form of risk transfer.* One does not partake in a risk-sharing scheme without participating in the risk-transfer process that ensues.

To illustrate, in the realm of Islamic financial practices, the *Takaful* (i.e. cooperative) insurance model's much touted risk-sharing structure is built on each policy holder transferring their risk of loss to the communal pool of financial resources in which they participate through the contribution of monthly premiums. Moreover, in the hedging sphere, even the staunchest critics of 'conventional' risk transfer, in general, and derivatives, in particular, seem to have espoused a more pragmatic, even if convoluted, position vis-à-vis 'Islamic' risk transfer in recent years. This can become evident in that they argue that risk transfer could be accepted if undertaken in some sort of cooperative insurance/hedging fund since it is not-for-profit and consequently the rules on *Gharar* are 'forgivable' (Al-Shubaili 2012: 48; Al-Suwailem 2012: 10).

Thus, for all intents and purposes, it should not be the concept of risk transfer that is problematic for *Shari'ah* scholars and academics but rather its modalities and use (hedging versus gambling) in the Islamic finance industry.[9] That being said, as we consider modalities and use, economics and statistics should also remind us that they do matter in terms of the overall viability of whatever framework it is that is being proposed (even if some elements of such are deemed forgivable by Islamic jurisprudence).

Essentially, at the onset, the effectiveness of the proposed insurance/hedging fund depends primarily on its size vis-à-vis the prospective exposure, and to a certain extent on the effectiveness of its management. Further, while the prospect of hurricanes, fires and car accidents affecting all policy holders in a traditional cooperative insurance scheme at once is an extremely improbable scenario, systemic economic events are not endowed with similar remoteness, especially in modern settings. Consequently, these often recurring suggestions for an 'Islamic' cooperative insurance/hedging fund should exhibit a greater cognisance that they are, at best, long-term recommendations that host myriad systemic stress eventualities, which one way or another would require backing by public funds.

Moreover, there are serious practicality issues with some of the Islamic risk-sharing suggestions being proposed at the contractual-level (i.e., contractual hedging) (Al-Baz 1999; Al-Rubaia 1992; Al-Suwailem 2006: 120–38; Herak 1988: 87) whereby, for instance, the supplier and the producers share the bounties of the profits of the producer and his/her losses in some form of a mixed-sum game framework (rather than the perception of prohibition of zero-sum games).

This is because, apart from losing the benefits of risk consolidation (i.e., combination and diversification), these real-sector operators ought to be more focused on their core operations rather than on the issues and costs associated with contractual hedging, including credit exposure to the producer/supplier, monitoring costs and moral hazard as well as issues related to asymmetry of information. In fact, the contractual hedging proposition becomes even more unrealistic in the era of globalisation wherein an organisation's list of partners is increasingly international in nature and contains many who harbour no Islamic finance inclinations.

Other risk-sharing suggestions offered in Islamic finance circles, such as the asset swap schemes, are also arguably offering expensive and legally uncertain artificial religious forms to address a legitimate economic issue. Moreover, it appears that these propositions do not account for the low probability of the 'double coincidence of wants' between real-sector counterparts in that it is unlikely that there is an exact same hedging need and a comparable asset for the swap in order for the transaction to come to fruition.

Perhaps in an effort to address this difficulty of matching the wants of hedgers, Hassan proposes the involvement of banking institutions at the contractual-level (mainly through *Murabaha* contracts) as facilitators for the hedging of market risks (Hassan 2012: 26–8), although, once more, his suggestions involve multiple transactions to produce, as he admitted, essentially the same outcome as generated by conventional hedging (with added uncertainty and fees).

Thus, in light of the above, one can argue against the claims made by Askari *et al.* that 'since risk sharing is the foundation and a basic activity in Islamic finance, it is governed by rules that, if and when observed, lead to lower transaction costs than in conventional finance' (Askari *et al.* 2012: 71). Essentially, it is not entirely certain what these rules are, how can they be objectively observed in order to promote the professed desire for fair sharing or how it is that they relate to the issues and costs that were outlined earlier. This should be contextualised in a financial environment where the costs of risk transfer (e.g., spreads), consequent of competition and better market intelligence, have gone down significantly and thus provide an effective and efficient means to hedge market-risk exposures.

3.5 Rationale for hedging

Prior to continuing on to the next chapter with its focus on derivatives, it is perhaps necessary, for the sake of completeness, to delve into the rationale behind the desire for the relative safety of hedging rather than speculating on the movements of the financial markets with unhedged market-risk exposures. For this, one starts with the assumptions behind the rationale for pursuing hedging practices; these are: First, sources of finance (debt and equity[10]) are more expensive to a business than internally generated funds; second, in addition to being more expensive, the external sources of finance are not perfectly elastic in that higher levels of funding are met with an increase in the overall marginal cost; and, third, taxes are traditionally a convex function of earnings (i.e., higher earnings are taxed at a higher tax bracket than lower income).

The first reasoning for pursuing hedging practices, which was alluded to previously, is that they reduce the probability of financial distress and its associated costs. These comprise legal costs, the reduction in the value of the firm, diversion of management time and focus and the cessation of strategic and operational control. Of particular importance, especially when viewed from a normative Islamic perspective, are also the costs that affect a firm's commitment to its stakeholders (including employees, management, suppliers, customers and tax beneficiaries) in a financial distress scenario. The case of managers and employees are particularly severe consequent of their undiversified financial exposure to the firm.

The second reasoning is related to the growth potential and the prospect for above-average profitability by the companies that hedge their market-risk exposures, some of which may have tighter financial constraints (i.e., lack of desire or ability to access the costly debt and equity markets). Specifically, it has been argued extensively in the risk-management literature that the use of hedging instruments to ensure the sufficiency of internal funds, by reducing the variability of free cash flows, to take advantage of attractive investment opportunities, is a common strategic decision by managers. This is also especially valid in the context of the observed decreasing marginal returns to investments (i.e., output is a concave function of investment) (Bernstein

1996; Froot *et al.* 1993; Geczy *et al.* 1997; Lessard 1991; Shapiro and Titman 1985; Smith and Stulz 1985; Visvanathan and Schrand 1998).

Thus to return to the potential risk-retention strategy as outlined earlier and proposed by some in the Islamic finance industry in order to legitimise returns, companies that seek to employ that particular strategy are effectively being pressed to choose between a finite reserve system to face an unknown exposure to market risk (timing, magnitude, etc.), expensive external debt and equity financing or loss of profitable investment opportunities (and consequently a lower firm value). The evolution of this dilemma, at the macro-level, is likely to entail a reduction in private sector investment and an overall sluggishness in the economic progress of Islamic countries (i.e., not exactly an adherence to the theory of *Maslaha*).

The third rationale for hedging is linked to the competitiveness of companies operating in the real sector. In essence, in today's globalised landscape, managers, particularly in multinational companies, need to be able to rely on stable financial inputs, such as market interest and foreign exchange rates and commodity prices, for their operational planning and pricing decisions. Additionally, competitiveness can be enhanced further through the utilisation of hedging instruments to lower financial expenses by way of accessing 'cheaper' capital markets around the world.[11]

Eventually, the ability to hedge market-risk exposures can result in competitive and stable pricing that can contribute to not only the protection, but also the maximisation, of market share. Additionally, insofar that competition results in lower prices to consumers, the reduction of market-risk exposure by companies can produce higher societal welfare (i.e., *Maslaha*). This reasoning is also relevant to Islamic banking institutions that face competitive pressures in their home markets as well as in their efforts to seek cross-border market share enhancements.

The fourth, and final, justification for hedging discussed in this section focuses on the taxation of enterprises. As mentioned earlier in the discussion on the assumptions, many countries adopt a progressive tax system in order to add an element of fairness to their tax receipts whereby higher earnings are taxed at a higher tax bracket than lower earnings. In this setting, an increase in the volatility of earnings consequent of the exposure of market risks poses a real possibility that the risk-retention strategy entails a net enlargement of the tax liability. That is to say, the taxation of the abnormally high income at an elevated tax rate and the taxation of abnormally low income at the lower tax rate will most likely result in higher average taxes than the ones paid at the average moderate tax rate that reflects the earnings from core operations.

3.6 Conclusion

The contemporary risk challenges faced by real-sector companies, and the banks that finance their operations, are much different from those that were encountered by the early Muslim community in the seventh century, a period that provides the juristic basis for the current perspectives on the subject matter by the *Shari'ah* scholars. The introduction of the volatile-natured interest rates as benchmarks for asset pricing (including assets in the Islamic finance industry), floating exchange rates for cross-border dealings and unstable prices for commodities that serve as indispensable inputs for the real economic sectors have been shown to exert tremendous pressure on the profitability and survival of ordinary businesses.

In this chapter, the topic of market risk as well as the various frameworks that are available for institutions to deal with it, was examined in detail. For this, while it was stated that risk is an indispensable component in the search for profit, it has been also contended, with reasoned economic argumentation that builds on Islamic jurisprudence, that the relationship between risk and return is not an 'all or nothing' arrangement as viewed by some in the Islamic finance industry. It is, in fact, a relative relationship with the degree of return being a factor of the extent of riskiness involved. With that, the arguments on risk management in Islamic finance should transcend the discourse concentrating on the importance of associating risk with return, which is a given in economic thought, and move into the sphere of maximisation of *genuine* return and the minimisation of risk through *legitimate* means.

Subsequently, one can proceed to differentiate, through proper identification and measurement, between the controllable core risks whose presence is an integral part of the existence of a particular firm (e.g., operations and primary market) and the non-core exogenous risks (e.g., market risks) whose random nature makes their retention a rather speculative endeavour. In terms of the risk strategy, it has been shown that the risk-reduction and consolidation (i.e., combination and diversification) strategies, although useful for an enterprise, can only be complements, not substitutes, to the efficiency and effectiveness of the market-risk transfer strategy.

That being said, it is acknowledged that at the heart of the risk-transfer process are derivative instruments that, by virtue of their predesigned negative correlations with the specific market-risk exposure, can provide hedging opportunities to real-sector entities, which can, in turn, reduce the probability of financial distress, under-investment, loss of potential financing savings and market competitiveness and lower overall firm value.

To be certain, transacting in derivative contracts whose pricing behaviour is related to another underlying variable is currently not wholly limited to the hedging sphere. Effectively, it can be contended that speculation in the financial markets with financial instruments in the commodity, interest-rate and foreign exchange rate markets, which have grown tremendously over the same period, is also a culprit in the increase of market risks. However, the realisation of this contention, which is partly true, provides little relief from the serious consequences of unmanaged market risks to businesses operating in the real sector. In fact, a more logical argument could be put forth that the speculation with open market-risk exposures in the financial markets, and the resultant increases in volatilities, are more of a reason to ensure the implementation of an appropriate risk-management framework, which in turn requires the usage of hedging techniques and instruments within a broader risk-transfer strategy.

To that end, the next chapter will examine the economics and the rationale for the utilisation of these derivative instruments with a particular focus on market-risk management in order to address the often made association between these instruments and the prohibitions of *Riba* (usury), *Gharar* (excessive uncertainty) and *Maysir* (gambling).

Notes

1. In the context of the subject matter it is assumed here that psychology includes religious convictions.
2. For Islamic banks, the theory of Islamic investment accounts is not matched by the current banking practices of Islamic banks that offer banking products economically equivalent to their conventional counterparts.

3. For our purposes here, equity price risk will not be discussed since it is mainly related to capital market investments as opposed to operations in the real economy.

4. Hedging is characteristic of actions taken in order to reduce risks.

5. An investor in a mutual fund or a private equity investment traditionally has higher return expectations than has a regular depositor in a banking institution. Also, the inclusion of equities to the mix of financing by Islamic banks is expected to contribute to the higher expectations consequent of the increased uncertainty regarding the payoff.

6. Although in the financial markets instruments can, and on occasions (e.g., Long-Term Capital Management (LTCM)) do, exhibit a fat-tailed distribution that increases the risk associated with a severe loss scenario.

7. See OIC Fiqh Academy Resolution No. 63/1/7.

8. See OIC Fiqh Academy Resolution No. 9/9/2.

9. Even within the *Takaful* cooperative insurance model, there was a realisation by the *Shari'ah* scholars of the need to engage in risk transfer for reinsurance. This was evidenced in the AAOIFI *Shari'ah* Standard No. 41 ('Islamic Reinsurance'). Effectively, the nature of the reinsurance, Islamic or conventional, is the transfer of risk that is deemed excessive for its reserve base.

10. The (additional) equity infusion into the firm is costly to current shareholders in terms of dilution of their control and benefits.

11. For example, a real-sector borrower can utilise a swap to borrow in financial markets where they have a comparative advantage (tenor, fixed/floating, currency, etc.) and can swap this exposure to their desired position (tenor, fixed/floating, currency, etc.) for an overall cost saving. There are potential diversification benefits to this strategy as well. Finally, these

hedging instruments can help a company become flexible to changes to its operations and market conditions over the life of the market risk exposure (e.g., changes in projected sales, the currency basket and raw materials).

CHAPTER 4

CONVENTIONAL DERIVATIVES: THEORY AND PRACTICE

4.0 Introduction

This chapter continues with the discourse on the topic of market-risk management in Islamic finance that commenced in the last chapter but with a focus here on the economics of the derivative instruments themselves as tools that facilitate the transfer of market risk. Specifically, the formulation of the pricing of the derivative instruments along with their relationship to prices in the cash markets for the underlying variables will be examined in a manner that anticipates the views of some of the contemporary *Shari'ah* scholars and academics regarding these tools that will be the focus of the next chapter. Moreover, the technicalities of the utilisation of derivatives as hedging tools will also be explored through individual assessments of these instruments.

4.1 Economics of derivatives

The basis for the creation and evolution of any financial instrument is inherently an economic one. Thus, to fully understand the technicalities of the derivative instruments, one should look at the economic theories that underlie their existence. To that end, economics is defined by Marshall as the 'study of mankind in the ordinary business of life; it examines that part of individual and social action which is most closely connected with the attainment and with the use of the material requisites of wellbeing' (Marshall 1910: 1). Robbins adds further granularity by stating that economics, as a science, 'studies human behaviour as a relationship between ends and scarce means which have alternative uses' (Robbins 2007 [1932]: 16).

An economic system, for its part, manages that relationship by focusing on the efficient allocation and distribution, across time and space, of resources between economic agents in a manner that strives for the attainment of the most valuable uses of those resources. It is within this conceptualisation that derivatives, much like equity and fixed-income securities, perform their main function of the temporal and spatial shifting of risk and return to different market participants.

A derivative is normally characterised as being a financial instrument created as a result of a bilateral contract or payment exchange agreement whose value is based on (or derived from) the value of another underlying variable such as a physical asset, a reference rate or a benchmark. The underlying variables in the case of the market risks that will be examined comprise benchmarks for interest rates (the London Interbank Offered Rate (LIBOR) or Treasury rates), foreign exchange rates and/or actual commodity prices.

However, despite sharing with equities and fixed-income securities an analogous economic function, derivatives are unique financial instruments for four main reasons. First, a derivative instrument can, through time, oscillate between being an asset having an ownership claim over a positive monetary value and becoming a liability with a negative charge. In terms of valuation, it should be emphasised that the notional amounts in the derivative contracts do not provide an accurate measure of the level of asset or liability (and any associated risk exposures) as is the case with the face value of the other securities. This is because the actual amount of the asset or liability implicit in a particular derivative contract is connected to its 'replacement cost' in the financial markets, which is, in turn, dependent on the prevailing interest rates, exchange rates and/or commodity prices. In other words, the valuation of a particular derivative instrument is related to the cost it would take a counterparty to purchase a similar contract in the financial markets with the same economic value as the one provided by the derivative instrument.

Second, as demonstrated by Nobel laureate J.R. Hicks (1931), derivative contracts contain an explicit time element in that there is traditionally a delay in the delivery of *both* the underlying asset and the transfer of cash in order to settle a liability claim. Specifically, a spot transaction in the cash markets, which is the basis for most of the contracts in Islamic finance, entails an immediate payment by the buyer (or a credit agreement) in return for prompt delivery by the seller. However, a derivative instrument normally involves the payment for and the receipt of an asset at a time that is different from the time that the contract is concluded. Thus, in broad terms, derivative contracts can be considered as facilitators of asset transfers over time and space between economic agents who have diverse sets of opportunities and constraints.

Third, a derivative instrument can be used exclusively as a hedging mechanism in the risk-transfer process outlined in the previous chapter. This is in contrast to other financial instruments that serve mainly as investment and resource mobilisation vehicles. In essence, while a derivative instrument cannot be used to reduce the market risks that are associated with the ownership or production of assets, they can assist in the transfer of these risks, as part of a wider market-risk management framework, to either another hedger with an offsetting exposure or a financial intermediary who is more willing and able to bear them.[1]

For this, a hedger can enter into a *short hedge* where the already owned, but perhaps incomplete, asset is expected to be sold at some time in the future (e.g., crops or oil) or for an asset that is currently not owned but will be owned after a period of time (e.g., a foreign currency receivable by an exporter). Alternatively, a *long hedge* is utilised for taking a position in a derivative contract to lock in the price of an asset or exposure that will have to be settled in the future (e.g., interest rates or fuel for aircraft).

To be certain, derivatives can be, and have been, used as investment products by market participants, excessively in some circumstances, who seek to benefit from the flexibility offered by these instruments and their lower transaction costs to synthetically create exposures with tailored risk and return preferences. However, it is the usage of derivatives as hedging instruments for market risks that is the focus of this chapter and indeed the purpose of the discussion in this book.

Fourth, while equities and fixed-income securities primarily provide an indication of the value of a particular company and its credit quality, respectively (and presumably also a signal of wider market sentiment), derivatives, because they derive their values from market variables, provide an exceptional opportunity for price discovery of many financial and commodity products in a centralised and more inclusive marketplace. Effectively, the open market bidding system and real-time price dissemination reduce the asymmetry of information between buyers and sellers participating not only in the same market but also in similar markets around the globe. For example, a farmer has an opportunity to learn of the prices paid for his crop in his home market as well as in other regions of the world.

The attainment of the aforementioned price discovery is a product of market intelligence and analysis (mainly by financial intermediaries) as well as the economic Law of One Price and the theory of arbitrage. For market intelligence and analysis, advances in communication and information technology (IT) in addition to the use of sophisticated mathematical and statistical techniques by ever-skilled market participants have resulted in a pricing system that is a much closer approximation of market equilibrium (that is never static).

The Law of One Price, for its part, is significant in that it not only prices the derivative instruments but is also the driving force in the pricing of the underlying variables (i.e., interest and exchange rates in addition to commodity prices). Basically, in efficient financial markets,[2] the Law of One Price states that all identical goods with the same payoff structure for one, or multiple, point(s) of time in the future should have the same price at the present time.

The facilitator for the attainment of the outcomes of the Law of one Price is the theory and practice of arbitrage that serves an important role by ensuring pricing convergence, based on economic fundamentals, of identical goods in different markets. In essence, arbitrageurs, in striving to make profits by utilising the base-rate market rates (e.g., LIBOR) for borrowing (lending) and simultaneously buying (selling) similar financial products in different markets in order to take advantage of any price discrepancies, are crucial to preserving the harmony between the cash and derivatives markets.

The significance of the Law of One Price and the theory of arbitrage in the hedging sphere is in the fact that they both allow hedgers to rely on derivative instruments and their stable correlation with the cash markets to appropriately transfer their market-risk exposures. Furthermore, the Law of One Price and the theory of arbitrage exert convergence pressures between the various derivative instruments (e.g., forwards, futures and swaps) whose payoff structures are equivalent and bear the same relationships to goods in the cash markets.

With that background, and in light of the on-coming examination of financial instruments, including the so-called 'Islamic derivatives', it is important to understand that the Law of One Price and the theory of arbitrage apply to any financial instrument being traded and/or any financial instrument that uses similar underlying variables for pricing in the financial markets.

In effect, given that, first, hedgers utilise derivative instruments, and their stable correlations with the cash market, to hedge market-risk exposures, second, any Islamic derivative instrument has to perform the same hedging function as the one performed by its conventional counterpart since the market-risk exposures are all-encompassing (i.e., the exposure to market risks is not peculiar to Islamic institutions), and, third, if the underlying variable in both the conventional and Islamic derivative instruments are identical (e.g., foreign exchange or oil), then the pricing of the conventional and Islamic derivative instruments *will be the same at any given time*. The added complexity of contemporary Islamic derivative contracts along with the inclusion of non-precious commodities, multiple contracts and numerous agents to the structure of the transaction will not change that economic reality. In fact, if anything, the latter are likely to exacerbate the market-risk management challenges for companies operating in the real sector (see Chapter 5).

Apart from the conceptual framework (i.e., Law of One Price and theory of arbitrage) that regulates the pricing of derivatives, the economics behind the actual attainment of the pricing of the derivative instruments should also be considered in order to enlighten the current legal-centric discourse in the Islamic finance industry on the subject matter, particularly in the focus areas of the prohibitions of *Riba* (usury) and *Gharar* (excessive uncertainty). Essentially, the pricing of any derivative instrument is centred on Black's (1976) cost-of-carry formula whereby market interest rates, the cost of storing an asset and its convenience yield are analysed by market participants in order to develop expectations regarding the future prices of the underlying assets.

For market interest rates, as discussed in Chapter 3, the prohibition of *Riba* in Islamic finance, while addressing the legitimate issue of indebtedness within a society, is less relevant when it comes to the pricing of assets and liabilities in contemporary financial markets. This is because interest rates are used in this context to account for the preferences and perceptions of economic agents as well as as a benchmark for the uncertainty associated with the holding period of a particular financial instrument. Specifically, the pricing of any financial instrument (including Islamic contracts) is dependent, in part, on the discounted cash flows over its life. The tool used to discount the cash flows of tradable financial instruments is traditionally the base rate, which is customarily either the market-determined LIBOR or the Treasury rates.

Notably, the base rate is also used for the pricing structure within the framework of the Law of One Price. This is done in two ways. First, the base rate is used to account for the borrowing and lending taking place by arbitrageurs to exploit any mispricing in the financial markets.[3] Second, given that the base rate is used to discount the cash flows of financial instruments, the theory of arbitrage ensures that the relationship between the spot prices and the prices for the instruments in the future is stable in that it depends on the timing and amount of the cash flows.

In addition to the market interest-rate considerations and insofar as the prices of the derivative instruments are based on the pricing behaviour of the assets themselves, the storage costs and the convenience yields are also considered important factors in the derivative pricing formula. Storage costs are mainly applied in the pricing of the derivatives associated with commodities (cereal, cocoa, oil, gold, etc.) by considering it as a negative income. Essentially, storage costs can be considered as either a discounted cash outflow occurring at particular time intervals or as simply a constant cost proportion of the market prices.

Convenience yields, on the other hand, serve a vital function in the pricing of derivative instruments in the commodities markets in that they distinguish between the value generated from owning the derivative instrument vis-à-vis actually possessing the underlying variable. Moreover, the convenience yields also serve as a barometer of market sentiment regarding the supply-and-demand forces that shape the pricing structure of a particular asset.

In effect, there are particular benefits (i.e., utility) in holding an asset as opposed to holding a financial instrument whose value is derived from that asset. An oil refinery, for instance, is likely to view having an inventory of crude oil to ensure continuous production in addition to profit from any temporary shortages as having a greater usefulness than simply having a derivative contract with crude oil as an underlying (i.e., synthetic inventory). Moreover, to account for the diverse benefits accruing to the various institutions storing the asset, the level of the utility of the convenience yield is a product of the equilibrium obtained from the competition between the various users of the asset.

It should be stated here that it is not self-evident in the writings of many critics of forward-based derivatives vis-à-vis their 'Islamic' alternatives, particularly *Salam* (forward sale) and *Bay Ajel* (deferred payment sale) contracts, that there is the recognition of this component in the pricing of derivative instruments. More specifically, the argumentation by Al-Suwailem (1999), for example, espousing the position that the Islamic temporal contracts of commerce have different payoffs than conventional derivatives lacks empirical evidence. On the contrary, the inclusion of the convenience yield in the cost-of-carry pricing formula, as indicated above, is precisely accounting for the issue of 'real exchange effects' that he seeks to address – although he does so in a manner that paradoxically criticises conventional derivatives. In other words, Al-Suwailem's remarks reinforce the convenience yield component in the cost-of-carry formula for derivative pricing.

An additional aspect of the convenience yield is its use as a mechanism to express the market expectations regarding, what Stevens calls, 'the adaptation of the probable supplies to anticipated requirements' (Stevens 1887: 62). In essence, the market perception regarding the economic fundamentals of a particular asset is internalised within the convenience yield as a measure of not only the utility derived from owning and storing the asset, but also the expectations regarding this utility in the future.

Notably, the importance of the storage costs and convenience yields is relevant only in the commodity sphere, as it formulates the relationship between spot prices and futures prices. The markets of monetary financial derivatives, however, such as those relating to interest and foreign exchange rates, do not contain storage cost or convenience yield elements; otherwise arbitrage opportunities will present themselves, resulting in the ultimate disappearance of these non-applicable variables.

That said, the pricing for these monetary financial derivatives does share with their commodity counterparts the interest-rate component in the cost-of-carry model even if it is distinctive in that the interest-rate component is adjusted in order to account for the differentials in the interest rates across the countries. This is to conform to the arbitrage-free interest-rate parity relationship of international finance.

The discussion of the economics of derivatives is significant in two respects. First, it indicates the value of utilising derivative instruments to achieve an optimal allocation and distribution of resources (including their associated risk and return) among economic agents across time. Second, it provides important insights that can serve to alleviate some of the *Shari'ah* concerns that often circulate in the discourse on derivative contracts, namely the perceived association between them and the prohibitions of *Gharar* and *Riba*.

For *Gharar*, it should be realised that the existence of derivatives actually reduces *Gharar* by allowing market participants to decrease not only the uncertainty with how the prices of assets are derived in the cash markets, but also the doubt associated with the pricing of assets at different times in the future. This is achieved, as outlined previously, by way of an all-inclusive (base rate plus storage costs minus the convenience yield) and transparent price discovery process that is made available to all relevant stakeholders (farmers, producers, customers and government bodies, among others). Indeed, with respect to the charges of dealing in *Gharar* consequent of uncertainty of the price in the future, Kamali (2000) has argued (through articulation of the opinions of Ibn Taymiyyah, Ibn Al-Qayyim, Musa, Sulayman and Hasan) that it has been accepted in Islamic jurisprudence to set a future market price for a contract on the condition that it is agreeable to both parties and of a level of clarity that eliminates any dispute.

In regards to *Riba*, it may be apparent at this stage that interest rates are employed in the context of the base-level cost of capital that is used to discount the cash flows of any asset or liability (including all assets/liabilities in Islamic financial markets), all the while adhering to the arbitrage-free pricing structure that ensures that market prices are in equilibrium. Notwithstanding the above, it is remarkable that the criticisms hailed at the derivative instruments consequent of its supposed handling of *Riba* (in the form of the base rate for pricing) are done at a time when there seems to be a wide agreement among *Shari'ah* scholars on the acceptability of the usage of LIBOR as a benchmark that integrates the economic choices associated with consumption and with saving through time.[4]

With that added understanding of the economics of derivatives, it may be now appropriate to proceed to the examination of the various derivative instruments existing in the global financial markets and how their individual traits have led to particular preferences by hedgers in utilising them to off-set their specific market-risk exposures. The implication of this discussion will become ostensible in the next chapter in which the attempts to associate these derivative instruments with pre-modern 'Islamic' contracts through the theory of *Qiyas* (analogical reasoning) will be delineated along with the legal-centric endeavours at financial engineering to replicate their payoff structure.

4.2 Conventional derivative instruments

All derivative contracts are built from two basic and fundamental building blocks – forwards and options.

Forward-based instruments include forwards, swaps and futures, while the option-based contracts not only contain options on tradable assets as a stand-alone instrument but also can be made 'exotic' through innovative structures that seek to construct an almost unlimited array of transactions and strategies.

Broadly speaking, a forward contract is a relatively simple contract that is negotiated between two counterparties whereby a binding commitment is made for specific terms of agreement for the purchase/sale of an asset in the future, which, in turn, is based on the particular needs of the counterparties. The terms of agreement are fixed for the duration of the contract and include the price at maturity (forward price), the contract size, the quality and the location and time of delivery.

Notably, the initiation of the contract is completed by agreement without any payment exchanging hands between the counterparties. At maturity, the long hedge receives the underlying variable in the contract from the short hedge in return for the forward price. If the parties agree, however, then the contract can be cash-settled and in such as case the cash-equivalent value, based on the prices in the financial markets, of the underlying variable is given by the short hedge to the long hedge in lieu of the asset itself.

The basis for the allowance of cash-settlement for hedging transactions is that the transaction itself is meant to manage the market risks associated with a particular exposure rather than to ensure delivery of a specific asset at a precise time. Essentially, a hedger, for a commodity risk exposure, for instance, is likely to want to continue with the existing relationship with its current suppliers based on an already established supply chain (with preferences for delivery location, grade, size, transport and so forth), even if those suppliers are not in a position to provide a viable hedging counterparty to the business in question.

Put differently, a hedging transaction should not force real-sector companies to alter their operational decisions in order to respond to market risks. In fact, the whole purpose of market risks' management is for businesses to effectively manage their market-risk exposures without the need to make costly changes to their modus operandi. In the realm of derivatives with a financial variable as an underlying, the delivery is either impractical (e.g., LIBOR) or just simply adds to the transaction costs in an era of electronic banking (e.g., currency).

That said, the cash-settlement feature in modern derivative instruments also allows pure speculators to enter the derivative markets, which is evidently a major concern for *Shari'ah* scholars (see Chapter 5 and Chapter 7). However, while it is acknowledged that the excesses of speculation have been prominent in the contribution to global financial instability, it should be recognised that the forcing of delivery, besides constraining the risk-management potential for derivative instruments by imposing operational inconveniences and transaction costs on true hedgers, will likely serve to only limit speculation in the derivative markets; that is, they will not eliminate it. This is because the costs of delivery by pure speculators, much like with pure speculative traders in the spot market, will simply be included in the transaction costs within a wider cost–benefit analysis of pure speculative endeavours.

In terms of valuation, at initiation, the forward contract has no value because in an arbitrage-free setting the maturity price is an approximation of the future spot price; otherwise, *arbitrageurs* would exploit the market differentials, which would return the forward contract to a zero valuation setting. Throughout the life of the contract the valuation of the forward contract will likely fluctuate in order to respond to spot market pricing changes of the underlying variable. The actual direction and size of fluctuation, for its part, is dependent on the degree of change in the economic fundamentals affecting that particular variable and the belief about potential changes in the future.

At maturity, if the forward price (i.e., contractually agreed to price) is higher than the prevailing price of the asset in the spot market then the long hedge (short hedge) makes a profit (loss) and vice versa. This zero-sum payoff structure between the counterparties should largely offset the market-risk exposure in a true hedging transaction. Put differently, the purchase of the forward contract that is negatively correlated to the market-risk exposure will counterbalance any gains or losses experienced consequent of the changes in prices in the spot markets in the future.

Moreover, for the purpose of Islamic jurisprudence that is quite averse to the accumulation of debt and the unjust exploitation that may result in the process, it needs to be emphasised that a forward contract is not considered to be debt in a true sense. This is consequent of three main reasons. First, at the most fundamental level, as discussed earlier, a forward contract does not have a value at initiation. Second, after initiation, a forward contract does not have a face value or a predefined, one-sided, cash-flow stream; it simply contains a commitment by the counterparties to transact on a variable with specific terms of agreement in the future. Third, despite the presence of counterparty risks, a forward contract does not have a predefined creditor/debtor structure at initiation; in fact, the exact party to benefit financially from the contract will only be made apparent at maturity. Thus, with that distinction, it may become apparent that the classification of forward transactions as debt by some contemporary *Shari'ah* scholars as well as the drawing of analogies between the derivative instruments and the financial exploitation that is a fundamental part of usurious transactions is an inaccurate characterisation.

In terms of the variables underlying the contracts, these can range from agricultural and physical commodities to currencies (i.e., foreign exchange forwards) and interest rates (i.e., foreign rate agreements (FRAs)). The commodity forward contracts are quite straightforward in that they outline the purchase of a particular commodity in the future at a particular price. The foreign exchange forwards entail the exchange of specific amounts of notional currencies between the counterparties at a designated date in the future.

A forward rate agreement, for its part, is a contract defining interest rates that will apply to the borrowing and lending of a particular notional principle in the future. The base rate often used is LIBOR but it can be any predefined interest rate that is correlated with the desired interest-rate exposure for one, or both, of the counterparties (e.g., profit rate). The reverse position in the forward contract is a fixed rate of interest that ensures an arbitrage-free interest-rate parity position for the duration of the contract at its initiation. The overall purpose of this form of transaction in a true hedging scenario is the implementation of an effective asset-liability management (ALM) policy in institutions exposed to interest-rate risk.

Besides contributing to the effective management of interest-rate risks in the financial markets, the FRAs also serve an important role in the price discovery process for financial assets by aiding in the determination of the interest-rate curve. Essentially, through interpolation from existing FRAs trading with specific maturities, the financial markets can derive market interest rates even for those maturities with no tradable derivative instruments. This benefit allows companies and financial institutions to properly strategise their financial structure in future periods based on the costs and opportunities existing in the financial markets. That is, the presence of the interest-rate curve, as derived from the FRAs, helps the market participants reduce the uncertainty (e.g., *Gharar*) associated with financial planning.

Futures, as the second form of derivative instruments examined in the risk-transfer strategy, are similar to forward contracts in that there is a binding commitment between two parties to buy or sell a specified underlying variable for a certain price on the contract maturity date. However, there are a number of differences between forward and futures contracts that should be clarified for an added understanding of these instruments.

First, the futures contracts are traded in a centralised exchange as opposed to in the over-the-counter (OTC) market where most forwards (and swaps; see below) are traded. The exchange, which is a voluntary association of its members, provides buyers and sellers of the futures contracts the infrastructure (location and IT systems), legal framework (rules and arbitration procedures) and clearing mechanisms to ensure a smooth and unambiguous transaction process.

Second, apart from the determination of the pricing of futures by the laws of supply and demand (as with all derivatives), the parties to a futures contract do not negotiate the terms of the agreement since these are standardised by the exchange where they are traded. These terms of agreement are: the quantity and quality of the underlying variable, the time and place of delivery and the method of payment. In the hedging sphere, the standardisation of the futures contracts with specific quantities, specifications as to quality and particular delivery dates around the year compels the hedging party to seek a contract that most resembles, but perhaps does not exactly match, the factors that define its market-risk exposure. This hedging behaviour in the futures markets can explain the early settlement tendencies by even the pure hedging parties in the futures markets.

To illustrate, an oil refinery with a long hedge on oil futures that is no longer needed will close out that position by assuming a short hedge position of the exact same contract in the futures market. Similarly, a financial institution with a terminated interest-rate exposure will seek to close the open futures contract (Eurodollar deposits or Treasury bills/notes/bonds) with another that offsets it. In effect, once the original market-risk exposure is terminated for a hedging party, it can proceed to offset its open position with a contract that is equal (quantity, quality, date, etc.) but the reverse (buy/sell) of its open futures contracts in order to assume a zero net exposure in the derivatives market.

With that, it is acknowledged that the standardisation of the futures contracts has also contributed to the emergence of a new class of traders in the futures markets that have no concurrent exposure to the cash markets and no intention to deliver or receive the underlying variables. Essentially, they are simply motivated by the profit potential from trading in the commodities/financial variable markets in the future and accordingly proceed to open and close futures contract positions in response to market opportunities that present themselves.

However, as stated previously within the discussion on forward contracts, the imposition of delivery is not the proper means to eliminate gambling behaviour in the financial markets. For besides the negative effects to the hedging community, especially since the contracts are not tailored to the specific exposures of the various hedging parties, the forced delivery will be simply considered as a transaction cost by the pure speculators much like the costs of the margin system are (see below). The eventual outcome will be a framework that comprises higher transaction costs with no discernible benefits.

Interestingly, the often quoted figures of very low delivery ratios for futures contracts is likely a result of *both* the lack of tailored contracts for hedgers and the presence of pure speculators – not a simple representation of a function of the latter. Along the same lines, for the cash-futures link, it is not the actual delivery that is important in the context of the pricing of the futures contracts but it is actually the prospect of delivery. This is because the presence of the prospect of delivery, and indeed the requirement for delivery for those who have not offset their contracts prior to maturity, serves the same role by forging the cash-futures link whereby the futures price is approximately equal to the cash price at the expiration of the contract. In other words, contrary to some beliefs about the futures markets by some *Shari'ah* scholars (see the next chapter), the derivatives markets do not exist in a vacuum of pure gambling that is completely detached from the activities and prices in the real economy.

The third difference between forward and futures contracts is that the counterparties do not actually trade with each other but rather enter directly into a futures contract with the exchange itself, which becomes the buyer to every seller and the seller to every buyer. This system was designed with the intention of reducing the risks of default by the counterparties as well as facilitating the clearance activities of the futures market participants. Thus, within the framework of futures, the counterparties are, in effect, liable to the exchange for performance, and if a particular counterparty defaults on a futures contract, the exchange honours the contract to the other counterparty by the absorption of the loss from its own reserves. To that end, the financial integrity of the exchange is sustained by a process called marking-to-market (see below) along with the establishment of margin accounts by the members of the exchange.

The margin accounts are accounts by the party with an open position in the exchange that benefits from and absorbs the losses from market fluctuations. At the initiation of the contract, the margin account usually requires funds totalling about 2 to 5 per cent of the value of the underlying assets of the futures contract and can be paid in cash or by pledging securities at a discounted value in order to avoid cash payments. Further, the initial margin is also a function of the volatility of the price of the underlying variable and the nature of the client entering into a particular futures contract (i.e., hedger versus pure speculator).

Specifically, a higher volatility in the market prices of the underlying variable and/or the adoption of speculative motives by the transacting party will necessitate higher initial margin requirements while lower pricing volatility and a bona fide hedging profile allow for a lower initial margin consequent of the lesser risks of default. Thus, the margin system should be thought of as a performance bond or as a good faith deposit and not as a premium (as in options) or as leverage (as in debt) for the transaction.

Fourth, the futures contracts are effectively rewritten every trading day at the new futures price consequent of exchange rules stipulating daily mark-to-market of open positions. Hence, as with the forward contracts' zero-valuation at initiation consequent of the theory of arbitrage, the futures contracts have a valuation of zero at the beginning of every trading day until maturity. This feature, in effect, makes futures contracts similar to a forward contract paid for on a unique instalment plan that is a factor of the movement of the market prices throughout the duration of the contract.

Essentially, the buyers (sellers) of the futures contracts

are expected to make (receive) daily instalment payments towards the eventual purchase (sale) of the underlying asset for the price stipulated in the futures contract. When the contract matures, the buyer and the seller of the underlying asset will have already paid/received the difference between the initial price in the futures contract and the futures price at maturity, which, as mentioned earlier, will equal the spot price prevailing in the financial markets in an arbitrage-free setting consequent of the prospect of delivery.

The third derivative instrument that will be examined is the swap contract. In a swap, the counterparties agree to exchange periodic payments based on a predetermined amount of principle at specified intervals that usually extend into the medium- to long-term timeframe. The payments, in turn, can either be fixed or they may float with an agreed-upon benchmark that varies over time.

Essentially, one set of the cash flows is the one associated with a party's market-risk exposure and the second set of cash flows is related to their desired exposure based on the status of their balance sheet and future operational expectations. These cash flows can be related to interest and currency rates as well as commodity prices. However, given that commodity swaps are not a large part of the swaps market and when they are utilised they are traditionally viewed as tailored investment products rather than as hedging instruments, the assessment of the swap market will focus on interest-rate swaps and currency swaps.

The 'plain-vanilla' interest-rate swap, that is the most common type of swap, involves the exchange of a fixed set of interest-rate payments for a floating set on a common principle amount by counterparties known as the fixed-rate payer (long hedge) and the floating-rate payer (short hedge). The floating side of the periodic payments is usually linked to LIBOR or some other variable interest rate, while the fixed rate, for its part, is broken down into two components: a Treasury note yield and a swap spread. Basically, the fixed rate is determined by using the yield on the most recently issued (and usually the most liquid) Treasury note with the same maturity as the swap along with the spread added on by the financial intermediary that accounts for its fees (hedging and operating costs plus profit) as well as the premium for the default and liquidity risks.

Notably, the principle is only 'notional' in that there is not the actual exchange at the beginning or at the end of the contract because there is no economic value to parties exchanging exactly the same amount of money at exactly the same moment in time. Moreover, it is market convention that settlements are made on a net basis in that, based on the movements of the market interest rates, the party owing the larger amount will simply pay the other party the difference.

Currency swaps are different from the interest-rate swaps in that the counterparties engage in the spot exchange of the principle at inception, the payment of the cash flow streams at specific dates for the duration of the contract and then there is the reversal of the swap with the re-exchange of the principle at the agreed-upon maturity, all of which are denominated in two different currencies. The contracts can be more flexible by defining the intermediary cash flows as being fixed-fixed, fixed-floating or floating-floating in the benchmark rates of the different currencies. Needless to say, the flexibility of the currency swaps, while meaning tailored hedging products, makes the pricing of the instruments more complex and precludes payment netting.

Thus, as demonstrated by the aforementioned description of the interest-rate and currency swaps, the essential variables in each swap contract are the level of the fixed rate, the manner in which the variable rate is determined, the scale of the transaction (i.e., notional principle), the currency of the cash flows, the dates of periodic payments along with the date of maturity and the events of default. These negotiated variables, which are a function of the preferences of the counterparties, serve as the fundamental elements for pricing and valuation.

With that, there are two basic approaches to the pricing and valuation of swaps. The first, and simpler, approach is to view the swap as the exchange of two hypothetical securities.[5] For example, in an interest-rate swap, the fixed-rate payer can be viewed as the seller of the fixed-rate bond in return for the floating-rate bond given by the floating-rate payer. Alternatively, in the second approach, the swap can be considered as a series of forward transactions extending until the maturity date. An exporter, for instance, who utilises currency swaps to manage currency risks is effectively entering into successive foreign currency forwards for specific durations (e.g., six months) with known but different fixed rates for each period that continue until the currency exposure is terminated.

Thus, with the assumptions that, one, the floating- and the fixed-rate securities sell at par at initiation (i.e., the cash flows are discounted at the relevant interest rate), two, the forward interest rates are realised, three, the term structure of interest rates is upward sloping, and, four, the presence of arbitrage-free market conditions (i.e., that any mispricing in the securities given their defining features will be eliminated by market forces), the interest-rate swaps fixed rate will be a present value of the average of forward rates for the duration of the swap.

For the currency swaps, the same set of assumptions apply with the addition that it is also presumed that the forward exchange rates, in addition to the interest rates in each currency's home market, are realised. As for cash flows, if the interest rates are different for the two currencies, it can be construed that the payer of the higher interest rates throughout the duration of the swap will have a positive final exchange and vice versa.

In terms of valuation, the value of any swap instrument (a.k.a. its 'replacement cost') is, one, the difference in the values of the two hypothetical securities, and/or, two, the present value of the difference between the application of the average forward rates (i.e., the fixed rate) and the floating rate to the notional principle. As a practical matter, the calculation of the value of a swap instrument can be undertaken by direct observation of prices and rates in the financial markets (e.g., OTC-traded FRAs or exchange-traded futures) or through the interpolation process, which, as described earlier, is based on inferences from available market variables. Notably, in an arbitrage-free setting, the hypothetical security or FRA-based pricing, whether done by direct observation or by calculation, will always be the same.

The discussion in this section thus far has focused on the forward-based contracts, which included an in-depth review of the economics of the forwards, futures and swaps. The remainder of this section will concentrate on an examination of the option-based contracts, as the second form of derivative instruments, with the aspiration that this should provide a more complete picture of the derivative markets.

The option contract is the foundation of all the option-based instruments, which can include very sophisticated derivative strategies[6] that are more innovative than those offered by forward-based contracts. The sophistication of the option strategies, and the concomitant growth in options trading, were an outcome of the Black-Scholes-Merton mathematical modelling that was developed in 1973 in papers by Black and Scholes as well as Merton in addition to the establishment of the Chicago Board of Options Exchange in the same year.

There are essentially two types of options: the call option and the put option. A call option gives the holder the right to buy a specific underlying variable by or at a certain date (depending on the nature of the option[7]) at a predetermined price. The put option, on the other hand, gives the holder the right to sell a specific underlying variable by or at a certain date at a predetermined price. Notably, the right by the holder of the option is not an obligation on his/ her part to 'exercise' the option. This is in contrast to the obligation by the writer of the option to honour the right of the holder to exercise the option in the framework that is stipulated in the contract (maturity, exercise price, underlying asset, etc.). In return for the rights contained in the option contract, the holder of the option pays a premium to the option writer as a form of compensation for the risk exposure.

Thus, the option contract is, for many reasons, fundamentally different from the forward-based contracts outlined earlier. First, while the obligations in the forward-based contracts are mutual, the responsibility for performance in the option contract rests solely with the option writer. This supplants the nature of the mutual risk transfer, and shared asset/liability classification, that is present between the counterparties in forward-based contracts. Second, entrance into a forward-based contract is cost-less for the counterparties (except for possibly the cost of the margin account for the futures market and the collateral in swaps and forward markets), while the commencement of an option contract entails an explicit fee payment from the option holder to the option writer.

Third, whereas the hedging strategies of the forward-based instruments are linear in nature, in that these instruments, for the most part, exactly offset market-risk exposures, the option instruments are non-linear in that they eliminate exposure to adverse market movements all the while allowing the option holder to benefit from favourable ones. In essence, option contracts are more akin to insurance than true hedging because their value to the holder, after the payment of the premium, is either positive or zero.

Aside from the contractual differences, the option contract offers a much different pricing and valuation structure than the one presented earlier under the various forward-based contracts. Essentially, the valuation of an option as per the Merton-Scholes model is dependent on, one, the market price of the underlying variable; two, the exercise price of the option; three, the time to expiration of the option; fourth, the volatility of the market price of the underlying variable; and, five, the base rate over the life of the option.

From these factors, two sets of values materialise in the valuation of option instruments: the intrinsic value and the time value. The intrinsic value of an option to its holder is the greater of either zero (if a negative value) or the difference between the market price and the exercise price (if a positive value). The time value is any premium that the market adds to the value of the option that is greater than the intrinsic value. This premium is greatly affected by the time to maturity and the volatility in the market price of the underlying asset. In effect, the longer that is the time to maturity and the higher the volatility, the greater the market premium for the option (and vice versa). Thus, as time passes, the only way that the value of the option remains constant or increases is by way of an increase in volatility in the price of the underlying.

Thus, one may discern that, apart from the non-linearity and the asymmetry of the payoff of the hedging function, the actual pricing of the options poses challenges to its effective use in the risk-management sphere. These challenges revolve around the valuation of the option that is to be used and its effectiveness in offsetting the adverse market-risk movements affecting the actual exposure to the underlying asset. For, while the relationship between the valuation of the forward-based derivatives and the price of the underlying asset is relatively constant throughout the duration of the contract, such a case is not apparent with options that are considerably affected by the factors stated earlier, not the least of which is volatility.

Eventually, the utilisation of options in a hedging strategy requires a much more dynamic risk-transfer approach that should be continuously adjusted in a process named 'delta hedging'. This process, which seeks to ensure a fairly perfect hedge, entails the continual adjustment of the hedging position to account for the effects that time and volatility (along with stochastic interest rates) exert on the value of the option. This, of course, imposes the need for constant monitoring and analysis by the hedger along with the necessary transaction costs to implement the required changes.

The above discussion on the utilisation of options demonstrated serious issues (maybe even shortcomings) with their usage in pure hedging scenarios, especially when compared with the linearity and relative certainty of the pay-offs of forward-based contracts along with the simplicity of their utilisation for market-risk management. In effect, the unique nature of the forward-based contracts endows it with a form of risk sharing between the counterparties rather than a one-way system that is based on a right to one party and one obligation by another. Moreover, the importance of volatility in the pricing of options has arguably imposed negative systemic implications in that it provides an incentive to the financial markets to generate profits from option-based strategies through manipulating volatility.

From the foregoing analysis, it can be construed that one would have an easier task defending the market-risk hedging argumentation by way of the utilisation of forward-based derivative instruments (i.e., linear risk and return payoffs) in Islamic finance settings than their option-based counterparts because of the undeniably speculative characteristics of the option-based strategies, even if they are used for hedging. This is stated despite claims to the contrary in some of the Islamic finance literature (for example, Kamali 2000: 181–2; Obaidullah 1998: 100).[8]

To be sure, it has been contended that there are situations (e.g., contingent liabilities) in which options are most effective in hedging, such as in, for example, the usage of options by contractors to hedge currency and commodity exposures as part of a bidding process (Bacha 1999: 8) or by farmers who are eager to hedge *both* the price and the quantity of their production (Al-Amine 2008: 201).

However, while these contentions are true to some extent, it is also apparent that speculation is not a remote eventuality in the usage of options as hedging instruments. In effect, for the bidding argument, the pure hedging assertions begin to weaken with the potential combination of a refused bid and a favourable value of the option position (i.e., in-the-money). As for hedging both the price and the quantity, apart from the importance of assuming core risks (in this case the quantity of crops by the farmer), as discussed in the previous chapter, it is not evident how a favourable price movement and a high-yielding crop season would factor into a pure hedging strategy using options.

In effect, if one concedes that the usage of derivatives in hedging contexts is undertaken in matters relating to an insurable interest by the hedging party wherein the derivative instrument provides indemnity to any sustained losses, then, as stated by Culp, the requirement 'that the hedger has an insurable interest means by definition, that the *net* [*sic*] of the indemnity contract and the natural position of the hedger cannot ever be positive' (Culp 2004: 73).

4.3 Conclusion

This chapter delved into the economics of the derivative contracts and the technicalities of their usage in the financial markets with a particular focus on hedging transactions. The significance of this discussion, and the greater understanding that it is trying to elicit, will become apparent in the coming chapters not the least of which the next one that concentrates on the conceptualisation of derivatives in the Islamic finance industry by the *Shariʻah* scholars and academics, which, in turn, played a major role in instigating a movement of superficial replication by market participants.

Suffice it to note at this stage that the current chapter has demonstrated that derivative instruments, by virtue of the Law of One Price and the theory of arbitrage, are an effective means to lessen *Gharar* (excessive uncertainty) in the financial markets in that, when used as tools for risk transfer, they reduce the uncertainties of future transactions between parties in a transparent manner.

Further, and with a particular reference to the prohibition of *Riba*, it has been shown that derivative transactions are not debt transactions with a unique debtor–creditor relationship. In fact, derivative contracts cannot serve the financing needs of any party since they do not provide funding at contract initiation. Essentially, they are a complement to financing (including operational arrangements) in order to make it more effective and efficient for the parties involved.

As for the interest component in the pricing of these instruments, it has been also shown that the interest rates are not used in a usury context in the credit markets; rather, much like the utilisation of LIBOR for *Ijara* (leasing) financing in Islamic finance, they are used for pricing to account for the preferences (liquidity, among others) of economic agents as well as a benchmark for the uncertainty (including inflation uncertainty) associated with the holding period of these financial instruments.

It is perhaps appropriate at this juncture to state that the focus (although not exclusive) in the remaining chapters will be on the forward-based derivative instruments consequent of their more amenable utilisation as contracts in a hedging context without the controversial charges of speculation that have often circulated with their usage. Essentially, while it is acknowledged that options contracts can be used for risk management, the nature of their payoff structure (i.e., non-linear) does make the argumentation for the acceptability of their usage in Islamic finance exclusively as hedging instruments more challenging. With that, we now turn to the view of contemporary Islamic finance of derivative instruments.

Notes

1. This does not factor in the potential benefits of risk consolidation (combination and diversification).
2. Efficient markets in this context entail no transaction costs, homogenous opinions, the rationality of economic agents, equal borrowing and lending rates and no restrictions on trading.
3. The borrowing and lending at the base rates is a theoretical construct that serves primarily as a means to include the opportunity cost of capital in determining the potential value of exploiting an arbitrage opportunity. The arbitrageur may or

may not be willing and able to operate at the base rate (e.g., a non-rated or lower rated *arbitrageur*).

4. A more elaborate discussion on this issue will be undertaken in Chapter 6.

5. In markets where the swap instruments are not active (e.g., emerging markets), the bond swap approach to valuation may be of greater use.

6. These include caps, floors, collars, corridors, straddles and butterflies, among many others.

7. There are also other types of options, such as the Asian options and the Bermudan options.

8. Obaidullah makes a sweeping, and erroneous, generalisation of options in that he concludes: 'We also show that this tool of risk management cannot be used for speculating on price differences' (Obaidullah 1998: 100). Kamali's assertion is more tempered, but still inaccurate, whereby he states: '[O]ptions trading cannot be equated with gambling or over-indulgence in financial speculation since it is basically designed to minimize speculative risk-taking, and for the most part operates as an antidote to gambling' (Kamali 2000: 181–2).

5.0 Introduction

The previous two chapters discussed the topics of market-risk management and the utilisation of derivatives as hedging instruments in conventional finance in order to assist in the efficient transfer of these risks (and returns) between economic agents. It has been argued that hedging, in general, not only reduces the possibility of financial distress and its associated costs, but also serves to assist in the creation of an enabling environment for capitalising on growth opportunities in competitive markets as well as potentially reducing the tax costs of businesses.

In this chapter, the discussion moves more prominently to Islamic finance with the detailed examination of the prohibitive resolutions elaborated by the three leading standard-setting bodies in Islamic jurisprudence, that is, the Makkah-based Islamic Fiqh Academy, the Jeddah-based Organisation of Islamic Cooperation (OIC) Islamic Fiqh Academy, and the Accounting and Auditing Organization for Islamic Financial Institutions (AAOIFI) in addition to the contributions of the various *Shari'ah* scholars on the topic of derivatives. More specifically, the contemporary market-risk-management practices by Islamic institutions will be explored in a manner that mixes the resolutions of the standard-setting bodies and opinions circulating in the Islamic finance space. Furthermore, the relevant elements of the discussion on market-risk management and the economics of derivatives as outlined in the previous chapters will also be examined in light of the foregoing exploration.

5.1 Resolutions by standard-setting bodies in Islamic jurisprudence

The discourse into the utilisation of derivatives in Islamic finance effectively commenced with the debate on the view of the *Shari'ah* regarding contemporary security and commodity markets (i.e., financial markets) by the Islamic Fiqh Academy of Makkah in its Seventh Session in January 1984. In its resolution on the subject matter, the academy noted the benefits of the financial markets in promoting *Maslaha* (public interest) by providing a permanent forum for buyers and sellers of securities and commodities to transact within the framework of supply and demand. Interestingly, the benefits highlighted were exclusively focused on the cash markets in the realm of investments without any reference to the original purpose of the derivative markets, which is risk management.

However, the derivative contracts were explicitly mentioned as part of the negatives, which according to the academy, were: First, the contracts in the derivative markets are not 'real' transactions in that the parties involved do not transfer (i.e., deliver and receive) the actual underlying assets; second, the seller is mostly selling what they do not own to another party in the future with the payment exchanged at that future date, which is in contrast to *Salam* contracts that require upfront payment (see below); third, the derivative contracts, which entail an artificial exchange, are sold and resold many times until maturity to many parties with the sole objective being the gambling on price differentials; and, fourth, the derivative markets serve the purposes of the large traders at the expense of small traders, mainly by spreading rumours and market manipulations, resulting in wealth destruction and economic crises.

In the latter part of the resolution, the academy did acknowledge that the benefits and the negatives of the financial markets co-exist in a manner that makes it difficult to provide a general ruling, but rather each type of transaction should be given a specific ruling. Surprisingly, and despite this acknowledgement, the academy proceeded with the following *general resolution* that pertains to derivative transactions: First, cash market contracts whereby the goods are owned by the seller and are transacted on a spot basis are allowed, with the exception being the *Salam* contracts for forward sales in which the payment is completed on the spot and delivery is stipulated at a forward date with no third party selling in the interim period; second, any spot or forward transactions involving bonds with interest are disallowed consequent of the prohibition on *Riba*; and, three, *all* forward contracts that have an underlying asset that is not owned by the seller are not permitted.

The Jeddah-based OIC Islamic Fiqh Academy, an equally powerful standard-setting body in the Islamic finance industry, for its part, examined the derivative instruments as part of its discussion regarding the financial markets in its Seventh Session in May 1992. Prior to outlining its Resolution No. 63/1/7 on the subject matter, it may be necessary to survey the research papers by some of the renowned Islamic jurists that shaped the final decision by the academy.

Of the seven research papers, six of them were mainly focused on options and appear to be in response to eight specific questions by the academy to the Islamic jurists. These questions were:

1. Is the option contract a known Islamic contract or is it a new type of contract? Moreover, if it is a new contract, what is the *Shari'ah* opinion on its permissibility?
2. What is the relationship between the option contract and other contracts, such as *Urbun* (earnest money), pre-specified asset sale, *Salam* and gifting?
3. What is the *Shari'ah* opinion regarding charging a premium by the seller for granting a purchase right to the buyer?
4. Can a simple right to the underlying be the object of the contract?
5. If these contracts are exchanged within the framework of an exchange that guarantees performance, what is the *Shari'ah* opinion on its role and the actual guarantee?
6. Can a put option be sold or is it a sale of an asset that is not owned by the seller despite its presence in the market?
7. Can the option contract be considered as a type of purchase stipulation (*Khiyar Al-Shart*), which would render it a permissible contract?
8. If the contract is not permissible, in whole or in part, how can it be altered in order to make it permissible?

The communication of these questions by the academy to the Islamic jurists, which appear to be partly based on the aforementioned resolution by the Makkah-based academy, is significant in that it not only pre-emptively influenced the direction of the submitted research papers, but also shaped the discourse that was to follow in the academy and beyond. The last question, particularly, was quite important in providing the juridical foundation, by way of *Qiyas* (analogical reasoning), for the partaking of financial engineering by market participants in the years that followed the resolution with the objective of finding a *Shari'ah*-compliant hedging instrument.

The six research papers on options (*Al-Ikhtiyarat*) concluded that these contracts, which were acknowledged as being new forms of contracts unlike any other pre-modern Islamic era ones (e.g., *Salam*, *Urbun* or *Khiyar Al-Shart*), were impermissible in Islamic jurisprudence. Specifically, the rather consistent findings echoed those of the Makkah-based Islamic Fiqh Academy in that it was stated that options should be prohibited because of:

1. the lack of ownership of the underlying asset by the transacting parties
2. the sale of a non-existent underlying asset at the time of the contract
3. the transacting in a contract that is independent of the underlying asset
4. the partaking in gambling behaviour by market participants by way of those contracts
5. the prohibition of the transfer of these contracts to third parties
6. the lack of delivery and receipt by the transacting parties.

The sole research paper on the forward-based contracts was one on futures by Justice Usmani,[1] also the chairperson of the AAOIFI *Shari'ah* Board, who famously stated in a paper delivered at the World Economic Forum Annual Meeting in 2010:

> When we speak of Islamic Finance or Islamic economic principles, it is generally assumed that these principles are emphasized by Muslim scholars only to satisfy the religious requirement of

Muslims, or that they are meant only for Muslims to the exclusion of all others. This is an incorrect assumption. Although Islam is basically represented by a set of beliefs, the benefits of its social, political and economic principles are not restricted to Muslims; they are meant for the common good of humanity at large. (Usmani 2010: 3)

In his analysis of the futures markets, Justice Usmani advanced the position that the parties transacting in the forward-based derivatives are either speculators seeking to gamble on price differentials in the underlying assets or hedgers seeking to monopolise an asset in order to increase their profit margins. Further, he asserted that the trading in the forward-based contracts is unlike the *Salam* contracts and is more akin to 'the sale of one debt for another' (*Bay' Al-Kali' Bil-Kali'*), which was reported to have been prohibited by the Prophet (PBUH). Finally, Justice Usmani raised the issue of ownership of the underlying asset that was posed earlier by the Islamic jurists examining the option contracts. Consequently, the final opinion, for him, was that these contracts should not be allowed to be a part of the Islamic finance industry.

This prohibitive opinion was elaborated further by Justice Usmani in later discussions on the subject matter in which he maintained that these transactions are invalid because: One, sales and purchases cannot be affected for a future date; two, delivery is not intended and, consequently, settlement occurs by price differentials only; three, even if delivery is intended, the seller does not have full control over the underlying asset, which can be a form of deceit to the buyer; and, four, the transactions are tied together, which is prohibited in Islamic jurisprudence (Usmani 1999, 2010). Eventually, and once more, he declared these transactions as being 'totally impermissible regardless of their subject matter. Similarly, *it makes no difference whether these contracts are entered into for the purpose of speculation or for the purpose of hedging'* (Usmani 1999: 2; emphasis added).

Returning to the ruling by the Jeddah-based OIC Islamic Fiqh Academy, Resolution No. 63/1/7 stated the following: For options,

> [O]ption contracts as currently applied in the world financial markets are new types of contracts which do not come under any one of the *Shari'a* nominate contracts. Since the object of the contract is neither a sum of money nor a utility or a financial right which may be waived, then the contract is not permissible in *Shari'a*. As these contracts are primarily prohibited, their handling is also prohibited.

As for forward-based contracts,

> this contract is not permissible because of the deferment of the two elements of the exchange. It may be amended to meet the well-known conditions of 'salam' (advance payment). If does so [*sic*], it shall be permissible. Moreover, it is not permissible to sell a merchandise purchased under 'salam' terms with advance payment, unless the merchandise has been received.

Further, in regards to the futures contract settlement by entering into an opposing transaction, the Academy decided that 'it is not permissible at all'.

The Accounting and Auditing Organization for Islamic Financial Institutions (AAOIFI), as the third main standard-setting body in Islamic finance, appears to have not deliberated the usage of derivatives by Islamic institutions at any sufficient extent, as evidenced by the lack of any *Shari'ah* Standards on this issue. This could have been consequent of the belief that this issue was examined at length by the

Makkah-based and the Jeddah-based Islamic Fiqh academies and that the aforementioned analysis was deemed thorough and correct in its assumptions and conclusions.

Alternatively, the decision of avoiding reference to derivative instruments may possibly have had its roots in the elaboration of prohibitive opinions regarding the utilisation of interest-rate benchmarks and currencies for speculation *or* risk-management purposes (see the next chapter). The eventual outcome to see is that this institution has chosen to exclude itself from the discourse on the subject matter despite being in a superior, and indispensable, position to closely interact with both the Islamic jurists and the market participants in order to bridge the gaps in the understanding of the challenges being faced by contemporary business and financial environments with a focus on financial reporting.

Prior to delving into the *Shari'ah* issues that were outlined earlier by the standard-setting bodies, it is important to take note of the explicit prohibition of any form of hedging through forward-based derivative instruments by Justice Usmani, which eventually contributed to their broad rejection by the Jeddah-based OIC Islamic Fiqh Academy, and also presumably led to the decision by AAOIFI to ignore derivatives all together. In effect, if the argument was simply regarding the fear of engaging in pure gambling and its effects on global financial stability, the issue would have been understandable, and to a certain extent manageable, even if one disagrees with the generalisation.

Apart from the gambling behaviour, it is rather surprising that such a strong conviction was demonstrated by these standard-setting institutions regarding an instrument that has been acknowledged by all their Islamic jurists and their Resolutions as being a 'new type of contracts' without specific proscriptions in the scripture, which takes it out of the purview of *Qiyas* with pre-modern contractual forms as a source for the analogy. In other words, it does not appear that the discourse on these instruments in the juridical sphere gave adequate consideration to, one, the question of whether or not derivatives are beneficial to society, and, two, the question of whether if they are found to be beneficial in some respects and detrimental in others (increased competitiveness and reduction in probability of bankruptcy consequent of hedging vis-à-vis global financial instability consequent of gambling behaviour), how should they be handled and regulated.

Essentially, the work of Al-Ghazali on the five essential elements (*Al-Durariyat Al-Khamsa*) in his *Al-Mustafa Min Ilm Al-Usul* (1993a), especially with respect to the protection of wealth (*Mal*), and also the work of Al-Razi and Al-Qarafi on the same subject matter, in addition to the wider jurisprudence on *Maslaha* (Hassan 1994), and *Daroura* (Abu Sulayman 2003), along with an open dialogue with the industry's stakeholders in a more inclusive discourse process, would have undoubtedly been of value to arrive at more thorough findings. This is especially true in the widely recognised disparity between the religious perceptions of Islamic finance by the *Shari'ah* scholarly community and the real challenges facing institutions in the contemporary business and financial environments.

Notwithstanding the perplexing and arguably religiously unsupported opinions (see below) regarding the prohibition of derivative hedging transactions, it is appropriate at this stage to explore the issues that were outlined earlier as the basis for the prohibition of derivative instruments by the three standard-setting bodies. These issues can be divided into four groups: The first group contains theoretical *Shari'ah* issues; the second group comprises contractual *Shari'ah* issues; the third group, which will be discussed in detail in the next chapter, is related to the nature of the underlying asset with particular reference to derivatives tied to currencies and interest rates; and the fourth, and final group, which will be explored in the following chapter, entails the examination of the charges of *Maysir* (gambling) that were deemed to be integral to the derivative markets, in a wider context that includes financial intermediaries.

5.2 Theoretical *Shari'ah* issues

The theoretical *Shari'ah* issues that have led to a prohibitive stance regarding the derivative hedging instruments revolve around two main points. The first point is related to the supposed exchange of debts by the counterparties in a derivative transaction that is akin to the prohibition on *Bay' Al-Kali' Bil-Kali'* (sale of one debt for another), which was deemed prohibited in Islamic jurisprudence. The second point, for its part, focuses on the possession and ownership of assets that are non-existent at the time of the transaction as well as the small prospects of effective delivery at maturity, the sum of which is thought to render these contracts as not being true and genuine.

For the first point, its basis, which led to the proscription of derivative instruments, is connected to a *Hadith* by the Prophet (PBUH) that was reported by Ibn Umar in which the Prophet (PBUH) forbade *Bay' Al-Kali' Bil-Kali'*. The authenticity of this *Hadith* has been a point of contention between *Shari'ah* scholars (Al-Amine 2008; Al-Masri 1991; Al-Suwailem 2001; Hammad 1986; Kamali 2007) over the years with the arguable outcome that its penetration into Islamic jurisprudence has less to do with the actual *Hadith* and more with the *Igma'a* (consensus) among the various *Shari'ah* scholars of the impermissibility of the sale of one debt for another. Effectively, it can be discerned that the consensus view among the *Shari'ah* scholars was formulated mainly consequent of the explicit prohibition of *Riba* as well as the fear of the emergence of societal discord if the debt contracts were not fulfilled, especially if the circle of participation was extended to multiple third parties by exchanging debt contracts.

To be certain, these viewpoints can be characterised as being quite valid in usurious situations where a debtor, unable to pay a particular debt on its due date, asks (or is forced by) the creditor to buy his old debt for another one that is much higher (in absolute and percentage terms) to be settled at a later date.[2] Another contentious situation can arise whereby a creditor sells his or her rights over a particular debt to a third party that may be in a separate disagreement with the debtor, causing conflict between all the parties. Needless to say, this last example can have, in addition to *Riba*, forms of *Gharar* if the debt itself is in dispute.

Apart from these scenarios, it is difficult to economically rationalise some of the arguments that seek to extend the prohibition of *Bay' Al-Kali' Bil-Kali'* to *any* future-centred transaction, such as in the derivative markets, on the grounds that they amount to the sale of one debt for another. This is especially true in an industry that has accepted the existence of *Salam* (forward sale), *Istisna'a* (commission to manufacture) and *Hawala* (debt transfer), which can all be characterised as being types of future-centred commercial transactions.[3]

Moreover, the examination of these instruments in the previous chapter should not have led to any comparisons between derivatives and debt, as is often done in Islamic finance circles, especially when one examines the forward-based contracts. As outlined earlier, these are a complement, not a substitute, to the credit markets in that they are not funding transactions, as such, since there is no exchange of principle.[4] Further, the forward-based derivatives examined offer no static and party-unique asset/liability exposure.

The prohibition of derivative instruments because they facilitate the trading of debt could be discerned to also likely be a result of the unawareness of the technicalities of the forward-based derivative markets rather than a true resemblance between debt and derivatives in the context of the proscription of *Riba*. For, besides the fact that these derivatives are not debt instruments, as stated earlier, forward-based derivatives themselves are *not* tradable financial instruments because they traditionally do not have 'rights of assignment' that facilitate their exchange in the secondary market. A counterparty that is seeking to exit from a forward or a swap agreement can only negotiate for the cancellation of the agreement directly with the counterparty whereby the replacement value is used as the basis for the negotiation. For futures, the cancellation is undertaken with the exchange based on the daily mark-to-market nature of exchange-based derivative contracts.

Options, for their part, which also do not have any semblance to debt financing transactions, are different with respect to trading characteristics in that they can be traded by their purchasers to third parties. That said, if the issue was in the tradability of these instruments to third parties, the options could have simply been declared untradeable by the Islamic jurists. As for the static asset–liability structure (even in the prospective 'out of the money' situations) for the buyer and sellers of options, it is not evident that this framework amounts to a creditor–debtor in a classical sense, and even if it were viewed as such by the Islamic jurists, the generalisation to *all* derivatives (i.e., including forward-based derivatives) is clearly an overreach.

In addition, there is little economic substance to the claims that all derivatives increase *Gharar*. In fact, everything that was presented in the previous chapter should have demonstrated that derivatives, in a hedging context, are tools that actually reduce *Gharar*. The details of the contracts are unambiguously predetermined and are either negotiated between the parties or are set by the derivatives exchange. Further, it is not exactly apparent how the forward-type contracts increase *Gharar* through the augmentation in the risk of default, either in economic theory or through empirical evidence, as argued by Al-Suwailem (Al-Suwailem 2001: 61), as opposed to, say, the *Salam* or *Istisna'a* contracts. Thus, it can be validly argued that the only uncertainty in the derivative markets is regarding the future movements of the prices of the underlying asset, which for true hedgers is an uncertainty that is reduced with the proper utilisation of derivative instruments (i.e., exposure offset).

In fact, as mentioned earlier, the ability of the counterparties to negotiate the dissolution of the contract based on the replacement cost, besides the flexibility offered, is quite transparent in a manner that is quite distant from *Gharar* and is in stark contrast to the usurious relationships in some credit markets. Thus, for all intents and purposes, it can be proclaimed that derivatives are a powerful tool for the reduction of market risks and *Gharar* in a debt-free environment.

Having said that, if, on the other hand, the issue is the belief that *Gharar* (excessive uncertainty) is a part of *Maysir* (gambling) and should therefore be prohibited on these grounds, it can only be stated that this does not belong within the debate on *Bay' Al-Kali' Bil-Kali'* (or, for that matter, within the debate on the other theoretical issues, as will be outlined below) and should be taken up in the discourse on gambling using financial instruments with the prospect of some type of regulations to ensure that these instruments are not used in gambling contexts.

The second main point that has led to the proscription of derivative instruments by the Islamic jurists starts with the state of existence of the underlying assets at the time of the contract and continues to the nature of the possession as well as constructive ownership and finally to delivery from the seller to the buyer as a means of concluding the transaction. For this, it is acknowledged by essentially all parties to the discourse (both for and against derivative instruments) that the nature of derivatives is, one, transacting for the purchase/sale of assets that will come into existence at a specific time in the future, and, two, transacting in an asset that is not actually owned or possessed by the parties at the time of the contract initiation.[5]

As for delivery, and as mentioned in the previous chapter, the delivery of the underlying asset may not actually take place since the hedging parties seek primarily to reduce their market-risk exposure within their current operational framework (i.e., suppliers, supply chain, etc.). This practice *of hedging* was acknowledged, in fact, by Al-Suwailem (a notable critic of derivatives) in that he states: 'This clearly shows that the primary objective of a forward is hedging not physical exchange' (Al-Suwailem 1999: 84).

With respect to the juridical basis for the requirement of the underlying asset's existence at the time of sale, it is reported that the Prophet (PBUH) has prohibited the sale of some non-existent subject matter, such as the unborn calf of an animal, milk in the udders of a cow and fruit on a tree before the fruit's appearance.

In terms of the issue of the actual asset ownership and possession, three *Ahadith* have been quoted on this matter; in the first *Hadith* it was reported by Hakim Ibn Hizam that he asked the Prophet (PBUH): 'A man comes to me and asks me to sell him something that I do not have. Should I sell it to him and then go and acquire it for him from the marketplace?' The Prophet (PBUH) replied: 'Do not sell what is not with you.' A second *Hadith* stated that the Prophet (PBUH) said: 'He who buys foodstuff should not resell it until he is satisfied with its measurement.' The third *Hadith* that has been deemed to be related to ownership is: 'Profits are justified for the one bearing the liability for losses' (*Al-Kharaj Bi Al-Dhaman*), which was viewed by Al-Suwailem as directly referencing ownership (Al-Suwailem 2007: 63).

The aforementioned *Ahadith* has resulted in quite a large, and diverse, body of literature over the past few centuries from all schools of thought regarding how to apply the principles regarding actual asset ownership and possession in the commercial affairs of Muslims. One contentious matter has been whether the interpretation of the *Ahadith* stresses ownership or simply possession. Other questions have included: How would an exposure in a contemporary setting to, say, market risks where there is no ownership or possession of a future underlying asset, fit into Islamic jurisprudence? Does the object of sale under the purview of these *Ahadith* include all assets underlying any transaction or just foodstuff (with specific reference to particular foodstuff)? Also, would the nature of the asset itself (i.e., fungible goods versus specific goods) alter the religious legal opinion? In addition, it appears that the deliverability of the underlying asset to the buyer was given importance in the course of an elaboration of a particular ruling.

Notwithstanding what can be described as an enormously juridical and technical debate, there seems to be general consensus that the effective cause (*'Illah*) of the *Ahadith* is the avoidance of *Gharar* in commercial transactions (in particular, the potential for deception by the seller with respect to the object of the sale), and to a certain extent *Maysir*. Further, it can become clear that the focus that has manifested itself from the discourse is on pre-payment and delivery as being the ultimate tests of the validity of the transaction from the viewpoint of Islamic jurisprudence.

That is to say, there appears to be the belief among some that in order to deliver an object of sale, the object has to be existent as well as constructively owned and possessed. Alternatively, there appears to be a belief concerning the need to abide by the rules of the anomalous *Salam* and *Istisna'a* contracts with pre-payment as a centrepiece that legitimises their existence as exceptions to the general cash market-natured rules of Islamic jurisprudence in commercial transactions.

Interestingly, in light of the above observation, it may be contended that this tendency for the preference for spot delivery or pre-payment is given paramount importance vis-à-vis what is arguably the true reason for the directive in Islamic jurisprudence in the first place, which is the fulfilment of contracts, as was explicitly mentioned in the Quran where God stated: 'O you who have believed, fulfil [all] contracts' (Quran 5:1).

In other words, while it is recognised that delivery is a form of fulfilling a particular set of commercial contracts, it is not the only way that *all* business and/or financial transactions can be fulfilled. For if the seller was unable to complete the sale as agreed with the buyer and returned the purchase price to them along with any costs incurred by the buyer in a manner that eliminated the prospect of '*Akl Al-Mal bi Al-Batel*' (misappropriating the property of others) and dispute, then there would be very little issues of *Gharar* or deceit that formed the basis for the prohibition in the *Ahadith*. This would be especially true if the market modalities and contractual terms were detailed and agreed to prior to the effectiveness of the contract, as is currently practised in the derivatives markets.

In fact, one can argue that there is a greater chance of *Gharar*, deceit and dispute by way of the pre-payment characteristics of *Salam* (forward sale) and *Istisna'a* (commission to manufacture) contractual forms, in spite of their delivery stipulations, than in the derivative markets transactions that are based on predefined and widely traded commodities.[6] That is to say, in these 'Islamic' forward contracts, the unique objects (i.e., an agricultural product from a particular person's garden) are not only non-existent, but also neither owned nor possessed in tangible form and, as a result, have greater risks that are associated with deliverability in a manner that avoids dispute than the rather standardised and liquid underlying assets in the derivative markets.

In terms of the matter raised earlier by Al-Suwailem, and other *Shari'ah* scholars and academics, regarding the interpretation of the liability of loss in the *Hadith* by the Prophet (PBUH) as being derived from ownership, it can only be stated that it is not self-evident that the word '*Al-Dhaman*' unequivocally means 'ownership'. In fact, if anything, *Al-Dhaman*, linguistically and economically, can be broadly related to exposure (that includes ownership, but not on an exclusive basis) rather than being related to possession of the actual legal title. This was established in the detailed writings of Al-Zuhayli (1998) on the subject matter of *Dhaman* wherein he made it quite clear, on inspecting the Quran, the *Ahadith* and work of the Imams of the four *Mazahib* and their followers (including the venerable Al-Ghazali), that the word and usage of *Al-Dhaman* is related to a commitment of responsibility.

Al-Zarqa, for his part, demonstrated in his distinguished work on Islamic jurisprudence that the usage of *Al-Kharaj Bi Al-Dhaman* is associated with an (economic) exposure that one must be able to confront in order to legitimately derive profits (Al-Zarqa 1998a: 1035–6). Once more, this can be related to actual ownership, but is not necessarily defined by it. To illustrate, in Arabic, when one states that they are the '*Al-Dhamen*' of someone else in paying their debt in case of default, it is understood that what is meant is that they are placing themselves in a position of exposure (i.e., the aforementioned possibility of loss) rather than in a position of ownership of any underlying asset.

Eventually, one may be able to discern that, in the context of derivatives, the whole convoluted discourse on the details of existence of the object of sale as well as its ownership, its possession and, eventually, its delivery (in addition to the rules of the anomalous *Salam* and *Istisna'a* contracts) has less to do with legal contractual formalities that are based on the *Gharar* and deceit argumentation and are more to do with the fear of engaging in gambling behaviour by way of fabricated and disingenuous transactions.

This estimation presents itself clearly in that it has been stated repeatedly in the majority of the negative opinions on the permissibility of derivatives that since the parties concentrate on the cash-settlement of differences in market prices at contract maturity then it *must* be a form of gambling. Correspondingly, the ownership of the underlying is the only legitimate means of having profit (and wealth in general) be related to the real economy, whereby anything less than proprietorship, including exposure in future settings in a stand-alone fashion, can be ascribed to the realm of gambling.

With that, it becomes apparent that the tests of prepayment and delivery were formulated without the adequate recognition that these requirements simply add to the transaction costs (financial and operational) and legal uncertainty of true hedgers with only the prospect of reducing – rather than actually eliminating – the gambling behaviour of the counterparties who are intent on speculating in the markets. Ironically, pure gamblers are likely to ignore these contemporary *Shari'ah* injunctions anyway and participate in the conventional derivative markets, thereby placing the burdens of these resolutions on the shoulders of true hedgers who strive to operate within the confines of *Shari'ah* principles in real economic sectors.

5.3 Contractual *Shari'ah* issues

The resolution by the Jeddah-based OIC Islamic Fiqh Academy, especially its last question addressed to the Islamic jurists, wherein it was asked: 'If the contract is not permissible, in whole or in part, how can it be altered in order to make it permissible?', captivated the imagination and argumentative spirit of *Shari'ah* scholars, lawyers and finance practitioners alike. Specifically, the repeated reference in that resolution to *Urbun* (earnest money) and *Khiyar Al-Shart* (contractual stipulations) in the discussions about options were deemed as an indication of the suggested boundaries in the discourse on these types of derivative contracts.

In a similar vein, the continuous judgement of the forward-based derivative instruments in relation to *Salam* contracts instigated an exercise that attempted to not only redefine the *Salam* contract in a contemporary setting, but also to extend the reference of *Salam* to include also other pre-modern Islamic contracts, such as *Istisna'a*, *Bay' Al-Mu'ajjal* (ex-post payments for already delivered products), *Bay' Al-Istijrar* (pre-payment of delivery instalments) and even *Murabaha* (instalment sale) and *Jo'ala* (service contracts) (Al-Amine 2008; Al-Suwailem 2006; Iqbal 1999; Iqbal and Mirakhor 2007; Kamali 2007; Khan 1988; Khan 1997; Moody's Global Corporate Finance 2010; Obaidullah 1998, 2005).[7]

Notably, this exercise was undertaken despite the fact that there were some commentators, such as Abd Al-Qadir (1982), Azzam (1985) and Kamali (2007), who attempted to stress that derivative contracts are quite novel to Islamic jurisprudence and should be evaluated based on their contemporary utilisation in the financial markets. Eventually, it can be perceived from the literature that the ultimate objective of the focus on the pre-modern Islamic contracts is to seek the appeasement of the *Shari'ah* scholars as well as to satisfy market demands by attempting to 'generate a similar economic profile to comparable conventional derivative instruments, albeit through a Shari'a compliant structure' (BMB 2010: 132).

It is perhaps important at this juncture to point out that the approach adopted by the Islamic jurists to derivative instruments is considerably different from the approach adopted in the examination of stock market activity. Specifically, the Jeddah-based OIC Islamic Fiqh Academy itself, with respect to the topic of 'Participation in Stock Companies' in the *same* Resolution that contained the prohibitive ruling on derivatives (i.e., Resolution No. 63/1/7), has decided: 'Since the essential thing about transactions is their licit nature, the establishment of a joint stock company with unprohibited purpose and activities is permissible.'

Accordingly, for equity participations, a series of rules were given to govern that financial activity. In essence, for the participation in stock companies, the conventional financial practice, even though not exactly analogous to the classical modes of partnerships in Islamic jurisprudence, was viewed in the Resolution as being, on the whole, a 'licit' activity; however, some rules were elaborated to ensure that its advantages were harnessed and its disadvantages were limited. In contrast, the work on derivatives, for some puzzling reason, commenced with an outright prohibition and continued on this rejectionist trajectory by the Islamic jurists.

Notwithstanding the above, on the options derivative instruments front, the discourse evolved mostly into a debate on whether *Khiyar Al-Shart* (contractual stipulations) or *Urbun* (earnest money), which were forms of extensions of pre-modern sales' contracts, can serve as a basis to permit options trading in Islamic jurisprudence. At one end of the debate, some commentators on derivative instruments, such as Kamali (1997), Obaidullah (1998), Abd Al-Qadir (1982) and Al-Jundi (1988), seem to prefer the *Khiyar Al-Shart* modality, while others, including Vogel and Hayes (1998), Al-Amine (2008) and El-Gari (1993), tend to believe that the *Urbun* model is more appropriate.

Interestingly, the conflicting opinions exist in spite of the professed position by some of those same writers that these pre-modern contractual extensions have little to do with contemporary option derivative instruments (El-Gari 1993: 16; Kamali 1997: 26–7; Obaidullah 1998: 80; Vogel and Hayes 1998: 156). With that, it is perhaps necessary to elaborate in more detail these two forms of contractual extensions in order to address some of the arguments that were used as a basis to prohibit the options derivative instruments.

The *Khiyar Al-Shart* contract extension, whereby one or both parties to a contract enjoy the availability of an option to confirm or rescind a sale agreement, has evolved as an accepted addition to the Islamic theory of contracting. Originally, the acceptability of *Khiyar Al-Shart* was based on a *Hadith* where it was reported that Hibban Ibn Munqidh complained to the Prophet (PBUH) that he was often cheated in sale transactions and the Prophet (PBUH) responded by saying: 'When you conclude a sale, you may say there must be no fraud and you reserve for yourself an option lasting for three days.'

Subsequently, a rather technical debate started on the following points (some of which were raised by the Jeddah-based OIC Islamic Fiqh Academy) that were specific to *Khiyar Al-Shart*: One, whether the three days were fixed or whether they were only given for illustrative purposes and that they could, therefore, be extended, depending on the nature of the transaction and the prevailing market custom; two, whether it is appropriate for the seller to demand a fee (i.e., option premium) from the potential buyer for the right to rescind a contract; three, whether the option itself, as a right, can be traded as a form of *Mal* (wealth or money) to third parties; and, four, whether the liability of loss during the *Khiyar Al-Shart* period falls upon the seller or upon the buyer.

As for the *Urbun* contract extension, its basis, rather than an actual *Hadith*, is mainly a report by Nafis Ibn Harith, an officer of the Calif Umar in Makkah, to the effect that he contracted with Safwan Ibn Umayyah for the purchase of a prison house for 4,000 Dirhams on the condition that the Calif agree to the transaction, otherwise Safwan would be given 400 Dirhams as a form of compensation for the inconvenience of a potential lost sale. Thus, *Urbun* can be conceptualised as a form of good faith deposit on the part of the buyer in return for some time and flexibility to finalise a sale transaction.

Notably, this was the essence of the ruling of the Jeddah-based OIC Islamic Fiqh Academy when it developed a consensus on the matter of *Urbun* in its Resolution No. 72/3/8 in June 1993, whereby it was agreed that '[d]own-payment (earnest) sales are permissible if the time frame of the contract is set, and the down payment is considered as part of the selling price if the purchase is carried through, and as the property of the seller if the buyer desists.'

In a manner similar to the points raised in the *Khiyar*

Al-Shart debate, the issues raised specifically for the *Urbun* contract extension included the following details: One, whether the premium, which is independent of the strike price in conventional derivative transactions, should be a part of the sale price of the underlying asset; two, whether the option itself, as a right, can be traded as a form of *Mal* (wealth) to third parties; three, whether the time period for the option's maturity is to be open or fixed; and, four, whether the seller also has a right to reject the sale (for general fairness and also as a basis for put options).

It can only be stated at this point that the imposition of the *Urbun* contractual extension in the debate on option-based derivatives is a unique case of financial creativity on the part of its partisans. For it is clear to market participants that a premium does not hold any semblance of a deposit in an option transaction. Specifically, a $2 premium on a an option with a strike price of $50 is never really characterised as a deposit on the purchase of that stock at $50 since, in reality, the outcome of the option contract is simply the calculation of the differential of the actual price of the stock in the market at contract maturity and the strike price. Further, even if the *Urbun* was part of the deposit, in some kind of effort to curb gambling activity, the suggestion has little economic substance behind it since the *Urbun*-based option pricing would likely be calibrated to account for the increased transaction costs that will depend on the price expectations of the underlying, the base rate and the time frame of the contract.

The difficulty of conceptualising a put option as a 'reverse *Urbun*' is but another manifestation of how diffi-cult the proposition of utilising earnest money has become. To illustrate, to profit and/or hedge against declines in market prices, El-Gari (1993) offers a rather elaborate finan-cial scheme that combines elements of *Wakala* (agency agreements), *Mudharaba* (investment agency) and *Jo'ala* (service contract). Vogel and Hayes, for their part, formulate some form of system that is dependent on a third-party (e.g., a bank) guarantee to compensate the 'seller' of the underlying when the buyer walks away, in a premeditated manner, because of a decline in pricing (Vogel and Hayes 1998: 228–30).

In due course, it does become self-evident that the discourse on options, which is essentially an economic subject matter, has been quite legal-centric in a way that evolved with the broader objective of simply finding any means to re-create conventional option contracts with an 'Islamic' wrapping. In effect, what can be observed is that the materialisation of the debate on option-based derivatives, by way of invoking the many different elements of the Islamic theory of contracting, has been elaborated without a commensurate reference to economic theories (effectiveness, efficiency, Law of One Price, theory of arbitrage, etc.). This, in turn, resulted in essentially partaking in a discussion that is focused on the legal details at the expense of the bigger economic picture, which is the facilitation of the commercial practices of Muslim entrepreneurs away from the prohibitions of *Riba*, *Gharar* and *Maysir*.

Effectively, one ought to be careful in their attribution of a particular pre-modern practice to a contemporary financial instrument. For it should be ostensible that the effective cause (*'Illah*) of the *Ahadith* by the Prophet (PBUH) is to benefit the Muslim community by ensuring commercial trust and reducing the asymmetry of information (or allowing for flexibility in the case of the Calif Umar) rather than allowing for market-risk management tools (or even investments), as such. Interestingly, the attempted rationalisation of the arguments in favour of using some of these pre-modern contractual forms have opened numerous other types of issues (time frame, right transfer, premium, etc.) that needlessly warranted further superficial rationalisation within the framework of *Qiyas* (analogical reasoning), causing even more ambiguity and discord on this important subject matter.

In light of the aforementioned controversy on the permissibility of options, it may be argued that a better approach would have been the one taken by Kamali, despite falling into the *Qiyas* trap himself with the debate on *Urbun* and *Khiyar Al-Shart* (with a preference for the latter), in which he concludes: '[T]here is nothing inherently objectionable in granting an option, exercising it over a period of time, or charging a fee for it, and that options trading, like other types of trade, is permissible (*Mubah*) and, as such, it is simply an extension of the basic liberty that the Qur'an has granted to the individual in respect of trading civil transactions and contracts' (Kamali 2000: 204). Notably, the foundation for Kamali's conclusion is the theory of general permissibility (*Ibaha*) in the *Shari'ah* in allowing individuals the freedom to tailor the contracts to their legitimate needs and benefits if in fact there is no partaking in what is explicitly prohibited in the scripture (e.g., *Riba*, *Gharar* and *Maysir*).

The discourse on the permissibility of forward-based transactions, for its part, followed a similar path to the one taken in discussing the option-based contracts. As mentioned earlier, the literature on the topic of forward-based derivatives contained many suggestive forms of pre-modern Islamic contracts that were thought, individually or in combination, to assist in the replication of conventional forward-based instruments. However, it appears that the arguments regarding the *Salam*-type contracts were the most prevalent and thus these will be the focus of the examination of the contractual *Shari'ah* issues of the forward-based instruments.

In its Ninth Session in April 1995 the Jeddah-based OIC Islamic Fiqh Academy (Resolution No. 85/2/9) defined a *Salam* contract as a forward sale transaction that stipulates immediate payment by one of the counterparties (buyer) and a delivery of a marketable good with definable features on a relatively specific date by the other counterparty (seller). The basis for that resolution is a report by Ibn 'Abbas wherein he stated that when the Prophet (PBUH) migrated to Madinah from Makkah he found that the inhabitants were engaging in a one- to three-year forward sales of agricultural products with price being prepaid at inception. To address this unique form of financing, the Prophet (PBUH) is narrated to have said: 'Whosoever engages in a *Salam* contract, let him specify a volume or weight for the object of sale, and a definitive term of deferment.'

The permissibility of the *Salam* contracts in Islam provides two notable distinctions from other contractual forms: First, the *Salam* contract is an exception to the norm since it is not a classic spot market transaction that is highly regarded in Islamic jurisprudence. Second, on the face of it, there can be elements of *Riba* in this transaction were it not for the inclusion of an underlying asset (or real activity) as the basis of financing.

Put differently, the *Salam* contract is, in actual fact, two contracts in one. On the one hand, it is a financing transaction on the part of the buyer of the underlying asset to the seller. On the other hand, the *Salam* contract is a form of risk-management strategy for the parties who are looking to transact in the underlying asset at some future time. For this, one may also assume that the party financing the *Salam* (e.g., a bank/financier or a trader in per-modern settings) is not necessarily interested in hedging a market-risk exposure as much as it is interested in benefiting from the profits generated from the forward sale.

Based on the above, it should be recognised that the consistent attempts by the promoters of the forward-based derivatives to alleviate the 'controversial issue' of the pre-payment of contract value as a basis for resolving the juridical issues surrounding these instruments is futile. In essence, the pre-payment of the contract value is an integral part of the asset finance component of the *Salam* contract in order to allow the seller to undertake the necessary investments to ensure the generation of the underlying assets (including providing for sustenance) in the future.

With that realisation, one can disagree with Al-Suwailem in his assertion that the essence of the pre-payment is to move the transaction from a prohibited zero-sum gambling nature to some other mixed-sum framework (Al-Suwailem 2006: 76).[8] This is because any movement in the market prices in the *Salam* framework is, in effect, a zero-sum outcome to the parties of the transaction. The pre-payment of the contract value does not negate that ex-post effect.

To continue with the *Salam* transactions, on the risk-management and investment/speculation fronts, the appearance of the proposed Parallel-*Salam* structure to facilitate the trading of non-existent assets, whether to the original seller (to offset the transaction) or to third parties, is needlessly stretching the *Salam* contract to fit the forward-based derivative model and causing more of a basis for rejection than consensus of acceptance based on the fundamentals of the transaction. This becomes obvious with the recognition that in the Parallel-*Salam* framework, it is 'required' that both *Salam* contracts with the same assets exist *independently* of each other.

Along the same lines, the suggestions by Al-Suwailem (2006) of devising contractual agreements along the lines of 'Value-based *Salam*' (quantity times unit price) and 'Hybrid *Salam*' (for rate of return risk), which do not seem to have generated sufficient interests from academia or the Islamic finance practitioners, can be viewed as being symptomatic of the difficulty of finding some form of Islamic contracts to hedge market risks.

A more rational and direct argument could have simply entailed highlighting the fact that, in light of asymmetry of information and transaction costs, contemporary financial markets can produce a much more efficient outcome for all of the parties, along with higher utilities, by dividing this contract into its two components. That is, the seller of the commodity need not convince the financier to assume the market risks of the underlying asset in order to conclude a financing agreement, the failure of which entails limiting the productive capacity of businesses.

Essentially, the financier may be more interested in the capacity (technical know-how, equipment, cost structure, etc.) of the seller of the commodity to actually produce the commodity at a particular date for a particular price, which in turn is factored into their profitability expectations. This could be because the costs of gathering and analysing market intelligence for the pricing behaviour of the commodity itself may be too great for the financier. Thus, the forced carry-on of the market risk by the financier in this scenario is likely to increase the risk premium to the transaction consequent of the elevated perception of uncertainty than would be the case through the efficient division of the contract into two components.

Likewise, the seller of the commodity does not have to strive to persuade the buyer to always finance ex-ante the seller's operations by pre-paying the contract value. The buyer of the commodity, if a true hedger, is likely to be only interested in the commodity itself (or its cash equivalent) at a particular date. If it is a trader/speculator, then they enter into the transaction with the seller of the commodity after formulating their profit expectations based on the gathering and analysis of market intelligence of the pricing behaviour of the underlying asset over the life of the contract. The capacity of the seller of the commodity to produce it adds an unnecessary risk element that he or she may not be in the best capacity to evaluate, which, much like the case described earlier, is also likely to increase the risk premium to the transaction consequent of the elevated perception of uncertainty than would be the case through the efficient division of the contract into two components.

Effectively, the commodity seller can, and should be able to, obtain a lower financing from the financier market to properly invest in the generation of the underlying asset (in a manner that is not too dissimilar to the concept of bank-financed *Istisna'a* contracts or even *Musharaka*). At the same time, they are more likely to obtain better pricing for their hedging endeavours within the derivative markets that centre on the evaluation of market prices of the underlying assets rather than the profile of its producers.

In effect, it may very well be conjectured that the Prophet (PBUH) in his *Hadith* that formed the substance for making an exception for *Salam* was likely to be less concerned with the nature of the underlying or even its delivery and more interested in sustaining a real economic activity in a manner that reduced the potential for *Gharar* and *Riba*, including any disputes and/or injustice that may arise in the process. Put differently, the *Salam* contract is simply a means to a higher end, not an end in itself.

5.4 Contemporary derivatives in Islamic finance

Despite the literature that favoured the permissibility of options, forwards and futures in Islamic finance, there does not seem to be a wide uptake regarding these three products in the Islamic markets. The confusion created by the acceptability of these products along with the lack of consensus by their proponents on which contractual forms to use (*Khiyar Al-Shart*, *Urbun*, *Salam*, *Istisna'a*, etc.) may have been a contributing factor for this lacklustre response.

However, the exception in the lack of enthusiasm in Islamic finance circles for the derivative instruments was the swap contracts, which were deemed quite useful for the management of foreign currency and profit rates' (i.e., interest rates') risk exposures faced by commercial and financial institutions that are increasingly being connected to the global financial markets. And, as can be expected, the discourse on the permissibility of the swap derivative contracts followed the same *Qiyas*-by-product path that was taken to argue the permissibility of the other derivative contracts that were outlined earlier.

Specifically, in order to elicit a favourable response from the *Shari'ah* scholars, the participants in the Islamic finance industry developed two main avenues for structuring Islamic swap instruments in order to generate similar cash flows to the ones offered by conventional derivative products with a wider aspiration of assisting Islamic institutions in hedging market risk. The two avenues are quite similar in that they use a 'Master Agreement' that utilises the *Murabaha* (instalment sale) financing scheme and the concept of *Wa'ad* (promise) in Islamic jurisprudence whereby a series of *Murabaha* and Reverse *Murabaha* transactions for the purchase/sale of non-precious commodities are entered into by the swap counterparties for the duration of the swap.[9]

Where they differ, however, is in that the first method envisions 'two unilateral promises' (that makes it a bilateral exchange of promises) to actually undertake a series of *Murabaha* transactions at designated points for the duration of the swap within the framework of *Maqassah* (netting). The second method, on the other hand, entails an execution of a 'unilateral promise' by only the out-of-the-money party to undertake the purchase/sale of the underlying asset from the in-the-money party at the agreed price in the contract. That is to say, both the parties give and hold the promises that are to be utilised, either paying or receiving, on the various settlement dates.

Throughout the process, a non-precious commodity and a series of commodity brokers, as agents of the counterparties, serve the vital roles of ensuring, *à la fois*, that, one, an underlying asset exists in the sale contract; two, the transaction combines a series of sale contracts that contain 'profit' (i.e., not interest or *Riba*); three, the exchange of one debt for another (i.e., *Bay' Al-Kali' Bil-Kali'*) does not take place; and, four, the underlying assets (i.e., non-precious commodities) are owned, possessed and 'constructively' delivered at the designated dates. The usage of fixed interest rates and floating interest rates (e.g., LIBOR) along with foreign currencies, if applicable, formalise this Islamic swap structure.

In terms of preference, even though the first method seems to have been preferred by the Islamic finance industry accounting for nearly 70 per cent of Islamic derivative products in 2009, the risks (market risk, indemnities, etc.) of non-precious commodity ownership (even for a fleeting timespan) in addition to the execution risk (i.e., unacceptability of two unilateral promises executed at the same time in the *Shari'ah*) were deemed too great for industry participants, which resulted in the increasing preference for the second swap method in recent years (BMB 2010: 134).

Eventually, the growth in the usage of these instruments along with the lack of standardisation of the various swap

contractual agreements that were used by industry partici-
pants led to the efforts by the International Islamic Financial
Market (IIFM) in Bahrain to partner with the International
Swaps and Derivatives Association (ISDA) in New York
to develop the ISDA/IIFM *Tahawwut* (Hedging) Master
Agreement (TMA) in 2010.

The touted key benefits of this agreement are, one, the
reduction of costs that are expended in the evaluation and
negotiation of the swap documentation; two, providing
balance and fairness to the counterparties; three, increasing efficiency, liquidity and certainty; four, establishing a
benchmark that provides a reference point; and, five, reducing the price divergence between Islamic hedging instruments and their conventional counterparts.

Effectively, the TMA, which is derived almost entirely
from the ISDA Master Agreement, uses the aforementioned
Murabaha contractual form along with the *Wa'ad* concept
to develop a framework that comprises: a single agreement,
governing law, representations, flawed asset and condition-
ality, and a close-out mechanism and netting. However,
where it does differ from the ISDA Master Agreement, apart
from the requirement that there is an underlying asset that
is religiously permissible (mainly zinc and aluminium), is
in that it stipulates that the contract should be entered into
for hedging purposes and that interest cannot be chargeable
in the transaction, and in the event that interest is granted
as part of court proceedings, it must be promptly given to
charity.

One should be able at this stage, based on the discussion
in the previous chapter, to question the validity of two key
components of the TMA: First is the requirement that interest not be part of the transaction. For, on the face of it, it may
be lauded in Islamic finance circles that the TMA structure
does not partake in any usurious activity. However, it is

also notable, from an economic and financial sense, that aside from the facts: One, the swap instrument is not a lending transaction from one party to the other, and, two, the underlying (profit rates and currency) are based one way or another on the base rate (e.g., Treasury or LIBOR) and that the 'replacement cost' of any swap (that is explicitly included in the TMA contract) is in itself determined, in part, by the base rate of interest no matter which valuation method is used.

Apart from the issue of *Riba*, the second questionable component is the deployment of the concept of *Wa'ad* (promise) in these instruments as well as the forced usage of non-precious commodities. Originally, the concept of *Wa'ad* was used by early Muslim jurists in charitable situations whereby, in the interest of sustaining the philanthropic contribution by the wealthy members of the society, it was deemed that the promise of a donation was to be binding on the donor unless a justifiable reason for its withdrawal is given.

After the establishment of the *Murabaha* contractual form within the realm of Islamic financial intermediation in the 1970s as the primary financing means for banking institutions to service their clients' asset purchases, it was realised that there are promissory elements by many parties that required some form of regulation. For, as opposed to the basic, and historically prevalent, situations where the seller agrees to sell a product to the buyer on the spot, based on instalments with the condition that the buyer becomes contractually obligated to make the payments on their due dates, the modern-day *Murabaha* financing schemes technically involve the buyer requesting a particular good to be financed by the bank and makes a promise to purchase it from the bank once the bank acquires it. If the promise by the buyer was not binding, in the event that they decide not to conclude the contract, the bank (and/or the original seller) can be exposed to a loss.

This exposure, along with the prospect of the associated injustice and disputes, was the basis that was used by jurists such as Al-Zarqa, Al-Qaradawi, Al-Shazli and many others in expanding the binding nature of *Wa'ad* to *Murabaha* contracts (Al-Masri 2003; Al-Qaradawi 1987; Al-Zarqa 1998b: 1032–5). However, the issue of how to distinguish a contractual obligation (*'Aqd*) from a *Wa'ad* presented itself soon after the elaboration of those opinions since these two formats, which are quite identical in the view of a court of law, were deemed to be unworkable in a parallel fashion in Islamic jurisprudence.

To address this challenge, it was ruled by the Jeddah-based OIC Islamic Fiqh Academy that a 'unilateral' promise is binding while a bilateral binding promise is not allowed because it amounts to an *'Aqd*. Notably, there have been many commentators, such as Al-Masri, who perhaps in following Ibn Taymiyyah's doctrine of the supremacy of the focus on real objectives (*Maqasid*) rather than superficial wording, have derided such arbitrary treatment of *Wa'ad* in the law of contracts as being 'illogical' and 'unacceptable' and denoting 'a misinterpretation of some jurisprudential texts' (Al-Masri 2003: 32). This is despite its well-meaning intentions, by the academy and *Shari'ah* scholars with similar opinions, of balancing the difficulty in assisting Islamic banks and their clients on one end and the prohibition on *Riba* on the other.

To return to the subject of the ISDA/IIFM *Tahawwut* (Hedging) Master Agreement, the same difficulty facing Islamic jurists in the *Murabaha* financial structures, and the subsequent solutions, resulted in the use of *Qiyas* (analogical reasoning) to apply both the *Murabaha* contractual form and the concept of *Wa'ad* to underlie the TMA structure.

The final outcome is that, possibly even more so than is present in the traditionary *Murabaha* sale transactions, it is quite difficult to intellectualise a 'Master Swap Agreement' that includes a wide array of unilateral promises between hedgers, commodity brokers and banks on multiple payment dates that are expected to be enforceable in a court of law according to Islamic jurisprudence principles that prohibits bilateral binding commitments. This is especially evident in that the *Shari'ah* explicitly bans the superficial multiplication of contracts to circumvent Islamic jurisprudence where it was reported that the Prophet (PBUH) prohibited the joining of two sales in one.

With respect to the innovative structuring of the swap through multiple sales contracts of non-precious commodities, there does not seem to be any recognition by the *Shari'ah* scholars, legal experts or the Islamic finance practitioners of the economic reality of this transaction. In essence, it should be obvious that if the commodity was genuinely placed in the structure of the swap to demonstrate a true purchase and sale transaction in the future along with the assumption of all the association risks of ownership by the parties, which is perceived to be a chief way to legitimately transact in the future by the majority of current *Shari'ah* scholars,[10] then the overall pricing behaviour of the swap will differ, sometimes significantly, from the one offered by the conventional swap contract with the same underlying reference rate or price (i.e., foreign exchange or interest rate).

This is because whatever non-precious commodity is used has a pricing behaviour of its own that is determined by way of the equilibrium between the forces of supply and demand in the financial markets where they are traded (London Metal Exchange, Bursa Malaysia, etc.). Moreover, in times of market stress, the liquidity of the Islamic swap transactions can be severely affected if there is insufficient liquidity in the market of whatever non-precious commodity is used.

It should also be appreciated that the real partaking in the purchase and sale of these commodities in the future for the purpose of generating some form of a tangible underlying is likely to result in distortions in the pricing of these commodities consequent of artificial elements of supply and demand, which, in turn, has negative implications to their users in the real sector who have no relation whatsoever to the swap contract. Thus, for all intents and purposes, the inclusion of the non-precious commodities, if undertaken in a true and genuine manner in some sort of bid to directly relate the transaction to the 'real sector', not only makes the swap defective for hedging purposes consequent of uncertain pricing patterns, but also is likely to negatively affect the real sector that Islamic jurisprudence is so much in favour of promoting.

The reality of incompatibility between economic theory and the current interpretation of the *Shari'ah* proscriptions in economic matters is equally harsh on the financial engineering suggestions made by the various authors in the Islamic finance literature. These include the writings by Iqbal and Mirakhor who espouse the position favouring the use of financial engineering to replicate conventional derivatives in an Islamic manner as a means to facilitate market-risk management (Iqbal and Mirakhor 2007: 209–20).

The modalities proposed by those distinguished authors range from *Jo'ala* (service contracts), *Murabaha*, and equity structures to *Sukuk* (Islamic bonds) issuances. In judging the appropriateness of these suggestions, at a basic level, it is not entirely understood how the invocation of all of these contractual forms, vis-à-vis conventional derivatives, resolves the substance of the self-imposed prohibitions that were placed by the standard-setting bodies, especially those relating to *Riba* (usury) and *Maysir* (gambling).

As for the genuine utilisation of the *Murabaha* (i.e., not in a swap format), it can become apparent that the utilisation of this contractual form through the use of commodities, serving as the collateral component of financing, in market-risk management transactions effectively transforms the currency or interest-rate exposure into either commodity price risk or credit risk (depending on how the transaction is structured). If the commodity price risk is assumed then the hedge largely becomes defective in managing the market-risk exposure. Further, the risk would be compounded if the commodity itself in the structure is not marketable.

For credit risk, it should be notable that the default of the counterparty does factor into producing disparities in the pricing of the derivative instrument, as in the case of forward versus futures contracts (see Kane 1980). This would be even more evident in a scenario where the potential losses from derivatives (i.e., difference between contract price and market price) are much less than the potential losses of the full principle of the *Murabaha* contract. Needless to say, the aforementioned issues associated with transaction costs and the negative effects to the real sector consequent of the artificial creation of trade transactions on usable commodities still apply.

Similarly, the challenges faced in implementing the suggestions of utilising equity participation certificates in some form of asset swap between institutions go beyond the author-admitted difficulty of finding matching securities to offset the market-risk exposures. This is because there are fundamental problems associated with asymmetry of information and adverse selection in this arrangement, which were made all too evident in the securitisation framework that contributed to the structural deformities that instigated the recent global financial crisis.

Finally, it appears that the proposition of actually utilising the concept of *Sukuk* for hedging transactions has its foundations in the use of the methodology that was discussed in the previous chapter for pricing swaps that assumes a hypothetical exchange of bonds by the counterparties. Nevertheless, within the current paradigm for interpreting the *Shari'ah* in the scholarly community, which will be disputed in the next chapter, this hypothetical exchange is impermissible because there are no *real assets* underlying the exchange. This alone would negate any reasoning to proceed with the hypothetical *Sukuk* exchange framework in lieu of the much more market-recognised swap structures.

Furthermore, any attempt to overcome the challenges of the restrictions placed on the usage of hypothetical securities by, one, actually transacting in the secondary *Sukuk* market in order to exchange real *Sukuk* as a means of offering a tangible asset to underlie the hedging transaction, or, two, having the counterparties actually issue securities in the primary market for the same purpose, would be a much more costly and inefficient method of managing market-risk exposures.

Specifically, with respect to the engagement of the secondary market, it will be quite difficult in the current illiquid *Sukuk* secondary market to find securities that offer the flexibility provided by derivatives to match the exact market-risk exposures by the counterparties. Moreover, even if the *Sukuk* secondary market was liquid, the utilisation of *Sukuk* for hedging purposes is likely to result in an increase in the prices of the *Sukuk* trading in the financial markets (i.e., lower yields) as a result of the increase in demand for these instruments. In time, the higher prices for

Sukuk would very likely trickle down to lower quality *Sukuk* issuance and trading in the financial markets. This would, effectively, be a form of wealth transfer from the hedging community to the issuers of *Sukuk* in the primary market.

Interestingly, the eventual outcome, which is probably not the one desired by the *Shari'ah* scholarly community, of this low-yield environment is that organisations will find it more beneficial to include increasing levels of *Sukuk* in their financial structure rather than the equity forms that are so well regarded in the Islamic finance industry (i.e., more debt and systemic risk).

As for the use of the primary market by the counter-parties to issue *Sukuk* to match the markt-risk exposures, the issuance of any security in the primary market entails prohibitive costs that can only be accepted in the context of resource mobilisation for an enterprise. Thus, the use of that route for market-risk management is rather unrealistic, especially with the recognition that finding another hedger with an exact offsetting exposure is quite improbable and that a financial intermediary, taking the opposite exposure, will undoubtedly include their cost of primary market issuance as a part of their fees.

Eventually, it becomes hard to imagine how any of these suggestions of financial engineering to address market-sheet management is related to, or can be used to hedge, the actual balance-sheet exposures faced by organisations as part of a wider framework that is built on the effectiveness and efficiency of the portfolio approach to asset-liability management. The increasingly complex nature of the global business and financial environments and its manifestation on the risk exposures of organisations, which require elements of flexibility and dynamism in the market-risk management strategy, make the aforementioned suggestions even more impractical.

Based on the above, it could be validly contended that these expensive, untenable and legally uncertain exercises (i.e., Islamic swaps and financial engineering) could have been prevented by simply invoking the theory of *Maslaha* (public interest) and/or the theory of *Daroura* (necessity) to exclusively allow the conventional derivative instruments within a hedging framework for companies that are choosing to operate under the auspices of Islamic jurisprudence. This is particularly relevant since it has been argued repeatedly that the derivative instruments, although having speculative elements, do not entail, one, *Riba*, because they are not lending transactions, as such, with static debtor–creditor relationships, or, two, *Gharar*, since their valuation is based on known economic theories and their pricing is undertaken in the financial markets in a transparent manner.

Essentially, in a similar approach to that utilised in the evaluation of the permissibility of the contemporary form of *Musharaka* (i.e., common stock ownership) whose market prices are determined, in part, by the base rate in developing the fair value of the company by looking at its book value along with the present value of all of its future cash flows, derivatives should be explored based on the contemporary forms of risk-management challenges that are facing religiously legitimate businesses that are operating in the real economy. Put differently, it is asserted that, if properly regulated with clear (and auditable (see the next chapter)) usage terms to minimise negative externalities, surely Islamic jurisprudence cannot prohibit something that is of benefit to humankind (i.e., more effective risk management, lower probability of default, improved effectiveness and efficiency, enhanced competitive capacity, increased investment, etc.).

That said, one must admit that the decision made by

some of the largest and most respected banking organisa-tions, including their *Shari'ah* Boards, to accept to oper-ate by some of the aforementioned contractual structures, which are by no means cost effective or legally certain, in order to confront the real and legitimate market-risk chal-lenges by the Islamic finance industry is quite perplexing. At the institutional level, it demonstrates the inability of academic institutions and Islamic banking organisations, and to a certain extent the IIFM and the Islamic Financial Services Board (IFSB), to penetrate (or to be allowed to pen-etrate) the decision-making process of the juristic standard-setting bodies. The irony of this reality is that an inclusive process of decision making would have been invaluable to a relatively young industry in that it offers a realistic rep-resentation of the opportunities and challenges facing the participants in the Islamic finance industry.

5.5 Conclusion

The examination of derivatives in Islamic finance in this chapter is built on the economic foundations that evolved from the discussion in the two previous chapters on market-risk management and conventional derivative instruments. Specifically, it has been argued that derivative instruments are powerful tools for hedging the non-core market-risk exposures in a manner that does not involve excessive uncertainty (*Gharar*) or usurious debt creation (*Riba*). This contention is, of course, contextualised as being part of a larger risk-transfer strategy that also allows for the benefiting from the prospects of risk consolidation (combi-nation and diversification) through a portfolio approach to risk management rather than the utilisation of contractual forms that are costly and that contain a larger amount of risk to the counterparties.

In essence, even though this chapter is a key chapter in the book, the rationale for the earlier two chapters revolves around the estimation that the study of market risks and derivatives would have not been complete without attempting to shed some economic light, which will continue in the next two chapters, on some of the controversial issues that surround the opinions of some *Shari'ah* scholars on the subject matter. This, obviously, is a much more challenging road to travel than the one offered by the superficial formulation of contractual structures that comply with *the form* of *Shari'ah* proscriptions rather than with their substance. However, the meeting of this challenge becomes necessary as one recognises that the prohibitions in Islam are focused mainly on the substance or the essence of the impermissible act. That is evident when one examines a comparable of banning alcohol and how it is not the colour of wine or the ingredients of the constitution that is the basis for the prohibition, but rather it is its intoxicating effect.

Thus, one may argue that the same analogy applies to the sphere of Islamic derivatives in that even if the ingredients of Islamic swaps are individually permissible, their presence leads largely to the same effects as those that are created by conventional swaps and should therefore result, if one takes the anti-derivative arguments to their literal ends, in being impermissible under the auspices of the *Shari'ah*. Notably, the facilitative arguments for superficial financial engineering, whereby it is deemed that Islamic financial engineering is necessary in order to produce 'Islamic' contracts, since, by equivalence, the Islamic slaughter of animals is the only means to produce '*Halal*' beef, is seriously ignoring the reasoning behind the God-given directives.

Effectively, as shown earlier, it becomes rather apparent

that the use of financial engineering, commodities and questionable legal contracts do not and will not affect the substance of the prohibition, as they are being perceived by the *Shari'ah* scholars, because the end result is mostly the same. In fact, it has been demonstrated that these reformulations of the conventional derivative contracts means the prospect of adverse consequences for their users as well as for society as a whole in that they hold the prospect of being defective hedges with negative externalities to real-sector operators consequent of the imposition of artificial supply-and-demand forces for whatever underlying commodity is used. If, however, the commodities are placed in the transaction only for cosmetic reasons (i.e., fleeting or ineffective ownership), as is currently the case with some Islamic hedging contracts, then one must really strive to examine the direction that the Islamic finance industry is headed in.

With that, the in-depth consideration of the religious basis for some of the negative perceptions in the *Shari'ah* scholarly circles of these contractual forms has arguably delineated the position that the main obstacle to the acceptance of the derivative instruments is perhaps the implicit unease felt by the *Shari'ah* scholars in accepting the nature of the underlying reference rate (e.g., LIBOR) or price (e.g., currency) in the derivative contract, which has a corresponding ambiguity in the recognition of the derivative contract on the financial statements of the hedging entities.

A second obstacle to effective acceptance is a product of the institutionalisation of the trading of derivatives along with the widening of the level and nature of the market participants, especially when these instruments are viewed within the background of the prohibition of *Maysir* (gambling) wherein there is a clear involvement of added levels of pure gamblers in the derivative markets. The focus will now turn to these two topics.

Notes

1. Justice Usmani's analysis is specifically on futures contracts; however, it can be assumed from his analysis that his opinions extend to the wider forward-based contract market.
2. It should also be acknowledged that in some cases the creditor may accept an extension of a lesser amount of the debt for a longer period, which would make the argument of a static juridical view of this prohibition a form of injustice to both parties.
3. The argument of one versus two deferred payments indulges technical matters that likely have little to do with the objective of the *Shari'ah* directives.
4. Except for currency swaps. However, they are usually not used as a funding transaction because of the initial cash outflows for each counterparty.
5. Except for some currency derivative transactions (e.g., currency swaps).
6. One has to remember that the *Salam* and the *Istisna'a* contracts were mainly used in close communities where members were well-cognisant of the characters and the abilities of the other parties. Such is not the case in today's global financial markets with the advent of moral hazard, adverse selection and asymmetry of information.
7. Interestingly, these forms of contracts exist, in their current format, only in modern forms.
8. Al-Suwailem maintains that the funding available to the seller provides him or her with a form of compensation for moderate price increases in the underlying asset. Also, the buyer is benefiting from a lower price than is currently in existence in the spot market. Both of these assertions are not made in the

technicalities derivative markets, as outlined in the previous chapter (cost of carry, etc.).

9. Within the *Murabaha* and the Reverse *Murabaha* Master Agreement framework, the terms 'seller' and 'buyer' are not static and become rather superfluous.

10. Otherwise, the imposition of the commodity would be circumventing the spirit of the directive that put it in the transaction in the first place.

CHAPTER 6

PERMISSIBILITY OF THE UNDERLYING VARIABLES AND THE RECOGNITION OF THE CONTRACT

6.0 Introduction

The previous three chapters provided evidence supporting the argument that market-risk management, particularly with derivative instruments, should be encouraged in Islamic finance. More specifically, the discussion on market-risk management should have demonstrated that the other risk-management strategies are complements to and not substitutes for the risk-transfer strategy. Along the same lines, it was explained that the risk-sharing arrangements proposed by commentators in the Islamic finance literature are built on risk-transfer modalities, and thus they cannot simply be touted as a superior form of risk management. Further, it was argued that derivatives, especially the forward-based contracts, provide the most effective and the most efficient technique for a portfolio approach to market-risk management.

In the two chapters that followed, the economic and operational particularities of derivative instruments were illustrated in a manner that sought to respond to the repeated attempts by some *Shari'ah* scholars and academics to link the usage of derivative contracts in hedging contexts to the prohibitions of *Riba* (usury), *Gharar* (excessive uncertainty) and *Maysir* (gambling).

In particular, in the examination of the contemporary Islamic derivative instruments, it has been argued that the continual attempts to advance the *Qiyas*-based reformulations of pre-modern contracts to fit the modern-day market-risk management environment are futile, consequent of the operational and financial constraints that are imposed on their users. This was evident in the analysis of the Islamic swaps that showed that these contracts oscillate between being unsound hedging instruments with negative externalities (i.e., defective economic contracts) and being religiously flawed in that they have been shown to follow the form rather than the substance of the *Shariʿah* prohibitions that instigated the efforts for their formulation in the first place (i.e., defective *Shariʿah* contracts).

Eventually, it was proposed that derivative contracts are neutral instruments whose ultimate positive or negative implications depend on their usage by market participants. This stance, in essence, requires that Islamic jurisprudence, and the *Shariʿah* scholars who shape it, strives to pursue a deeper and more complete analysis of all the issues and technicalities of the complex topics that surround contemporary market-risk management.

This chapter continues the discussion of the previous ones with a particular focus on the permissibility of the underlying variables of the derivative contracts, which was viewed as one of the main factors leading to their outright prohibition by the standard-setting bodies and the resultant superficial replication of conventional derivatives in seemingly *Shariʿah*-compliant forms by operators in the Islamic finance industry.

For this, the remaining sections shall focus on the

interest-rate and foreign exchange rate risk-management endeavours consequent of two main reasons: First, as noted in Chapter 3, there is growing recognition in Islamic finance circles of the importance of the management of interest-rate risk and foreign exchange risk to the future health of the industry. Second, this particular area in the discourse on the permissibility of derivative instruments has not elicited a significant amount of thought, even by some of the earlier mentioned commentators who have a favourable view on the acceptance of derivatives in the Islamic finance industry.

6.1 Permissibility of the underlying variables: interest rate benchmarks

The examination of the permissibility of the underlying variables in derivative contracts commences with a discussion on the use of benchmarks. The benchmarks under discussion here are those that affect the financial statements of the entities exposed to their movements by virtue of being connected to the global economy and that consequently can be used as underlying variables in the derivative contracts to offset that exposure. In particular, the benchmarks that appear to be most contentious in Islamic jurisprudence are the interest-rate benchmarks (e.g., the Treasury rate curve, the London Interbank Offered Rate (LIBOR), the Kuala Lumpur Interbank Offered Rate (KLIBOR), the Saudi Arabia Interbank Offered Rate (SAIBOR), etc.) and the currency benchmarks (i.e., the movement in the value of the currency itself).

Incidentally, these two benchmarks are unique in that they not only form the bulk of market-risk exposures for most entities, especially financial institutions, but that they also directly confront the greatest of prohibitions in the economic doctrine in the *Shari'ah*: the prohibition of *Riba*.

With that, one, essentially, has two choices in attempting to deal with the challenges posed by the volatilities in the movements of interest rates and currencies.

One choice is to side-step the perception of the existence of *Riba* in derivative transactions that are designed to hedge interest-rate and currency exposures. This essentially means avoiding the exploration of the causes and effects of the interest-rate and currency volatilities and the possible tools to overcome to the challenges posed by their existence. Accordingly, the supporters of this choice either decide to preclude derivative instruments all together or alternatively camouflage it somehow (insertion of a commodity, *Wa'ad*, etc.) to give it the appearance of a legitimate, *Shari'ah*-compliant, transaction.

The second choice is to attempt to examine the supposed relationship between the hedging endeavours of entities and the engagement in usurious transactions that are a type of injustice and that consequently form the focus of the prohibition in Islamic jurisprudence. This section and the next elaborate the intent of proceeding along the path of the second choice since it has become apparent after the examination in the preceding chapters that the first choice has resulted in self-contradictory and economically deficient outcomes (e.g., superficial financial engineering and negative externalities).

One can begin with the vagueness surrounding the permissibility of the utilisation of the interest-rate benchmarks to manage this particular type of market-risk exposure. Once more, the Jeddah-based OIC Islamic Fiqh Academy Resolution No. 63/1/7 in 1992 shall serve as a starting point, where it states that the 'sale and purchase of the index are not permissible for they are pure gambling and constitute the sale of something fictitious (something that does not exist)'.

Fourteen years later, the Accounting and Auditing Organization for Islamic Financial Institutions (the AAOIFI), presumably upon realising that the Jeddah-based OIC Academy Ruling has been deemed ambiguous in an industry that has been increasingly using LIBOR as a benchmark for some Islamic transactions (e.g., leasing and *Sukuk*), decided to issue its *Shari'ah* Standard No. 27 in 2006 that attempted to both allow for and regulate the use of LIBOR in the Islamic finance industry.

In effect, the AAOIFI *Shari'ah* Standard No. 27 permitted the following forms of usage of indices:

> [5/1] It is permissible in the Shari'a to use indices to discern the magnitude of change in a certain market. . . . [5/3] It is permissible to use an index like LIBOR, or a certain share/commodity price index, as a basis for determining the profit of a Murabaha pledge. . . . [5/4] It is permissible to use the index to determine the portion of the variable Ujra (rent) that represents the return.

As for the prohibitions, the AAOIFI *Shari'ah* Standard No. 27 stated:

> [6/1] Shari'a prohibits trading in indices or taking advantage of their changes in the financial markets, through payment or receipt of money on the mere occurrence of certain readings of an index, and without selling or buying the real assets which the index represents or any other asset. Such dealing is prohibited even if it is practiced for the sake of hedging against potential risk. . . . [6/5] It is prohibited in Shari'a to connect the amount of a cash debt, at the time of lending, to the price index.

Moreover, in a bid to not appear out of harmony with the Jeddah-based OIC Islamic Fiqh Academy Resolution, the

AAOIFI *Shari'ah* Standard No. 27 has specifically mentioned the OIC Islamic Fiqh Academy ruling in the appendix to its own Standard after having explained the rationale for its approval. The rationale being:

> Developing indices is permissible in Shari'a because they constitute a method of forecasting and a means of observing the state of circumstances (inferences). Resorting to inferences is a well-recognized practice in judicature and financial transactions. *Ibnul Qay'yam* [*sic*] in his book on Judicial Methods presented a number of proofs on permissibility of using inferences. Permissibility of using indices to forecast the market situation is derived from acceptability of using inferences for judgment. As indicated above, Shari'a does not object to using inferences to make current or future judgment based on past events, or to initiate practical actions in the light of probable developments. Selling or buying indices is prohibited because it is nothing more than payment or receipt of money for the mere existence of a certain reading or figure. Such an act constitutes a form of gambling and an illegal act of gaining money. Hence, prohibition of selling or buying indices has been well emphasized by the Resolution of the [Jeddah-based] International Islamic Fiqh Academy which states that is not permissible to sell or buy an index because this constitutes pure gambling. It is an act of selling an imaginary object that never exists. (AAOIFI 2010: 493)

The roots of the aforementioned rationale by AAOIFI, which does demonstrate a shift in how the Islamic scholarly community conceptualises interest-rate benchmarks, may have very well been influenced by the writings of Justice Usmani, the chairman of the AAOIFI *Shari'ah* Board, who wrote an opinion in 2002, possibly in recognition of the difficulties that were then facing Islamic financial institutions, within his *An Introduction to Islamic Finance*, which argued:

> Many institutions financing by way of *murabahah* [*sic*] deter-mine their profit or marked-up on the basis of the current interest rate, mostly using LIBOR (Inter-bank offered rate in London) as the criterion. For example, if LIBOR is 6 per cent, they determine their mark-up on *murabahah* equal to LIBOR or some percentage above LIBOR. This practice is often criticized on the ground that profit based on a rate of interest should be as prohibited as interest itself. No doubt, the use of the rate of interest for determining a *halal* [*sic*] profit cannot be considered desirable. It certainly makes the transaction resemble an interest-based financing, at least in appearance, and keeping in view the severity of prohibition of interest, even this apparent resemblance should be avoided as far as possible. (Usmani 2002: 48)

One has to admit that, based on these arguments, it is hard to rationalise the persistent refusal by the *Shari'ah* schol-ars to allow derivative instruments in hedging contexts for interest-rate exposures; their prohibition is clearly not related to the expressed reasons for the rational, namely pure gambling, illegal act of gaining money, or the sale of an imaginary object that never exists. Moreover, it is not entirely understood how the statement of discerning the magnitude of the change in a certain market, which was preceded by pointing to the need to measure market situa-tions to forecast future developments before they take place in order to facilitate investment decisions (in section 2/2 of the AAOIFI ruling), could be related to anything other than developing expectations for investment purposes and man-aging the risks associated with those expectations. These include the interest-rate (and currency risk) exposures, which have been shown to be mostly non-core in nature, that are consequent of the entrance into contracts that are a part of an entity's normal operations (i.e., core functions) and that consequently form an integral component of its financial statement as well as its asset-liability management framework.

Furthermore, such an inconsistent position does pose its own set of questions, the answers to which are important in order to begin to produce a cohesive juridical position that can be a formidable basis to the current policy of prohibiting interest-rate derivative contracts for hedging purposes: First, how could LIBOR be prohibited on the basis of its being an imaginary object that never exists and at the same time be allowed for usage in determining the profit rate in *Shari'ah*-compliant transactions? In effect, according to this *Shari'ah* stance, one cannot receive cash flows or revenues or even be subject to the associated liability of such consequent of the passing of an imaginary event.

Second, how is hedging classified as pure gambling? This is, once more, a significant query since the hedging–gambling association is a recurring theme in rulings by the standard-setting bodies. This is despite the fact, as has been argued at length in previous chapters, that hedging is actually the opposite of gambling in that the hedging parties choose not to 'play' the financial markets and, as a result, be at the mercy of their rises and falls.

Third, in a manner similar to the second question but with a focus on *Riba*, how is it that the usage of interest-rate benchmarks is determined by the standard-setting bodies as a key means for transforming commercial transactions from being legitimate to being *Ribawi* (usurious) financial ones because it is an 'illegal act of gaining money' and at the same time that they be permitted in the Islamic finance industry by one of the chief proponents for the prohibition of interest-rate derivatives, *even for hedging purposes*?

Effectively, the position of the standard-setting bodies on derivatives with a monetary underlying goes against the arguments advanced by Justice Usmani himself in his book in 2002 wherein he stated: 'But one should not ignore the fact that the most important requirement for the validity of *murabahah* [sic] is that it is a genuine sale with all its ingredients and necessary consequences. . . . [M]erely using the interest rate as a benchmark for determining the profit of *murabahah* does not render the transaction as invalid, *haram* [sic] or prohibited, because the deal itself does not contain interest' (Usmani 2002: 48).

Eventually, it becomes clear, yet again, upon closer analysis of the discourse on interest-rate derivatives that the fear of gambling behaviour, not the prospect of indulging in *Riba*, by the users of these derivative instruments is ever present in setting the context for the rulings by the standard-setting bodies. Nevertheless, this fear is still perplexing because the answers for alleviating it are implicit in the prohibitive opinions of the *Shari'ah* scholars themselves.

More specifically, it appears that the invocation of *Maslaha* (public interest) in contentious contexts, such as the usage of LIBOR in rent contracts with very little direct relation to interest-rate movements in the capital markets, is permissible if there is a legitimate commercial transaction in the real economy. Other analogies used in the Islamic finance industry include the allowance for using the profit margins of alcoholic beverage producers in determining the profit margins of *halal* beverage producers. Needless to say, this divergent stance begs the important question: How are pure hedgers precluded from using LIBOR to hedge their interest-rate risk exposure that is derived from legitimate and genuine transactions in the real economy?

Notwithstanding the above, even the restricted acceptance of the use of interest-rate-based benchmarks in an
Islamic economy could not mask the unease in its presence
in the Islamic finance industry as evidenced by the continuing calls by *Shari'ah* scholars and Islamic economists for
the development of an Islamic benchmark that is disassoci-
ated from any appearance of usury. Justice Usmani himself,
having elaborated his rationale for the acceptance of LIBOR
in certain contexts, was one of the main advocates calling
for an Islamic benchmark for *Shari'ah*-compliant pricing
and discounting in the Islamic finance industry (Usmani
2002: 49). To be sure, he was not the first and will certainly
not be the last to delve into an issue that is still far from
settled.

The discourse into the development of an Islamic benchmark appears to have started in the early 1980s with the
debates surrounding the pricing of assets in an Islamic
economy. It could be conjectured that the impetus for that
exercise is the belief among some academics that Islamic
assets should somehow be priced differently from conventional assets, arguably because the current interest-rate-
based benchmarks are not only Islamically impermissible,
but they are also economically deficient.

The notable suggestions that ensued comprised the use
of the rates of return on comparable projects (Zarqa 1983),
the rate of profit in the economy (Azhar 1992), the market
average rate of return (El-Ashkar 1995), the rate of returns
on deposits of different maturities (Khan 1991), the 'true'
opportunity cost of venture capital (Ahmad 1994: 15; Zarqa
1983: 190)[1] and the rate of return on government paper collateralised against development and infrastructure projects
that are deemed to be analogous to the return on the real
sector of the economy (Haque and Mirakhor 1999; Iqbal
and Mirakhor 2007: 221–2).[2]

The aforementioned propositions that call for Islamic benchmarks are important to highlight insofar as it seems that the invocation of *Maslaha* in allowing the usage of interest-rate benchmarks, such as LIBOR, for hedging legitimate interest-rate exposures appears to be impeded consequent of the views by some *Shari'ah* scholars that there is a very real prospect of instigating an Islamic benchmark that would re-orient all of the opportunities and challenges to permissible channels. Consequently, taking a look at the substance of some of those Islamic benchmark propositions may be warranted in order to ascertain the soundness of that belief.

With that, one can commence with the assertion that if the Islamic finance industry is keen on developing a benchmark that can be used as a base rate that is more reflective of its substance and operations, then it is wholeheartedly believed that they should be encouraged to do so with the caveat that it should be built on empirically tested economic argumentation. A starting point can be to formally acknowledge that the constant appeals by some in the Islamic finance industry for a zero rate of time preference (i.e., no time value of money) are not supported in the *Shari'ah* and are simply not a practical means, grounded in theory, to explain the behaviour of economic agents with resources through time. For it is apparent that Islamic jurisprudence allows parties to factor in the uncertainties associated with the time element in some transactions such as *Murabaha* and *Salam* whereby the pricing for the settlement of a spot transaction is different from the pricing in transactions that involve payment, in money or product, through time.

To that point, it should be recognised in the Islamic finance discourse on market-risk management that, in terms of the practicality of the usage of a base rate in the capital markets, the rationale for the existence of a base rate is that the variability in the movement in the pricing of a particular asset or liability should be studied in reference to some benchmark or some minimum rate of return that the investor has to exceed.

To be certain, one may be able to tailor that minimum rate of return to be derived from the movement of the returns of comparable projects or asset classes for better measurement and evaluation of outcomes; however, these are unlikely to be lower than the lowest rate of return in international markets (LIBOR, Treasuries, zero-beta portfolio, etc.) consequent of many factors, not the least of which is diversification. In fact, almost any asset in an economy is priced on a base rate-plus framework whereby even tailored minimum rates of return are placed in a particular category, or risk premium group, in the base-rate-plus framework.

Moreover, in situations where interest-rate risk is a factor in a particular exposure, even if solely derived from the real economy (i.e., credit markets, deposits, receivables, etc.), time is a source of a quantifiable dimension of risk because it is the summation of the length of the exposure facing an entity to the risk of default and thus the possibility of greater volatility to its profitability. Thus, an entity that is faced with choices that relate to the receipt and the payment of resources over time needs to be able to decipher how their interest-rate risk exposure relates to the base rate (and the yield curve) in the financial markets for the precise time frame of the exposure (i.e., one week, one month, three months, etc.).

Notwithstanding the above discussion into the development of an Islamic benchmark, in the realm of market-risk management, it is of paramount importance to highlight the fact that *one traditionally hedges their exposures with the exact same variables that impose volatility on the financial statements of the hedging entities in the first place.* Thus, if market-risk exposures to a particular entity originated within the context of an economically sound Islamic benchmark, then it would be important for that entity to use *that* benchmark for hedging purposes.

However, if the movements in the interest rates, as manifested by LIBOR, for example, statistically explain the bulk of, if not all of, the interest-rate exposure then LIBOR itself (and not LIBOR mixed with some commodity price volatility) should be used as the benchmark to underlie the derivatives hedging contracts in order to offset the original exposure. Put differently, the choice of the benchmark to underlie derivative contracts for hedging purposes is a matter of exposure and not a matter of a debate on which benchmark should normatively be used by the hedging community to counterbalance market-risk exposures.

With that foregoing exploration of the use of interest-rate benchmarks as an underlying variable in derivative hedging transactions, one can turn to the issues surrounding the usage of foreign exchange rate movements for market-risk management purposes.

6.2 Permissibility of the underlying variables: currency benchmarks

As was done in the previous section, the examination of the permissibility of transacting in currencies as variables to underlie derivative instruments for hedging purposes shall start with the resolutions articulated by the various standard-setting bodies. For this, the Jeddah-based OIC Islamic Fiqh Academy, in deliberating the issue of the inclusion of currencies in forward transactions, during its Seventh Session in May 1992 – that is, Resolution No. 63/1/7, decided that the 'purchase and sale of currencies are not permissible [in the forward markets]'. This view was reaffirmed later in their Resolution 102/5/11 in November 1998 wherein it was stated: 'It is not permissible in *Shari'a* to sell currencies by deferred sale, and it is not permissible, still, to fix a date for exchanging them.'

Thus, the overall directive can be characterised as being favourable of the position that entities with operations that entail cross-border trade and investment over time should be required to assume (individually or collectively) the open currency risks that are associated with the transaction. Consequently, if two firms, one in Malaysia and the other in Saudi Arabia, decide to conclude a transaction, then they would have to negotiate as to who will assume this market-risk exposure (or how it could be shared between them).[3] The possibility of utilising the risk-transfer strategy by way of derivative contracts, with currencies as underlying variables, in order to assist entities with inclinations towards the implementation of *Shari'ah* directives, is apparently precluded.

The AAOIFI, for its part, despite the absence of any Standard focused specifically on derivative instruments, did formulate the *Shari'ah* Standard No. 1 – Trading in Currencies, adopted by the AAOIFI *Shari'ah* Board in May 2000, which states:

> It is prohibited to enter into forward currency contracts. This rule applies whether such contracts are effected through the exchange of deferred transfers of debt or through the execution of a deferred contract in which the concurrent possession of both the counter values by both parties does not take place. It is also prohibited to deal in the forward currency market *even if the purpose is hedging to avoid a loss of profit on a particular transaction effected in a currency whose value is expected to decline.* (AAOIFI 2010: 14–15; emphasis added)[4]

Having delineated the most pertinent resolutions by the standard-setting bodies with respect to the forward dealings in currencies, it may be appropriate at this juncture to discuss the justification for the formulation of the opinions contained therein in order to develop a greater degree of understanding of the basis and reasoning behind the prohibitive judgements that were articulated. For this, it has been explicitly declared by the standard-setting bodies that the basis for the general prohibition in the dealing of currencies in the forward market is the literal translation by *Shari'ah* scholars of some of the *Ahadith* by the Prophet (PBUH).

One of the *Ahadith* was reported by 'Ubadah Ibn Al-Samit as stating: 'Gold for gold, silver for silver – until he said – equal for equal, like for like, hand to hand, and if the kinds of assets differ, you may sell them as you wish provided that it is hand to hand.' In a second *Hadith*, it was reported by Abu Sa'id Al-Khudri that the Prophet (PBUH) said: 'Do not sell gold for gold except equal to equal and do not sell what is deferred for a spot exchange.'

Upon a closer examination of the literature surrounding these *Ahadith*, it appears that, despite some early divergence in their interpretation by some leading *Shari'ah* scholars (Al-Amine 2008: 84–6; Islahi 2005: 52), most *Shari'ah* scholars agree that the '*Illah* (efficient cause) for their elaboration concentrates on the prohibition of *Riba*, with its two forms being, one, *Riba Al-Fadl*, where items are exchanged on the spot, in different quantities (e.g., 1 oz. of gold for 1.1 oz. of gold on the spot) and, two, *Riba Al-Nasi'ah*, which entails the exchange of items for a deferred period (e.g., 1 oz. of gold for 1.5 oz. of gold in the forward market). Moreover, it has been decided by the Makkah-based Islamic Fiqh Academy in its Fifth Session in February 1982 that in conforming to the rules of *Qiyas* the items in the *Ahadith* are mentioned in the context of their utilisation as *Thamaniyya* (money) and, thus, money, whatever its form, becomes purview to the restrictions outlined in the *Ahadith*.

The use of *Qiyas* in the above context, in time, has evolved into the usage of the *Ahadith* to develop a juridical opinion with respect to *'Aqd Al-Sarf* (currency exchange contract), with *Sarf* being defined by Al-Zuhayli as: 'the exchange of one monetary form for another in the same genera, i.e. gold for gold coins, gold for silver, silver for gold, etc., whether it is in the form of jewellery or minted coins. Such trading is allowed since the Prophet (PBUH) permitted the exchange of properties for which *Riba* applied hand-to-hand in equal quantities in the same genus, or with difference in quantities in different genera' (Al-Zuhayli and El-Gamal 2003: 281). In short, the conceptualisation of *Riba Al-Fadl* and *Riba Al-Nasi'ah* applies to trading in money as characterised by currencies.

Thus, with an emphasis on the prohibition of *Riba Al-Fadl*, it is not permitted to enter into a contract to trade currencies of the same *Jins* (genre) for different amounts in the spot market (i.e., USD 10 for USD 11). Similarly, while it is permitted to agree to exchange in currencies of different *Jins* in different quantities on the spot (i.e., 7 Egyptian Pounds for 1 USD), it is not acceptable to transact in currencies of different *Jins* for different quantities in the future (i.e., 7 Egyptian Pounds for 1 USD in the future) consequent of the *Riba Al-Nasi'ah* proscription.

There are, of course, a few points of contention here that should be elucidated with respect to the all-encompassing interpretations given in a seemingly wholesale fashion to any form of transacting in currencies in the forward market, even if it is done in order to manage market-risk exposures. The first, which has been argued repeatedly in the previous chapters, is that derivative transactions are not debt instruments with a unique debtor–creditor relationship between the parties, which is the context in which the aforementioned *Ahadith* are to be understood.

Essentially, the proscription was targeting the banning of the use of the items that can be regarded as money as in *Ribawi* (usurious) contracts despite having the appearance of innocuous purchase-and-sale transactions. In fact, these *Ahadith* are likely related to the often quoted verse in the Quran on *Riba* where it states:

> Those who consume interest cannot stand [on the Day of Resurrection] except as one stands who is being beaten by Satan into insanity. That is because they say, '*Trade is [just] like Riba.*' But Allah has permitted trade and has forbidden Riba. So whoever has received an admonition from his Lord and desists may have what is past, and his affair rests with Allah. But whoever returns to [dealing in usury] – those are the companions of the Fire; they will abide eternally therein. (Quran 2:275; emphasis added)

In this context, the proscription in the *Shari'ah* of two sales in one becomes an effective enforcer of the *Riba* prohibition to confront seemingly clever structuring of usurious transactions by scrupulous money lenders under the guise of trade. Effectively, with the requirement of items in spot transactions of the same genre being of the same quantity and the proscription of joining two sales in one, the prospect of *Riba Al-Fadl* is eliminated because it becomes a value-less transaction to the parties of the contract.

Notably, a dissimilar situation arises in the endeavours to implement the religious commands with regards to *Riba Al-Nasi'ah* in the forward markets whereby, in a pure debt setting, a party pre-pays another party a particular form of money (gold, silver, USD, Malaysian Ringgit (MYR), Saudi Arabian Riyal (SAR), etc.) and agrees to be paid back at a particular point (or points) in time in the future either the same or a different form of money with an added premium. Here, it should be appreciated that the items included in the *Ahadith* were not only standardised, but they also had prices that were generally stable during the time of the Prophet (PBUH) and the period of the first four Califs where it was observed, for example, that the ratio of gold to silver at that time was a constant 1:10 (Chapra 1996: 1).

To return to the topic of the utilisation of derivative instruments for market-risk management purposes, it is perhaps difficult to comprehend the argument that purports that currencies should be viewed as gold and silver, as existing in seventh-century Arabia, and should, therefore, not be traded in the forward markets. At a basic level, the inclusion of the time factor ought to be properly contextualised in the above *Ahadith* in that the prohibitions contained therein are likely to have a deeper meaning than the one contained in the propositions calling for the institutionalisation of a zero time value of money (i.e., spot price should always equal forward price in an Islamic economy). For, as discussed in the previous section, it is evident that the classification of *Riba*, in contemporary settings that include the consideration of *Maslaha* (public interest), is moving in the direction of granting more credence to the nature, or substance, of the transaction.

Thus, it can be argued that the unease in Islamic jurisprudence should be focused on the trading of currencies in the forward markets in a 'naked' manner whereby there is no clear linkage to the real sector that can serve as a foundation to justify the transaction. Essentially, this view can be considered to espouse a sound position that promotes the proper consideration of the origin of the exposure in the first place, which in true hedging transactions is generated from activities tied to the real sector.

That is, it is neither a lending transaction within the framework of *Riba* nor a contract of *Maysir* (gambling) trading in variables that are built on a superficial exchange of money. To that end, if one closely examines the acceptance of the *Salam* contract, which is by its very nature a forward contract (with a financing element), in Islamic jurisprudence by the Prophet (PBUH) when he arrived at Madinah, they may not find a large degree in divergence in how a transaction on the face of it may be viewed as prohibited, but is ruled as acceptable consequent of the legitimacy of the practical need.

Accordingly, it may be contended that the contextualisation of the juridical issues surrounding the utilisation of currencies could have been done in a more comprehensive manner that accounts for how the worlds of commerce and finance have evolved; for surely it is not the intention of God to limit the currency transactions, even if they are done on a forward basis, which underlie legitimate trade among humankind. With that, it could be inferred from the discourse on the subject that the apprehension of the *Shari'ah* is actually rooted in the dealings of money between individuals in a manner that is formalised by a contract where there is no reference in the contract to any specific, genuine and real-sector transaction (hence the advent of the commodity *Murabaha* structures).

For that, we turn to the nature of money in Islam to shed light on its usage, particularly in the form of interest-rate and currency benchmarks, in the derivative markets.

6.3 The nature of money in Islam

The conceptualisation of money in Islamic jurisprudence is a controversial matter where the discourse is almost completely centred on the prohibition of *Riba*. This, along with seemingly rigid interpretations of the scripture by some the *Shari'ah* scholars, in mostly descriptive terms, with little engagement with economic theory in what is essentially an economic subject matter, does complicate the discussions on any topic related to money. With that, it should be stated that monetary economics with its focus on exploring the behaviour of economic agents with money (Brunner and Meltzer 1971; Keynes 1937; Lavington 1968; Marshall 1923; Tobin 1956, 1965) is outside the scope of the discussion at hand. There are some of its elements, however, that will be used to contextualise some of the opinions that have been transmitted with respect to money in Islamic thought.

At this stage, it is best to begin with a deeper understanding of the concept of money and what is meant by the slippery term along with the reasoning for its existence. The unit of account characterisation presents itself first where from the dawn of time humans have sought to account for what is theirs. In time, the simple calculation of the wealth of an individual and his or her income, as an economic agent who seeks to undertake rational decision-making, necessitated the existence of a common denominator, or a single *numeraire*, in order to gauge the values of objects (not only their count) with greater precision.

To this, Simmel offers a particularly rich conceptualisation in the usage of and rationale for the unit of account function of money by teaching his readers that:

> [t]he superstructure of money relations erected above qualitative reality determine much more radically the inner image of reality according to its forms. The mathematical character of money imbues the relationship of the elements of life with a precision, a reliability in the determination of parity and disparity, an unambiguousness in agreements and arrangements in the same way as the general use of pocket watches

has brought about a similar effect in daily life. Like the determination of abstract value by money, the determination of abstract time by clocks provides a system for the most detailed and definite arrangements and measurements that imparts an otherwise unattainable transparency and calculability to the contents of life, at least as regards their practical management. The calculating intellectuality embodied in these forms may in its turn derive from them some of the energy through which intellectuality controls modern life. (Simmel cited in Simmel and Frisby 2004: 445)

To be certain, the relevancy of the eloquent viewpoint imparted by Simmel is dependent on the dynamic relationship that exists between the unit of account characteristics of money with the second defining trait of money: medium of exchange. Specifically, the rationale for the utilisation of money as a unit of account can be considered to be largely a factor of the realisation by economic agents in society that its standardisation leads to systemic efficiency, consequent of less pricing uncertainty, if it is used as a medium of exchange in trade and investment.

This is especially true in increasingly specialised economies that depend on trade along with institutionalised payment practices that affect the exchange process that takes place. In effect, the reduction in the pricing uncertainty is a product of having the market forces achieve a balance in what Weber calls 'conflict of interests and compromises' between economic agents in a society with respect to the price of money vis-à-vis other objects (Weber cited in Weber *et al.* 1978 [1922]: 108).

Interestingly, consequent of the focus on the prohibition of *Riba* in Islamic jurisprudence, the literature on the use of money as a medium of exchange is particularly rich in Islamic thought. Among the notable Islamic writers who understood, and wrote on, the important role that money plays in promoting commerce are Ibn Rushd (Averroes) and Al-Ghazali. For Ibn Rushed, 'Justice in transactions lies in approximating equivalence. So, when realizing equivalence between different things was found to be almost impossible, dinar and dirham were made to evaluate them, that is, measure them' (Ibn Rushd 1998 [n.d.]: 135; Islahi 2005).

Al-Ghazali, for his part, viewed the existence of money as being derived from the need for:

> A measure on the basis of which price can be determined, because the exchanged commodities are neither of the same type, nor of the same measure which can determine how much quantity of one commodity is a just price for another. Therefore, all these commodities need a mediator to judge their exact value. . . . Allah Almighty has, therefore, created dirhams and dinars (money) as judges and mediators between all commodities so that all objects of wealth are measured through them. . . . [T]hat is why Allah has created them, so that they may be circulated between hands and act as a fair judge between different commodities and work as a medium to acquire other things. . . . Therefore, there was needed a thing which in its appearance is nothing, but in its essence is everything. (Al-Ghazali, n.d: 348; see also Usmani 2010)

These writings, especially in their explicit reference to 'justice', can be discerned to follow, and elaborate on, the specific instructions of the Prophet (PBUH) for the prohibition of the earlier described *Riba Al-Fadl*, whereby it was narrated by Muslim on the authority of Abu Said Al Khudriy that Bilal visited the Messenger of Allah (PBUH) with some high-quality dates, and the Prophet (PBUH) enquired about their source. Bilal explained that he had traded two volumes of his lower quality dates for one volume of the higher quality dates in the market. The Messenger of Allah (PBUH) said: '[T]his is precisely the forbidden Riba! Do not do this. Instead, sell the first type of dates, and use the proceeds to buy the other.'

Thus, the functions of money as a unit of account and as a medium of exchange in Islamic thought are believed to transcend the exclusive focus on the realm of the preference for systemic efficiency and also include the requirements for clarity and justice in the economic dealings between individuals. In effect, the prohibitions of *Riba Al-Fadl* and *Gharar*, as elucidated by the Prophet (PBUH), hold an intimate relationship in providing guidance for greater human well-being through transparent cooperation.

Up to this point, and having discussed the unit of account and medium of exchange roles of money, there does not appear to be much contention between the conceptualisation of money in Western thought and the conceptualisation of money in Islamic thought. However, as the discourse evolves into the third and final role for money, namely storage of value, the divergence in the conceptualisation of money begins to emerge. Once more, there are indications in the literature of the presence of a fear in *Shari'ah* scholars of engagement in *Riba* since it was consistently viewed by them that the dealings of money between individuals, if unregulated, amount to indulgence in *Riba* since the extension of credit is traditionally undertaken through monetary forms.

That being said, it is not self-evident how the fear of the exchanging of money and the saving of money as a store of value for transactions and investment (not necessarily in the credit realm) turned in contemporary settings to a focus on the purchase and sale of commodities as a means to ensure the avoidance of *Riba*.

One may surmise that the earlier mentioned verse in

the Quran stating '[b]ut Allah has permitted trade and has forbidden *Riba*' (Quran 2:275) was interpreted by some *not as an indication by God that trade and usury should not be thought of as one and the same for those who seek to pursue usurious money lending under the banner of trade, but rather that God was specifying economic dealings to be exclusively divided between individuals as either trade or Riba* (i.e., as being mutually exclusive and collectively exhaustive). The appreciation of this difference in interpretation is fundamental in order to understand the constant push for commodities to underlie any Islamic finance product where no clear asset is discernible even if the transaction is actually linked to the real economy (e.g., market-risk management).

With that, one may both agree and disagree with the statements by some *Shari'ah* scholars and academics regarding the use of commodities in Islamic finance as an objective test of legitimacy (Al-Amine 2008; BMB 2010: 132; Iqbal and Mirakhor 2007: 209; Usmani 2010).[5] True, money should not be treated as a commodity to be used with no real commercial rationale that is clearly linked to the real economy, the end result of which is probably associated with either *Riba* or *Maysir*, but, at the same time, the view that is expressed by several commentators that money cannot be a store of value, because 1) it is not an asset, 2) that can be an object of trade, 3) since it has no utility, is perhaps dependent more on philosophical reasoning and less on economic substance. For if this is the case then what is essentially being proposed entails the complete reformulation of economic theories and an overhaul of the accounting practice (as will be discussed in the next section). That is not to say that this extreme measure is impossible; however, its serious undertaking requires more than a passing philosophical argument by its adherents.

It may be necessary at this stage to discuss the characterisation of the storage of value function of money in Islamic
thought, which requires delving into some of the perspectives that deal with the property rights of individuals (and
entities) in Islam. For this, it should be affirmed at the onset
of the discussion that there is no text in the scripture that
defined the concept of *Mal* (property); however, the major
schools of Islamic jurisprudence (*Maliki, Shafi'i, Hanbalis*
and *Shafi'i*) do define *Mal*, broadly, as any *'Ayn* (corporeal) and *Manfa'a* (usufruct) that can bestow on its owner
current or potential benefit. Consequently, in carrying this
definition to a medium of exchange framework, economic
agents can be thought of as exchanging assets for their benefit. This includes the purchase of money from other economic agents in return for imparting with a particular *'Ayn*
or *Manfa'a* that is owned.[6]

Notably, the bought and sold money does not have to be
any specific commodities or precious metals (or even any
object at all for that matter). This becomes evident when one
observes the often quoted description by Paul Samuelson of
the embodiment of money in society, whereby Samuelson
states that money is 'an artificial social convention', since
when, for whatever reason, any particular substance begins
to be used as money, people will begin to value it (Samuelson
1998: 55).

To be certain, it was not the Western economic thought of
the twentieth century that bestowed on money this abstract
qualification. For it was advanced by some of the leading
Shari'ah scholars, including Ibn Hanbal, Ibn Hazm and Ibn
Taymiyyah, the belief that custom and usage are actually the
chief factors that determine the endowment of a particular
item with the coveted title of 'Money'. One can surmise that
this is probably consequent of the fact that, again, there is
no specific text in the scripture that requires the Islamic

community to use gold and silver, or any particular object for that matter, as money.[7]

Thus, with the agreement that the medium of exchange function is, in effect, defined by whatever custom and usage in society has been determined as worthy of the highly respectful money status, one should also accept that in the post-Bretton Woods system, the money that society has agreed upon is pure paper currency that entails people holding government-issued pieces of paper because they are certain that others will accept the same. This certainty is derived from the collective agreement, even if an implicit one, that they (or more precisely their issuing authority as a representative) will limit its issuance and will share any *seigniorage* that accumulates in the process.[8]

Interestingly, this modern-day convention was acknowledged by the Jeddah-based OIC Islamic Fiqh Academy, in its Third Session in October 1986, in that it stated in its *Shari'ah* Rules Governing Paper Money and Currency Rates Fluctuations Resolution (No. 21/9/3) that '[p]aper money is real money, possessing all characteristics of value, and subject to Shari'a rules governing gold and silver vis-à-vis usury, *Zakat* [*sic*], Salam and all other transactions.'

With that background into money, whatever its form, it may be difficult to conceptualise the argument that money as an imaginative construct that is built on social convention and has no utility.[9] This is because this assertion does not articulate a concrete and defendable position as to why money is held by individuals in the first place. To address that conundrum, and without indulging too much in the diverse economic theories surrounding that query, it may be simply stated that money, being a unique asset unlike any other, provides utility that emanates from the particular circumstances of its users and their specific needs for its presence in their lives.

To that point, Hicks, remarking on the nature of money, once wrote: '[O]ne of the advantages that are got from the use of money is that people do not have to pass it on immediately; they can choose the time of their purchases to suit their convenience. *If they use this facility moderately, it is useful to them; and it does no harm to other people*' (Hicks 1971: 21; emphasis added). The moderate use of money and its potential harm will be explored below; however, at this stage, it should be noted that there is inherent utility in the holding and use of money, otherwise one could discard money with little regard to their own welfare.

In effect, money is one of the centrepieces in what affects the behaviour of individuals with respect to choices of consumption over time (including the transfer of consumption capacity to inheritors). This follows from what Marshall taught us early in the twentieth century when he remarked: 'A prudent person will endeavour to distribute his means between all their several uses, present and future, in such a way that they will have in each the same marginal utility' (Marshall 1910: 119).

Thus, while one may concur with some of the *Shari'ah* scholars that money should not be desired for its own sake, it is, however, not sensible to assume a position that money should not be viewed as an objective and as a means to increase human welfare, if done in a legitimate manner. Effectively, money, being a store of value, is an integral component of wealth.

To be certain, money is not the only component of wealth; there are many asset groups that can assist in allowing for the attainment of the most efficient temporal distribution of consumption choices (i.e., wealth management). In fact, it is recognised that other asset groups dominate money in their ability to manage wealth over time, including wealth transfer. Yet, individuals still hold money, as a store of value, even if it is costly for them to do so, consequent of inflation, and in Islamic contexts, the payment of *Zakah* (alms) on liquid funds. This is because money is unique in that it offers functions that other assets cannot provide, namely a cost-efficient medium of exchange.

With that, it may be contended that the *Shari'ah* scholars and other writers who continue to hold unfavourable views on the use of money as a store of value should perhaps re-examine the aforementioned *Hadith* regarding Bilal and the sale of his dates. For, it can be apparent, in monetary terms, that the Prophet (PBUH) instructed Bilal to cede ownership of his lower quality dates for the ownership of money as a commercial act that precedes the one entailing the relinquishing of money in return for the ownership of the high-quality dates. Notably, these two exchanges did not have to be simultaneous, since Bilal could have sold his lower quality dates on Monday, for example, and purchased the high-quality dates a week later (possibly consequent of disagreement on the purchase price on Monday). During that week, Bilal had ownership of the money from the sale of the lower quality dates, essentially as a store of value, until he effected the high-quality dates' transaction.

Interestingly, in this transaction, the use of money was not associated with capital, investment or lending, as is often portrayed in the literature in Islamic finance when one speaks of money (Kahf 2006; Khan and Mirakhor 1994; Usmani 2010). In effect, the elaboration of the aforementioned example of Bilal is significant because it demonstrates that the use of money is primarily related to choices of consumption over time rather than being tied to an expression of a narrow view of money as a means for *Riba*. Specifically, in the case of Bilal, it was a choice of a spot transaction or one that is completed one week later.

In trade, these choices are almost limitless between the

numerous operators in the real economy, and the amount of money held for those transactions is a factor of many associated and interrelated variables. These may include: the wealth of the individual, the planned volume of transactions and the timing of receipts and payments as well as the size, extent and activity of the financial markets, among many other factors. Thus, the discussion into the store of value characterisation of money can be concluded by stating that money is considered to be a store of value because trade, by its very nature, is a process that takes time, and, thus, anything that serves as a medium of exchange must be held as a store of value.

There are, of course, concerns regarding hoarding money with the adverse effects on the economy and in terms of the welfare of economic agents within it. This, if one would recall, relates to the statement quoted earlier by Hicks in which he stated that money contains many advantages to people. Hicks wrote: '*If they use this facility moderately, it is useful to them; and it does no harm to other people*' (Hicks 1971: 21; emphasis added). The fear here, which is not peculiar to Islamic jurisprudence in that it has been an active issue of concern in monetary economic theory, is that the hoarding of money is likely to suppress economic activity and consequently reduce welfare in society.

As a background, many writers on monetary economic theory have shown that the hoarding of money in modern contexts could be marked as a reaction by individuals to exogenous economic factors, such as economic shocks, poorly developed financial markets and a dearth of investment opportunities. This should be contextualised by stating that economic agents, despite the views to the contrary in some of the Islamic finance literature, have an incentive to economise their holdings of money, as part of their portfolio, in a non-zero interest-rate (or profit-rate) environment since money has traditionally a negative rate of return consequent of inflation and other pressures (e.g., *Zakah*).

However, in Islamic jurisprudence, it can be clearly observed that there is a view by some of the *Shari'ah* scholars and commentators that the holding of money amounts to hoarding as a deliberate malicious act of economic injustice by some individuals who seek to circumvent the real economy in order to generate returns on money lending and/or illegitimate activities (Abu Saud 2002; Al-Ghazali n.d.; Al-Suwailem 2012; Siddiqi 1982; Usmani 2010). This indiscriminate view of hoarding exists despite the fact, as was stated earlier, that money is inferior to other asset classes for wealth management over time. If anything, it is more rational for profit-maximising individuals to hoard other asset classes, especially those corporeal assets that offer more cost-efficient returns that are highly favoured by contemporary *Shari'ah* scholars.

To be certain, this distrustful position in the holding of money is not without justification. It is closely associated with the literal interpretation of this verse in the Quran: 'O you who have believed, indeed many of the scholars and the monks devour the wealth of people unjustly and avert [them] from the way of Allah. *And those who hoard gold and silver and spend it not in the way of Allah – give them tidings of a painful punishment*' (Quran 9:34; emphasis added).

However, it should be recognised that a more certain path to developing an interpretative conjecture (and consequently an economic policy) in Islamic jurisprudence depends on *both* the details as well as the contextual understanding of what is being communicated by God. In essence, it is not the nature of what is being amassed that should be the focus of the discourse on money in Islamic finance, but rather it is the act itself of illegitimate amassing (i.e., malicious hoarding) that is forbidden in Islam.

That is, hoarding, no matter what asset, if undertaken illegitimately, because it entails greed, selfishness and deception, is an act of injustice and should therefore be forbidden.[10] In fact, if one wants to be devious, they can simply rely on the literal translation by the *Shari'ah* scholars to give themselves the juristic approval to circumvent the prohibition on ill-intended hoarding through a focus on the rational, profit-maximising amassing of all asset classes, except gold and silver (or even money, for that matter).[11]

Notably, in the circumstance of economic uncertainty and a dearth of investment opportunities within poorly developed markets (i.e., economic explanations for hoarding behaviour), one can hardly imagine that Islam, as a religion, supports the imposition on people to invest and expose themselves to losses or be condemned to 'painful punishment'. Indeed, this would be very much against logic and reason as well as the juristic consensus in support of *Al-Durariyat Al-Khamsa* (five necessities) as elucidated by Al-Ghazali (1993a).

The above discussion on the nature of money in Islam is intended to address the steady association in the discussion on the subject between the explicit prohibition of *Riba* in the scripture, and money, which, in turn, manifested itself in the negative perceptions about transacting in monetary variables (interest rate and currency) that underlie derivative instruments. Here, one should realise that, in the context of *Riba*, the usurious credit contracts are a type of asset class to creditors, albeit an impermissible one, which evolves from transacting in money.

In other words, it is the prohibition of usurious lending that should be the focus in terms of proscription, not money, or financial instruments whose value is related to money (e.g., derivatives). For, in the realm of commerce, the purchase and sale of a prohibited item (e.g., wine or pork) are realised with money, yet one does not usually charge money with the commitment of the prohibited act since it is the act itself that is prohibited.

The aforementioned distinction is significant insofar as it allows for the existence of financial instruments, such as derivatives with a monetary underlying, in order to serve as market-risk management tools. The relevancy of this becomes apparent in hedging contexts where there is little, if any, relationship with the credit markets or any gambling activities.

With that, and given that derivative instruments are monetary contracts that serve to hedge balance-sheet exposures by employing a contrarian market-risk-transfer methodology, it is important to also shed light on some of the side effects of the prohibition of these instruments, especially in relation to the formal recognition of the derivative contracts. The recognition of the derivative instruments becomes most prominent in this context.

6.4 Recognition of the derivative contract

The importance of delving into the formal recognition of the derivative contracts in the financial statements of the entities that use them stems from the quintessential reason for their existence. Effectively, in a hedging context, any particular derivative instrument is designed to ensure that the economic factors that contribute to the worsening of the balance-sheet position of a hedging entity are largely offset by the rise in the value of the derivative instrument. That is, the gain (loss) on the balance sheet of the entity as a result of the market-risk exposure will be offset by a loss (gain) on the derivative instrument. This defining element of the usage of derivative instruments for market-risk management necessitates the presence of accounting rules that acknowledge this practice and ensure that it is communicated to the readers, including the regulators, of the financial statements in the most transparent manner possible.

For this, the International Accounting Standards Board (IASB) issued the IAS 39 (*Financial Instruments: Recognition and Measurement Standard*) that outlines the requirements for the recognition, de-recognition and measurement of financial assets and liabilities, including derivative contracts. In effect, the standard stipulates that the initial recognition is recorded once an entity becomes a party to the contractual provisions of the derivative instrument and this recognition of the derivative instrument shall continue on its financial statements until the rights, obligations and control ceases to exist. In terms of measurement, the derivative instruments are to be recorded at fair value, which is the amount for which the asset could be exchanged, or the amount for which a liability could be settled, between knowledgeable, willing parties in an arm's length transaction (e.g., market quotation for replacement cost).

Remarkably, if the derivative instrument is used for hedging purposes, the IAS 39 allows the usage of Hedge Accounting. The importance of the IAS Hedge Accounting provision is in its extension to the hedging community the 'privilege' of overriding the normal accounting treatment for derivatives (fair value through profit or loss in the period incurred) and/or providing the ability to adjust the carrying value of assets and liabilities. The reasoning behind the offering of this privilege is that the derivative hedging instruments should not have an accounting life of their own, but they should rather be considered as a part of a unified package of an operational and/or financial commitment *plus* an instrument to serve as a hedge to that commitment.

The above treatment is significant insofar as the hedging instruments generate cash losses and gains over their

life while the transactions they are designed to hedge produce only paper gains and losses until they are recognised
in a later period, which in turn results in greater volatility, and thus uncertainty, in the income statement of the
hedging entity. In essence, hedge accounting as noted by
PricewaterhouseCoopers 'seeks to correct this mismatch
by changing the timing of recognition of gains and losses
on either the hedged item or the hedging instrument.
This avoids much of the volatility that would arise if the
derivative gains and losses were recognised in the income
statement, as required by normal accounting principles'
(PricewaterhouseCoopers 2005: 7).

In order to qualify for Hedge Accounting, an entity has
to comply with onerous requirements that oblige the existence of formal documentation at the commencement of the
recognition of the derivative contract. This is in addition to
the achievement of stringent effectiveness tests for the life
of the hedge in a manner that confirms the strength of the
relationship between the underlying risk exposure and the
derivative instrument. If either of these requirements is not
present, Hedge Accounting may not be used.

Specifically, the formal documentation that is demanded
is rooted in the requirement that the hedging entity identify
and certify their risk-management objective, the hedged
item, the hedging instrument, the nature of the risk being
hedged and the methodology that will be followed for
the effectiveness tests. In particular, the hedge should be
highly effective at the inception of the contractual relationship and is expected to be within the range of 80 per cent
to 125 per cent until it is de-recognised (prospectively and
retrospectively).

This approach that centres on providing an effectiveness band does leave some room for ineffectiveness in case
the correlation between the derivative instrument and the

relevant risk exposure experiences some changes consequent of mismatches in the underlying variables (e.g., different maturities), changes in counterparty risks and/or if
the underlying variable in the derivative contract is a proxy
for the actual item affecting the balance-sheet exposure (e.g.,
oil futures for jet fuel cost variation). Notably, it should be
clear from the aforementioned requirements that the push
for the utilisation of commodities to underlie the Islamic
derivative instruments may very well disturb their effectiveness within the IAS 39 framework, and may thus diminish
the prospect of the usage of that privilege, consequent of the
exogenous volatilities imposed.

The effectiveness tests, for their part, comprise of three
methods, whose choice of utilisation should be included in
the documentation at the inception of the hedge. The first
method concerns the comparison of critical terms, which
consists of comparing terms such as notional principle,
amounts, term, pricing dates, timing, and quantum and
currency of the cash flows, as well as being concerned with
confirmation that there are no features that would invalidate
an assumption of effectiveness. The second method is the
dollar offset method that entails the quantitative assurance
that the change in the fair value or cash flows of the derivative instrument corresponds to the change in the fair value
or cash flows of the market-risk exposure. The third method
is the undertaking of a regression analysis of the relationship between the derivative instrument and the underlying
exposure in order to statistically test effectiveness.

The privileges to hedgers also extend to the taxation
sphere in that the taxing authorities in some jurisdictions
offer preferential tax treatment in the recognition of gains
and losses that result from the utilisation of derivatives
for risk-management purposes. For example, the Internal
Revenue Service (IRS) in the United States has elaborated

tax regulations that do not force the application of the mark-to-market rules to hedging transactions and that allow instead for a closer matching between the gains and the losses of the derivative instrument and the underlying risk exposure.

The foregoing discussion into Hedge Accounting and taxation is actually important to the discussion at hand. This is because it provides a view into the practicalities that surround the recognition of the derivative contracts in a manner that appreciates the rationale for their existence (i.e., offsetting risk exposures). Notwithstanding the above, it is remarkable that the AAOIFI had not sought to establish some form of an accounting standard for derivative usage.[12] This, as mentioned in the previous chapter, could be consequent of its opinion that the matter was settled in the *Shari'ah* scholarly community and accordingly did not warrant deliberations of accounting and auditing technicalities.

Alternatively, the AAOIFI may have thought that it had made its position clear with the injunctions against the usage of currencies (*Shari'ah* Standard No. 1) and benchmarks (*Shari'ah* Standard No. 27) for hedging purposes. Nonetheless, this position is not completely comprehensible since the growth in the utilisation of the Islamic swaps in the Islamic finance industry should have clearly propelled it to at least consider the implications of its usage by industry participants.

Then again, it could be the case that AAOIFI deemed the Islamic swap contracts (i.e., the ISDA/IIFM *Tahawwut* (Hedging) Master Agreement (TMA) and other variants) a matter of transacting in commodities that renders them within the purview of the accounting treatment that is normally accorded to the ordinary purchase and sale of assets. If this is indeed the case, AAOIFI's position is problematic for two main reasons: First, as per accounting convention, it forces the participants of dynamic hedging in the Islamic finance industry to hold the underlying commodity contracts as held-for-trading, which necessitates measurement at fair value with the changes in the valuation reported in the income statement until the maturity of the contract.

This becomes a rather prohibitive stance because, as alluded to earlier, the volatility of the commodity market price is effectively added to the movement of the Islamic swap consequent of the changes of the underlying risk exposure (e.g., interest rates and currencies). Both will, accordingly, manifest themselves through increased uncertainty over the stability of earnings of the hedging entity (i.e., higher risk premium). Notably, this treatment may also have negative implications on the capital adequacy prospects for Islamic banking institutions.

Second, AAOIFI's position precludes the possibility of utilising the stringent requirements (documentation, effectiveness tests, etc.) articulated by the IASB in order to benefit from the privileges of Hedge Accounting. Specifically, the requirements for Hedge Accounting may very well offer an important perspective regarding the efforts to avoid *Maysir* (gambling), which appears to be a major concern for the standard-setting bodies and some of the sceptical *Shari'ah* scholars and academics. For this, the IAS 39 requirements could provide insights into the necessary, and testable, evidence that the management of entities would need to show in order to prove that their derivative usage is not within the realm of gambling in the financial markets.

In effect, Hedge Accounting can be easily tested and monitored by the board of directors, *Shari'ah* supervisory boards, regulators, shareholders and other stakeholders of the entities that are seeking to utilise derivatives in their market-risk management endeavours in order to confirm that the entity is not engaging in gambling activities that increase the risks of financial distress as well as having other negative externalities with regards to the stability of the global financial markets.

With that prospect in mind, it should be stated that the current implicit AAOIFI acceptance of the usage of Islamic swaps by the participants in the Islamic finance industry offers little accounting oversight over seemingly clever treasurers and chief financial officers (CFOs) who decide to use these commodity-based instruments to generate excess returns within pure gambling contexts. To be sure, the usage of Islamic swaps is usually preceded by an approval by the *Shari'ah* supervisory board of the entity that hopes to use them, which is invariably given within a hedging mandate.

However, as opposed to the stringent rules of the Hedge Accounting requirements, the hedging mandate can be easily circumvented by those in the Islamic finance industry who are intent on using the instruments as investment tools to potentially increase their profitability performance, and consequently salary bonuses, since the gains and losses for these instruments are treated as ordinary gains and losses in the financial statements. The above is not a hypothetical situation or an unlikely scenario; there is ample literature on agency theory and moral hazard that supports the presence of those risks and that implores the need to appropriately prepare for and manage them.

Interestingly, the decision by AAOIFI to completely disregard any policy directive or accounting standard related to derivatives does offer a glimpse into the advancement of religious-based normative accounting principles in the Islamic finance industry at the expense of the neutral accounting requirements that focus on providing greater transparency for effective decision making. This arguably exists despite the fact that a study undertaken by the professional services Deloitte Touche Tohmatsu Ltd recently showed that 79 per cent of the Islamic finance industry leaders surveyed claimed to support a convergence initiative of the AAOIFI Standards to the International Financial Reporting Standards (IFRS) (Deloitte 2010: 25).

To be certain, it is acknowledged that accounting theory does have elements of normative principles in that the recognition, measurement and disclosure requirements may provide incentives for 'proper' financial behaviour by firms (i.e., making it harder to engage in tax evasion, money laundering, income smoothing, etc.). However, this facet of accounting theory is not deemed to be in a position to overpower the chief role of accounting of providing neutral and technical information that centres on promoting rational decision making by the readers of the financial statements.

Moreover, it becomes a perilous path to continuously push for the view that it is improper to record an impermissible asset or liability, such as some transactions (e.g., derivatives) that record the dealings of money between economic agents. This is because of the impracticality of its implementation in a global setting wherein it has become established in the legal corpus that the courts (and even some regulatory bodies such as capital market authorities) focus on the legality of the contracts, not its permissibility. In other words, an impermissible liability is viewed and will be ruled as a liability if it is entered into by knowledgeable, willing parties in an arm's length transaction.

The articulation of the foregoing discussion on accounting is worthy of consideration because the understanding that it is trying to elicit offers the prospect of commencing a process whereby the air of uncertainty is removed with regards to the recognition of the 'monetary' derivative instrument in the financial statements of the entities that use them. This, in turn, may very well plant the seeds for the practical implementation of the arguments whose evidence was outlined in the present and previous chapters on the acceptability of the risk-transfer strategy in Islamic finance, especially for interest-rate and currency risk exposures, with derivative hedging instruments as its main tools of application.

6.5 Conclusion

The significance of examining the viewpoint of the *Shari'ah* on the permissibility of the underlying variables in the derivative contracts stems from the charged and sometimes divergent opinions of some *Shari'ah* scholars and academics regarding monetary benchmarks that are related to interest rates and currencies. The common theme, as has been communicated repeatedly in the Islamic finance circles, is that the dealings in interest-rate benchmarks and currencies in the forward markets amounts to the indulgence in a concoction of *Shari'ah* prohibitions that include *Riba*, *Gharar* and *Maysir*.

The aforementioned viewpoint, in turn, can be estimated to have manifested itself in the lack of any technical directives by any of the standard-setting bodies for the recognition of the derivative contracts by the companies that use them, even if they are used exclusively for market-risk management. Notably, this stance exists despite the growing usage of Islamic derivative instruments (primarily swaps) as hedging contracts in the Islamic finance industry.

To address the unease of the *Shari'ah* scholars in accepting financial instruments with monetary benchmarks as underlying variables (and the resultant policy vacuum in their recognition), the pertinent parts of the scripture were examined in this chapter along with the myriad juridical opinions that relate to the various commercial and financial transactions that centred on money. In the examination process, multiple arguments were articulated that, as was done in the previous chapters, contextualised the discourse with the relevant economic theories in order to bring out a more comprehensive and thorough understanding of this complex subject matter.

For this, it has been contended that the religious sensitivity in the dealings of money between individuals, whether in the form of interest-rate or currency benchmarks, emanates chiefly from fear of engaging in *Riba*, with the injustices associated with hoarding as an associated concern. Interestingly, this sensitivity endured notwithstanding the almost complete transformation of the commercial and financial practices of economic agents, including the Muslim populace, consequent of the advent of new theories and practices that offer a host of novel opportunities and challenges.

In other words, it is not evident that, as is often stated by some commentators, God limited the economic practices of Muslims to either trade (with an underlying corporeal asset) or *Riba* with nothing permitted in-between. It is likely, instead, that our divine gifts of logic and reason were meant to help Muslims distinguish between the permissible and the proscribed transactions in a framework that adheres with the *Maqasid Al-Shari'ah*.

Remarkably, in the middle of all of the anti-derivative rhetoric by some of the distinguished *Shari'ah* scholars and academics, there is a clear appearance of these divine gifts at work with the ostensible pragmatism in their opinions on matters that were until recently deemed closed and settled (e.g., usage of LIBOR in commercial transactions). Yet, for some odd reason, there is this obstinate belief among some of those same individuals that the usage of derivatives for hedging purposes should not enjoy the fruits of contemporary enlightenment in some form of a bid to protect the

Islamic finance industry from the contaminated effects of the usage of the derivative contracts.

Given the presence of the wide-ranging evidence throughout the previous chapters that supports the permissibility of the utilisation of derivative contracts for hedging purpose, it may be necessary to devote the last substantive chapter prior to the conclusion to exploring a recurring concern in the discourse on derivative instruments in the Islamic finance literature: the prohibition of *Maysir* (gambling).

Notes

1. The basis for that suggestion seems to have originated from Lamberton in his book entitled *The Theory of Profit* (Lamberton 1965: 113–14). However, Lamberton simply espoused the position that the discount rate for a particular asset/particular asset classes should be the rate of return on *similar* assets/asset classes with commensurate risk characteristics. His position should probably not be used in the context of developing one comprehensive benchmark in the pricing of assets.

2. In the context of the benchmark suggestions by the authors, it is not understood how the pricing of collateralised government paper is different from the pricing of regular treasury securities in light of the statement by the authors that '[t]he return on such an index needs to be adjusted for a risk premium which would be negative for the government paper because the governments are assumed to be insulated from credit and default risks' (Iqbal and Mirakhor 2007: 221). Moreover, the rationale for inclusion of benchmarks such as the International Finance Corporation (IFC) emerging market index, which may contain non-*Shari'ah*-compliant stocks, is also not fully comprehended, especially when the objective is to generate an Islamic benchmark.

3. Of course, this assumes that all of the parties, including non-Islamic institutions, will agree to this proposition

4. Interestingly, sections 2/4 and 2/5 in the AAOIFI Standard No. 16 'Foreign Currency Transactions and Foreign Operations' puts the burden of foreign currency exposure in *Murabaha* transactions, the main lending form in the Islamic finance industry, on the Islamic banks. This policy was formulated in a bid to reduce the uncertainty of the borrowers from banks, which is commendable. But the coupling of that policy with the prohibition on hedging instruments is incomprehensible because it needlessly places the open exposure on the banking institution shareholders as well as depositors/investment account holders.

5. Obviously, one of the problems in the focus on commodities as a legitimate form of exchange is that it starts a contentious debate of what items are *Ribawi* (usurious) commodities and cannot be a centre of exchange and what items can be permissibly traded.

6. In the context of usufruct, one is selling the use of a something, including their labour, to the other party in exchange for the purchase of money.

7. Nonetheless, there were writings by some *Shari'ah* scholars, such as Abu Hanifah, Al-Ghazali and Ibn Khaldun, which favoured the position that gold and silver are money by nature and consequently other metals used as money were relegated to the *Fulus* category (coins of other substances) (Islahi 2005).

8. *Seigniorage* is the revenue accruing to the issuing authority when the exchange value of money issued exceeds the money's production cost.

9. Justice Usmani, quoting Imam Al-Basri, makes an argument that the utility of money is derived when it leaves the individual in exchange for another object (or service) (Usmani 2010).

10. Similarly, it is not what is being stolen that is prohibited in Islamic jurisprudence, it is the act of stealing itself.

11. Of course, they can use the lack of specificity in the divine instruction in the verse to show that they did not contravene the prohibition on not spending the money 'in the way of Allah'.

12. Or IFSB for capital adequacy standards, for that matter.

CHAPTER 7

MAYSIR, HEDGING AND DERIVATIVES

7.0 Introduction

The preceding chapters concentrated on market-risk management, as a framework, and derivative instruments, as tools within that framework. Throughout the discussion, it has been shown that risk management is encouraged in Islamic thought; this can particularly include the market risks that do not come under the direct control of the enterprises that have chosen to follow the economic doctrine of the *Shari'ah*. It has also been delineated, while challenging the contemporary restrictive stances, that derivative instruments have very little, if anything, to do with the prohibitions of *Riba* and *Gharar*; and if used in a hedging context are actually far from the prohibition of *Maysir* (gambling) in that enterprises that utilise them choose not to hinge their fortunes on the movements of interest rates, currencies and commodities in the global financial markets.

Nonetheless, the necessity in the articulation of the content of this chapter emanates from the widely held viewpoint among many writers in the Islamic finance literature (as noted in the previous chapters) that the usage of derivative instruments is analogous to partaking in gambling behaviour. To be certain, Islamic finance is not unique in its hostility to derivative instruments; as will be outlined below, they have had a history of opposition in the last two centuries in Western society. This came to the fore, after some period of tacit acquiesce, subsequent to the latest global financial crisis that was instigated, in part, by the Credit Default Swaps (that interestingly does not have a strong relation to market risks).

That being said, what is perhaps distinctive in the discourse on derivatives in the Islamic finance space in recent decades is the invocation of persistent juridical perspectives that profess seemingly indisputable epistemological stances regarding what is in actual fact an indefinite and complex subject matter. The end result that can be observed is the all-encompassing simplistic stance that derivatives are tools of *Maysir*. This is no matter what the context and without response to how derivatives exactly relate to the actual prohibition in the religion – that being the act of gambling.

7.1 A conceptualisation of *Maysir* in Islamic and Western thought

The prohibition of *Maysir* (gambling) is considered one of the pillars of the economic doctrine in the *Shari'ah*. Indeed, as should have been self-evident in the previous chapters, within the discourse on the subject matter of the book, one can clearly observe that *Maysir* is an overarching concern for most of the participants in the discourse on market-risk management and derivatives in the Islamic finance industry.

To be certain, this concern is understandable given the direct reference to the prohibition in multiple verses in the Quran wherein it was stated in one verse: 'They ask you about intoxicants and *Maysir*. Say, "In them is great sin and [yet, some] benefit for people. But their sin is greater than their benefit."' (Quran 2:219). Two other pertinent verses in the Quran, for their part, declare: 'O you who have believed, indeed, intoxicants, *Maysir*, [sacrificing on] stone alters [to other than Allah], and divining arrows are but defilement from the work of Satan, so avoid it that you may be successful. Satan only wants to cause between you animosity and hatred through intoxicants and gambling and to avert you from the remembrance of Allah and from prayer. So will you not desist?' (Quran 5:90–1).

The rationale for the prohibition of *Maysir*, for its part, can be said to be mostly related to, one, unearned gains and, two, anti-social behaviour (Al-Masri 1993; Haroun 1953). Indeed, the root of the word '*Maysir*' in the Arabic language (i.e., '*Yousr*') can be embodied by the word 'facile' in the English language that the *Merriam-Webster Dictionary* (2012) defines as something that is 'easily accomplished or attained'.

The relationship to anti-social behaviour in Islamic thought can become apparent after the reference to 'animosity and hatred' in one of the aforementioned verses in the Quran. Essentially, *Maysir* is one facet that can be considered as being related to, but still somewhat distinct from, theft, cheating, bribery and so forth in that vein, which is directly addressed in the Quranic verse: 'O you who have believed, do not devour one another's wealth unjustly but only [in lawful] business by mutual consent' (Quran 4:29).

To be certain, Islamic jurisprudence is not unique in its objective of seeking to eradicate gambling behaviour in society; one can clearly observe that the same rejectionist stance is endemic in the history of Western thought with an accompanying diverse and deep discourse in the realms of religious studies, law, politics, sociology, psychology, mathematics and economics on this intricate subject matter. Notably, with a focus on the economic realm, the discourse on gambling in Western thought, especially in the last two hundred years, much like its contemporary Islamic counterpart, have transcended the traditional argumentation that centre on games of chance and have broached other contentious (or uncontroversial, depending on the perspective) topics such as insurance in addition to commodity and stock trading.

However, where the two discourses differ is in the level of depth of Western thought on the subject of gambling consequent of the more involved presence of a multitude of interested parties shaped by multifarious perspectives. These have been traditionally formed around institutional arrangements that covered the spectrum of opinions and beliefs – from the speculative-favouring organisations (e.g., commodity exchanges, investment banks and hedge funds), passing through the risk-management-centred consortiums (hedging community, monetary authorities, etc.) and on to the policy-oriented establishments (government, religious groups, etc.). Throughout, diverse academic interest has spurred with myriad perspectives built on many theories and empirical evidence.

This, of course, provides an excellent opportunity for observers seeking to enrich the debate on gambling in Islamic thought, in general, and Islamic finance, in particular, beyond the commendable work by many writers on the subject matter of gambling within the purview of the *Shari'ah* in recent decades such as Al-Masri (1993), Al-Saati (2007), Haroun (1953) and Rosenthal (1975). However, since the topic of gambling is rather complex and the discourse surrounding it is nowhere a point of resolution or consensus, the discussion in this chapter will be limited to areas that were deemed important in the context of the debate on the permissibility of derivatives in Islamic jurisprudence for market-risk management.

One can begin with the definition of a wager or a bet

within the larger context of gambling. For this, the definition of a wagering contract elaborated by Henry Hawkins in his ruling on *Carlill* v. *Carbolic Smoke Ball Company* [1892] seems to have taken hold in common law, wherein he stated:

> It is not easy to define with precision what amounts to a wagering contract, nor the narrow line of demarcation which separates a wagering from an ordinary contract; but, according to my view, a wagering contract is one by which two persons, professing to hold opposite views touching the issue of a future uncertain event, mutually agree that, dependent on the determination of that event, one shall win from the other, and that other shall pay or hand over to him, a sum of money or other stake; neither of the contracting parties having any other interest in that contract than the sum or stake he will so win or lose, there being no other real consideration for the making of such contract by either of the parties. It is essential to a wagering contract that each party may under it either win or lose, whether he will win or lose being dependent on the issue of the event, and, therefore, remaining uncertain until that issue is known. (Hawkins cited in Finch 1896: 30)

The statement articulated by Hawkins defining wagering contracts is interesting on many levels and does have a high degree of relevancy for the present discussion on derivatives. To commence with, it acknowledges the often overlooked matter in the literature in Islamic finance that there is difficulty in the differentiation between a wagering contract and an ordinary contract, since any contract, as MacNeil has put it, is a 'projection of exchange into the future' (MacNeil 1974: 712–13).

That is to say, the future is always uncertain and this uncertainty propels economic agents to create contracts (and actually contribute to the evolution of contract law) for their dealings with one another whether they are for religiously legitimate transactions such as *Ijara, Musharaka* and *Murabaha* in the Islamic finance industry or a wagering contract that encapsulates the rules of the game that surround the spin of the roulette wheel. In fact, the central role of uncertainty continued to be apparent in contract law almost a century later on the other side of the Atlantic Ocean where in *Spartech Corp.* v. *Opper* [1989], heard before the US Court of Appeals, it was stated by the court that 'a principal purpose of contracts and contract law is to allocate the risk of the unexpected in accordance with the parties' respective preference for or aversion to risk and their ability or inability to prevent the risk from materializing' (Kreitner 2007: 97).

With that, one should be able to recognise that the first significant trait in Hawkins's definition of a wager underlines the fact that the parties to the contract hold opposing views regarding a future uncertain event and that the payment of monetary consideration from one person to the other becomes an obligation once the event that surrounds the opposing views is determined. On the face of it, this does endow the wagering contracts with a monetary zero-sum feature whereby, in the absence of any other mutual exchange, the interests of the parties to the contract are diametrically opposed and, consequently, the contract itself can only be considered as one regulating a pure win–lose transaction.

To be sure, the nature of gambling contracts as zero-sum games that dictate winnings and losses between contesting parties have been recognised much earlier in Islamic thought with the notable contributions of writers such as Ibn Taymiyyah and Ibn Al-Qayyim, and others, who have built their restrictive stances on gambling contracts, in part, based on this mathematical characteristic (Al-Suwailem 2006; Kamali 2000).

The second defining attribute of wagering contracts is in the fact that parties enter into a wagering contract for its own sake. In effect, as explicated by Hawkins, there is no other 'interest' or 'real consideration' for one gambling party that impels them to seek a counterparty for their wager other than the prospect of monetary gain (and/or perhaps the thrill of a game with monetary stakes). Thus, in a manner that complements and contextualises the afore-mentioned zero-sum feature, the pure win–lose scenario of the game becomes the full story, as it were, of the transaction with the hopes of the players being solely linked to the gains taken from the counterparty and, conversely, their fears being exclusively connected to the losses given to the counterparty.

The shared apprehension for the two previous features of wagering, which has been communicated repeatedly in the literature on the subject matter in both Islamic and Western thought (as highlighted earlier in this chapter and in pre-vious chapters), revolves around the unearned gains from social unproductive endeavours as well as the anti-social behaviour that can result consequent of wagering. This is understandable since any particular party can only gain monetarily, and thereby avoid monetary losses, if, and only if, the other party loses. Once more, this assumes that there is no other consideration for entering into these contracts.

More specifically, for the unearned gains, the professed concern is that wagering encourages a wasteful vocation that artificially creates risks in society that can wrongly be viewed as a facile alternative to participating in the human welfare-oriented and wealth-generating (to the individual and to society) productive commerce that is built on dis-ciplined ethic and hard work. In fact, the perception of gamblers is often so negative that the parties to wagering contracts were often labelled as 'social parasites' (Patterson

1918: 386). As with respect to the anti-social behaviour, it was perceived that wagering contributes to the advent of harmful aspects in society that include vice, crime (including corruption of public officials, fraud and market manipulation), impoverishment of losers and their dependents, dissipation and psychological problems (including suicide).

The final attribute of a wagering contract, as per the definition of Hawkins, is that it is determined by a particular event. For this, wagering contracts are traditionally known for being quite precise in the definition of the event and the monetary consideration being transferred as a result. Thus, in effect, the only uncertainty, which is the chief trait in the wagering contract, resides in the passing of the event itself and/or in the manner of its passing.

Moreover, it should also be highlighted at this juncture that the dominance of Hawkins's definition of wagering is arguably in its implicit recognition that, as opposed to the opinions of many writers on the subject matter of gambling (Al-Suwailem 2000: 11; Borna and Lowry 1987; Brenner and Brenner 1990; Freeman 1907; Hobson 1905), it is not the element of chance, whether 'pure' or 'mixed', in the passing of the event within these contracts that detains them within the realm of gambling.

Notably, chance, which has been a central feature in the discourse on gambling, has been defined by Newman in his seminal book *The World of Mathematics I* as:

> Phenomena (events or variations) that are not exactly determined, or do not follow patterns described by known exact laws, or are not the effects of known causes. That is to say, the domain of chance varies with our state of knowledge – or rather of ignorance. Such ignorance may be fundamental because the relevant exact laws of causes are unknowable; it may be non-essential or temporary, and exist because the exact

laws do not happen to have been discovered or the ignorance may be deliberately assumed because the known exact laws and causes are not of such as character that they can profitably be used in the particular inquiry at hand. (Newman 1956: 1,469)

In essence, the implications of the lack of exclusivity of chance in wagering contracts are that it broadens the scope of contracts that could be given the wagering label. Thus, a contract between players to a game of chess, for example, where the winner would be paid a certain sum of money from the loser, would still be labelled as a wagering contract within the context of the definition by Hawkins despite the arguable reduction in the role of chance in the outcome of the game vis-à-vis the skill of the players. Put differently, wagering contracts are not simply confined to the traditional games of lottery or those existing at casinos; they can include a whole range of contracts between individuals.

Effectively, as has been realised (and even internalised) in the late nineteenth century and early twentieth century in the public policy and legal circles in the United States and Europe, which in a sense is being replayed today with the contemporary *Shari'ah* prohibition on derivatives,[1] it is acknowledged that wagering contracts could very well include seemingly ordinary contracts with legitimate underlying variables, such as derivatives, in the financial markets with the uncertainty of the event being the rise and fall in prices. This, of course, also applies to the 'Islamic' derivatives that entail multiple contracts with commodities as an underlying between the parties in the Islamic finance industry *if, in fact, they collectively meet the definition of a wager as articulated by Hawkins.*

That said, and with the agreement that the usage of derivatives can be done in gambling contexts, it should also be recognised, as has been repeatedly argued in the previous chapters, that one should not be hasty in the simplistic adoption of a prohibitive stance on derivative contracts without a greater appreciation of all the facts that surround their existence and the social utility that is provided by that existence. In effect, the whole purpose of seeking to define some contracts as wagering contracts in public policy was not some sort of attempt to delve into technicalities in the legal sphere, but rather it is to serve as a normative attempt to ensure societal well-being through the rejection of the *act of wagering*.

Thus, the focus on the contract served as a means to a higher end, not as an end to itself. This characterisation can become self-evident upon the examination of the discourse on the subject in the legal sphere with judges in Western societies considering the underlying causes and traits of the contract (including 'intent' and 'insurable interest') in addition to the background of the parties to the contract (i.e., not simply contractual structure and language) in order to formulate an opinion that, in turn, established a public policy stance by the state for a particular period of time.[2]

In other words, it is not the contract that defines the act of gambling; rather, it is the act of gambling (with due consideration to the multi-layered definition by Hawkins) that manifests itself in the wagering contract. This, of course, does have implications to the subject matter here in that it effectively calls for the discourse on this topic in the Islamic finance industry to transcend the comforts of the simplicity of contractual analysis and to venture into the complexity of a more thorough examination of the context of usage of derivative contracts (market-risk management vis-à-vis playing the market for gambling purposes) in order to appropriately devise a juridical and policy position on their usage.

This should ideally be done in a comprehensive manner that accounts for *both* the positive and negative externalities to society. The greater ambition here, of course, is the possibility of adopting, following the large corpus of evidence in the Quran, the opinions by the Prophet (PBUH) and the tradition of *Maslaha* (public interest), a pragmatic utilitarian approach to *Shari'ah* rulings within the realm of *Mua'amalat* (i.e., not *Ibadah*, or worship) in a manner that promotes social welfare through the maximisation of societal benefits and the reduction of harm.

7.2 *Maysir, Gharar* and the indeterminacy of the zero-sum prohibition

Having expounded on the concept of *Maysir* and its manifestation into a wagering contract, it is deemed important to address the recent trend in the Islamic finance literature to define the 'act' of *Maysir* by linking it to any zero-sum arrangement in an absolute monetary sense. The aim of this anti-zero-sum movement is conjectured to be an attempt by some writers to add objective certainty (almost in a checklist fashion) to the basis for contemporary *Shari'ah* opinions regarding modern-day financial contracts as opposed to what can only be discerned to be the intolerable subjective contextualisation in the elaboration of permissibility.

This position can be exemplified by the multiple writings by Al-Suwailem on the subject matter of *Maysir* (and indeed *Gharar*, which he views as being largely the same on zero-sum grounds),[3] wherein he stated: 'The economic significance of the zero-sum measure provides insights into the Islamic view of economic behaviour. Elimination of zero-sum arrangements can be viewed as a paradigm governing Islamic principles of exchange' (Al-Suwailem 1999: 98).

Needless to say, the risk of this attempt at objectivism in matters of religion is that it has been shown to be emulated by other commentators in their subsequent writings on derivatives (Hassan and Mahlknecht 2011: 376; Jobst and Sole 2012; Jobst 2007; Kunhibava 2011; Obaidullah 2002). The eventual danger, of course, is that this new contract classification paradigm may seep into the decision-making process of *Shari'ah* scholars as a foundation for a juridical stance in the standard-setting bodies on *any* zero-sum contract without the necessary appreciation of the assumptions (and contradictions) that were apparent in the formulation of such a perspective in the first place.

With that, it appears that the contemporary Islamic finance literature on *Maysir*, often with a reference to derivatives, has elected to impart with the path of humility that was followed by Hawkins (as noted earlier) in acknowledging the difficulty in the designation of a particular contract with the wagering label and the need to consider a wider set of factors in order to arrive at a proper conclusion. The chosen course, instead, seems to have been built on the belief that one can distinguish, based on the absolute monetary zero-sum traits of the contract (i.e., not the act) in question, whether it is considered prohibited or not. In the face of such a sure-footed conceptualisation of *Maysir* as any zero-sum game, it is perhaps imperative to investigate some of the assumptions in the multiple writings of Al-Suwailem (who has been one of the chief critics of derivatives in recent years based mainly on zero-sum argumentation) that were used to construct that particular epistemological stance.

To commence with, one of the dominant assumptions made by Al-Suwailem, and perhaps unsurprisingly given a writer who often interjects game theory into the Islamic finance discourse, is that the zero-sum characterisation of *Maysir* contracts are self-limited to 'strictly competitive games' with a paramount focus on *monetary payoffs* consequent of the consent of an add-on assumption that revolved around the concept that from a strategic sense, strictly competitive games and pure zero sum games are equivalent (Al-Suwailem 1999: 62, 65, 67; 2006). Accordingly, besides the fact that these assumptions confound the conceptualisation of the way that the game is played strategically and the nature of the payoffs (monetary versus utility gain/loss), one can establish without too much difficulty that the acknowledgements by Hawkins in the previous section of the potential role of 'interest' of the parties (such as in insurable interest, for example) or any other 'real consideration' in contextualising an opinion on a particular contract (i.e., wagering versus ordinary) is explicitly dismissed by Al-Suwailem.

The power of such a simplifying assumption cannot be overstated and really does demonstrate the importance of examining the basis for conjectures in the economic realm with real effects on the welfare of individuals, especially those used as a pretext to prohibit certain practices, such as derivative and insurance contracts, under the banner of religious adherence. The strength of the prohibition in this case was communicated by Al-Suwailem with a reference to the potent and often quoted Quranic verse proscribing the 'devour[ing of] one another's wealth unjustly' (Quran 4:29) (Al-Suwailem 1999: 65).

To continue with the Al-Suwailem conjectures, having shown that all zero-sum games are prohibited in Islamic jurisprudence, what appears to be allowed according to him are non-zero-sum games espousing cooperative arrangements. Specifically, he maintains: 'A necessary requirement for a transaction to be permitted [in Islamic jurisprudence] is the possibility of cooperation, as in nonzero-sum games. It is left to players to achieve cooperation in such games through rational decision making. Strictly competitive games, however, exclude this possibility by design, and thus, no matter how rational players are, one can win only at the expense of the other' (Al-Suwailem 1999: 63).

However, the above statement does become quite abstruse with the dual additional proclamations in the work of Al-Suwailem wherein he states, first, that '[t]his is not to say that only cooperative games are permissible' (Al-Suwailem 1999: 63), which, in effect, signals to the prospect of accepting zero-sum games in some contexts, and that, two, '[f]rom Shariah [*sic*] point of view, generally speaking, the acceptability of such mixed games depends on the likelihood of the cooperative, positive-sum, outcome' (Al-Suwailem 2006: 73), which apparently interposes some elements of probability theory into the mix of assumptions that underlie the zero-sum stance.

Notably, the aforementioned proclamations (especially the latter), show, with a unique sense of irony, that the search for definitional objectivity by Al-Suwailem for the concept of *Maysir* (vis-à-vis perhaps the wider and more humble definition by Hawkins) exclusively through the zero-sum paradigm is not as certain as it may have been hoped to be. That being said, the use of subjective probability theory does offer a glimpse into the more diverse choice of positions adopted by Al-Suwailem with respect to what can arguably be other zero-sum transactions. This includes the acceptance of *Urbun* (earnest money) modalities, but not options, and the rejection of conventional insurance, but not *Takaful* (cooperative) insurance (Al-Suwailem 1999: 77, 80; 2007).

In the case of the former, it appears that 'intent' does factor into the analysis despite its subjectivity (Al-Suwailem 2007: 90). The case of the latter, for its part, in a zero-sum framework, is rather intriguing since it is not entirely understandable how the cooperative insurance arrangement changes the zero-sum nature of contracts between it and its policy holders, as perceived by Al-Suwailem (e.g., premiums paid and indemnities received in the insurance industry), since it appears that any context outside the contract itself is irrelevant in Al-Suwailem's conceptualisation of *Maysir* and *Gharar* (see below).

Notwithstanding the above, it can also be observed from the writings of Al-Suwailem on the conceptualisation of zero-sum games that utility theory does take a rather ambiguous role in his analysis. For, on the face of it, he does clearly acknowledge utility theory, as he outlines the religious refutations to zero-sum games; this can also be evident in Al-Suwailem's (1999) acknowledgement of the utility theory-laden concepts of normal exchange, regret theory, loss aversion and marginal utility. Indeed, his own definition of zero-sum games being 'strictly competitive games, without implying that utilities of the two parties are identical' (Al-Suwailem 1999: 62) is explicit in its recognition of the role of utility in zero-sum frameworks. Nonetheless, for some paradoxical reason he chooses to limit utility theory only to the descriptive acknowledgement corner with very little usage of it in his analysis to build his argumentation for the rather serious affair of religiously proscribing contracts that formalise zero-sum arrangements (i.e., derivatives).

More specifically, the work of Al-Suwailem can be observed to concentrate almost exclusively on monetary payoffs in an absolute sense (e.g., ex-post monetary payoff of a coin toss) or relative to expected values based on probabilities (e.g., a 20 per cent chance of finding a lost camel valued at 1000 Dinars grants it an expected value of 200 Dinars) to draw the conclusion that zero-sum games are normatively inferior to non-zero-sum games (Al-Suwailem, 1999, 2006). Needless to say, while such a simplifying assumption can assist in an academic exercise of extending game theory, *on the strategy front*, to multiple settings

(Gintis 2009; Harrington 2009); its usage in the realm of economics, however, requires special care because it provides an incomplete framework for the analysis of human decision making with respect to resources.

In fact, the need to expand the horizon of decision making was realised as early as 1738 through the pioneering work of Daniel Bernoulli in the resolution of the St Petersburg Paradox that exposed a game with an infinite expected value, denoting the possibility of a wager with an infinite price. The source of the paradox was the supposition that the expected value is all that mattered in rational human decision making. Accordingly, the solution to the paradox, and arguably the advent of modern economic theory, came from Bernoulli's simple statement of: 'The determination of the *value* [*sic*] of an item must not be based on its *price* [*sic*], but rather on the *utility* [*sic*] it yields' (Bernoulli 1954 [1738]: 24).

As a background, the concept of utility can be related to usefulness, desirability or satisfaction. This intuitive conceptualisation of utility imparted by Bernoulli was transformed by the influential work by von Neumann and Morgenstern (1953) as well as Friedman and Savage (1948) into a mathematical construct of preferences by economic agents, who are assumed to operate in a framework where they will instinctually rank and choose their preferences based on the highest utility for each.

Thus, within the realm of risk management, when one speaks of risk aversion or loss aversion, they are, for the most part, actually speaking the language of utility. In fact, the section outlining the rationale for hedging, and all the associated literature, in Chapter 3, is largely constructed on the foundations of utility theory in that particular events are being favoured (higher utility) while others are being disliked (lower utility). With that, it may be necessary to briefly discuss the concepts of risk aversion and loss aversion in order to further appreciate the power of the assumptions made by Al-Suwailem.

To commence with, the theory of risk aversion, as developed by Arrow and Pratt in their extension of utility theory to the domain of decisions under uncertainty (Arrow 1951, 1971; Pratt 1964), was unique in that it formulised a notion that was recognised in circles of economic academia much earlier. In effect, the theory of risk aversion postulates that an uncertain income tends to be valued less by economic agents than its mathematical expectation. This, consequently, will lead these economic agents to seek solutions for reducing the uncertainty burden (insurance, fixed-income securities, derivatives, etc.).

Put differently, economic agents tend to choose a surer 'certainty equivalent', even if it is for a less amount than an expected value that is at least partially dependent on chance (or wholly dependent on chance, depending on the particular perspective on the source of risk). This behavioural trait is what endows the majority of economic agents with the often-mentioned risk-averse title. In the context of market-risk management by way of derivatives, it can be observed that firms choose a more certain hedged outcome (even if it is for a lower overall income), rather than 'play the market' (even if it has a higher expected value).[4] The theory of loss aversion developed by Tversky and Kahneman (1986), for its part, adds another angle to behaviour under uncertainty by showing that rational economic agents would seek to avoid losses, even if that entails assuming more risk.

With that, and based on the above formulation of the concept of utility and the theories that surround its existence, once one amalgamates Al-Suwailem's perspectives on the subject matter, namely, one, the need for active risk taking in investment decisions (Al-Suwailem 2000: 4), two, the impermissibility of reliance on chance to achieve desired outcomes (Al-Suwailem 2000: 9), and, three, the rejectionist stance of derivatives that, in actual fact, allow economic agents, who are mostly risk averse, to transpose the chance of expected value based on the randomness of the market risks to a safer certainty equivalent, it becomes apparent that the conclusions drawn by Al-Suwailem regarding the prohibition of derivatives based on zero-sum argumentation evolve into a full circle of indeterminacy.

That being said, and in returning to the discussion of the derivative contract *Shari'ah* proscription consequent of its *monetary* zero-sum trait that was interpreted to be linked to *Maysir*, there is no reason to suspect, as Al-Suwailem (1999) proclaims, that parties to a zero-sum game, as in a derivative contract, for example, must have one risk-averse counterparty and one risk-taking counterparty or two counterparties with neutral risk preferences (Al-Suwailem 1999: 74).[5] At the very least, this conjecture exhibits the neglect of the prospect of having a mutual gain for two hedging parties to a derivative transaction (that exists albeit uncommonly) who are both risk averse. In fact, it has been shown that by employing hedging modalities both parties enjoy higher indifference curves (i.e., mutually higher utilities) (Culp 2004: 79).

Considering the above, a real contention can be made that the probability of the existence of two hedging parties in the derivatives markets is dwarfed by the presence of speculators, many of whom are of the gambling type. To this, it should be stated that legal theory never prohibited the existence of contract law under the pretext of eliminating wagering contracts; rather it chose various means to facilitate the existence of ordinary contracts and attempted to reduce the incentives to engage in the wagering ones.

Such a stance can be observed to exist unequivocally

in Islamic jurisprudence and has, interestingly, even been acknowledged by Al-Suwailem himself in his reference to the work of Ibn Al-Qayyim with respect to the contentious *Gharar* characterisation of the sale of hidden (e.g., underground) fruits and vegetables wherein Ibn Al-Qayyim argues: 'To consider this (particular transaction) as *gharar* is not to the *faqih* [*Shari'ah* scholar] (as such). It is experts who decide whether it is *gharar* and gambling or not' (Al-Suwailem 1999: 79). Thus, after all, it may be conceivable that the 'experts' armed with less stringent and more realistic assumptions on human economic behaviour may provide insights that show that derivatives may in certain contexts not be regarded as *Maysir* (and *Gharar*).

That being said, it is acknowledged that the early Muslim scholars did have it right in their description of *Maysir* as a zero-sum game in terms of monetary payoff. This *description* is not disputed and has, in fact, been recognised as one attribute in the still-in-use common law definition of wagering contracts by Hawkins many centuries later. What is being disputed here, however, is the reverse argumentation by Al-Suwailem that attempts to cast any zero-sum game as *Maysir* (and *Gharar*). Indeed, this is what El-Gamal was attempting to convey in his work on *Gharar* wherein he rejected Al-Suwailem's attempts at the formalisation of the prohibition of *Gharar* along zero-sum lines by affirming that 'there are many examples of pure zero-sum games which are not forbidden based on gharar, and other contracts which are forbidden because of gharar, but which are not near-zerosum' (El-Gamal 2001: 30).

The focus in this section has been on the work of one distinguished academic: Al-Suwailem. This is consequent of the clear recognition of the influence of his work on the discourse of *Maysir* (and *Gharar*), in general, and derivatives, in particular, as evidenced by the imprints of his conclusions in the Islamic finance literature that followed. It is common to critique an academic endeavour (including the present one); the emphasis here has been in the appropriateness and soundness of assumptions that underlie the work of Al-Suwailem that called for the prohibition of derivatives based on the perception of zero-sum traits.

It has been argued that these assumptions were, one, mis-placed since they actually target the use of zero-sum games in strategy contexts, and, two, incomplete in that they really did not tell the entire story behind the existence of zero-sum contracts (e.g., derivatives and insurance) in the first place or the behaviour of economic agents that surrounds their existence (i.e., utility). Essentially, one must be care-ful in the modelling of their work as an objective law of science when, in fact, it is built on many assumptions, a large number of which vary in the degree of appropriate-ness and soundness. This applies even more forcefully in the realm of jurisprudence where academic conjectures can lead to outright religious prohibitions. To this, it should be affirmed that the present book, even in its stance on the permissibility of derivatives, is an argumentation based on available evidence that was presented throughout this and the previous chapters.

With that, and after arguing in this and the preceding section that a wagering contract, which is an elusive con-cept to define, entails multiple traits that include but are not defined by zero-sum monetary payoffs; how can society distinguish between speculation that is part of everyday life and gambling that has been shown to be the source of social malcontent? This is an important question insofar as it is significant to define the acceptability of the type of envi-ronment that hosts market-risk management endeavours by way of derivatives along with the classification of the parameters for their usage. In essence, the discussion into the permissibility of derivative instruments would not be complete without due consideration being made to the environment that facilitates risk transfer, which includes the contentious matters of speculation and financial inter-mediaries. This is what the next sections will seek to address.

7.3 Investment, speculation and gambling: the environment of risk management

The difficulty in the exact conceptualisation of gambling is equally present in the conceptualisation of its less sinister (or not sinister at all, depending on the perspective) cous-ins: speculation and investing. Effectively, one can largely estimate gambling behaviour, and they may be able to largely view preservation of capital to maintain purchas-ing power as investing. It is the delineation of the limits of the wide reaches of speculation that sits between those two concepts that poses the greatest difficulty for the social sci-ences (economics, law, sociology, etc.) and apparently also Islamic jurisprudence.

Essentially, there is wide recognition, even in Islamic thought as evidenced by the literature (e.g., Al-Masri 1993) that every affair, economic or otherwise, in life is a form of speculation consequent of the uncertainty of the future. However, one does not know with a high degree of preci-sion the lines that separate all these three concepts in the realm of economic theory since they all commence with a particular resource endowment and the desire to increase it through time as per some sort of target or objective. That being said, at least some form of classification, even if of the general type, may be warranted in order to address the near constant barrage of accusations of financial mischief thrown at derivative instruments in the Islamic finance discourse.

With that, the search for the definition of speculation,

which is perhaps harder to define than its gambling cousin, commences with the examination of the attempts by many writers to allocate particular attributes to the elusive concept. For Adam Smith, one of the fathers of modern economic theory, a speculator is one who:

> [e]xercises no one regular, established, or well-known branch of business. He is a corn merchant this year, and a wine merchant the next, and a sugar, tobacco, or tea merchant the year after. He enters into every trade when he foresees that it is likely to be more than commonly profitable, and he quits it when he foresees that its profits are likely to return to the level of other trades. His profits and losses, therefore, can bear no regular proportion to those of any one established and well-known branch of business. (Smith 1778: 140)

The above reference to speculation by Smith (1778) does add some guidance to the path of distinction between investing and speculating on the *decent* portion of the normative scale, as it were, of economic activities. In effect, the force that propels speculation to forego its roots in the relative safety of investing appears to depend, in part, on the level of opportunism through a proactive engagement with the various markets that hold prospects of higher profits vis-à-vis the passivity in the acceptance of the status quo with perhaps some mild improvements. This, it is conjectured, can be thought of as the key that begins to unlock the mysteries of the boundaries of speculation with investing and gambling at either side of it. To be able to turn the key, however, it is important to at least get a distinction (once more, even if not exact) of the middle ground on the normative scale based on the profit-generation inclinations.

For this, and in recognising the commentary of the notables: Emery, Schumpeter, and Kaldor when they were remarking that price change is a chief objective of the speculators (Emery 1896: 96; Kaldor 1939: 1; Schumpeter 1939: 679), it may be argued that the characterisation of the middle ground on the normative scale depends, in essence, on the behaviour of economic agents with respect to price changes. That is, it is the nature and extent of opportunism with regards to price changes that is a crucial trait of a speculator whether this exists in the real economy in the pricing of goods and services (closer to investing), the financial sector in the pricing of securities that trade on the secondary markets (perhaps somewhat in the middle) or in the pricing of odds by counterparties (closer to gambling).

Thus, while one is discussing the boundaries of speculation (and indeed the prohibition of *Maysir*), it is of high importance to note here that it is not so much the line of business of the speculator (including their background) or the instrument that they use (or its ownership traits) that defines in an unequivocal fashion where their economic actions belong on the normative scale. Rather, *it is in the ability of these actions to demonstrate what they perceive to be the best manner of generating profit from their ex-ante resource endowment.*

For, as was shown by Chancellor (1999), history is replete with a plethora of individuals and businesses (e.g., real-sector operators, traders and financial intermediaries) that have used a multitude of tools (e.g., Tulips, equities, fixed-income securities and derivatives) with varying degrees of ownership that instigated crises consequent of gambling behaviour with profound social, economic and political consequences. This, again, relates to the points that were elaborated in Chapter 5 wherein it was contended that ownership (and the associated issues of delivery and possession) is not a sole endower of transactional legitimacy; nor is the act of entering into a derivative contract, absent any contextualisation, a true indicator of committing a religiously prohibited deed.

Notwithstanding the above, it is acknowledged that there are some traits that are generally associated with the propensity of gambling behaviour that can add (and have actually added) to the depth of academic research on the subject matter; these are: turnover (Glaser and Weber 2009; Simonson 1972), classification of the economic agent (Bessembinder and Seguin 1993; Chang *et al.* 2000; de Roon *et al.* 2000; Wang 2003) and usage of credit (Chancellor 1999; Kindleberger and Aliber 2005). However, even though the merits of many of these designations are not disputed, it should be recognised that these general indicative traits are just that: They are generalisations, not definite classifiers.

One may be tempted to add to the above list the type of instrument used by the speculator, which may indicate their propensity to leave the anchor tying them to the realm of investing in a bid to wade into that of gambling. Indeed, this appears to be the crux of the *Maysir* argumentation by some of the *Shari'ah* scholars who professed a judgement against derivatives. In essence, the view (and the hope) is that the elimination of the instrument leads to the elimination of the act.

To this, it may be simply stated that derivatives are merely tools, albeit versatile ones, for a wide variety of purposes. True, apart from risk management, they may be used to speculate and gamble (with profound consequences) on the changes in prices in the financial markets. However, it should also be notable that this practice is not too dissimilar to that of using equities (e.g., remember Saudi Arabia Tadawul exchange in 2003–6) or real estate (e.g., remember Dubai in 2005–9) in an irresponsible manner for an economic gain. In effect, the nature of the instrument and/or the underlying variables has become almost an irrelevant consideration to those parties who are intent on gambling.

The positive thing that emerges from the discussion in this and the previous chapters is that it revolves around the permissibility of derivatives for market-risk management endeavours that are verifiable by modern accounting theory and market practice. Specifically, they should arguably be used in the context of transferring the non-core market-risk exposures of real-sector entities (and financial institutions that facilitate their existence), which can, in turn, reduce the probability of financial distress, underinvestment, loss of potential financing savings and market competitiveness and lower overall firm value. The anchor, consequently, to the investment sphere is stronger than any that has been examined thus far (ownership, delivery, possession, instrument, turnover, credit usage and classification of economic agent).

The above also concurs with the clear pre-eminence of the real sector in Islamic jurisprudence that can be observed to manifest itself in the commentary that exists in the Islamic finance literature with respect to gambling, in general, and derivatives, in particular (Al-Suwailem 2006; El-Gari 2010; Kamali 2000; Khan 1997; Moody's Global Corporate Finance 2010; Salamon 2000). Effectively, some of the contemporary commentators in Islamic finance do make a distinction between the constructive risks that are created as part of real economic activities (including speculative risks) and the artificial risk creation by the gambling parties that is exogenous to the real sector (Al-Suwailem 2006: 40; Kamali 2000: 147).

With the aforementioned generalised conceptualisation of the environment that hosts the market-risk management endeavours of real-sector entities (including the association between gambling, speculation and investment) in place, the discussion now turns to a related subject, which is the role of the financial intermediaries who facilitate hedging practices as speculators in the financial markets.

7.4 The role of financial intermediaries as speculators

The discussion thus far has concentrated on the usage of derivative instruments as hedging tools for market-risk management in scenarios that are linked to the real economy. Notably, it was argued that the market-risk exposures for real economic activity also include those being faced by financial institutions, such as Islamic banks (e.g., interest rates/profit rates and currency), which enable real-sector entities to create wealth in society in a value-added manner. Throughout the discussion there have been allusions to the role of financial intermediaries, or risk-transfer specialists as they are referred to by Culp (2004), who, even though not hedgers themselves, have been shown to be indispensable for the effective and efficient undertaking of market-risk management activities in society consequent of the diversity in the needs that exist between the various hedging counterparties.

One starts with an articulation by Marshall on the role of speculators in producing a socially valuable service. He states:

> Man cannot create material things. In the mental and moral world indeed he may produce new ideas; but when he is said to produce material things, he really only produces utilities; or in other words, his efforts and sacrifices result in changing the form or arrangement of matter to adapt it better for the satisfaction of wants. All that he can do in the physical world is either to readjust matter so as to make it more useful, as when

he makes a log of wood into a table; or to put it in the way of being made more useful by nature, as when he puts seed where the forces of nature will make it burst into life. It is sometimes said that traders do not produce: that while the cabinet-maker produces furniture, the furniture dealer merely sells what is already produces. But there is no scientific foundation for this distinction. They both produce utilities, and neither of them can do more: the furniture-dealer moves and rearranges matter so as to make it more serviceable than it was before, and the carpenter does nothing more. (Marshall 1910: 63)

The words of Marshall are particularly relevant to the subject of derivative contracts in that the financial intermediary, as a speculator who specialises in the transfer of risks that emanate from the real economy, can be thought of as serving a function that is not too much different from the role of a financier operating as an intermediary between depositors/investors and entrepreneurs/fund seekers. In effect, they use the benefits of economies of scale to lower their search costs to generate a more certain knowledge base (in a relative sense to the hedging community) in order to reduce forecasting errors.

Essentially, and as recognised early in the twentieth century by Fisher (1906), the role of the financial intermediary can be thought of as being built on the recognition of the inverse relationship between risk and knowledge. Furthermore, the utility produced to society, above and beyond the potential for risk reduction consequent of the increase in the knowledge base, also includes increased liquidity, lower trading costs, enhanced market depth and immediacy in execution.

In undertaking their function, the financial intermediary, after utilising the full potential of the portfolio approach to risk management by way of the combination (i.e., better statistical inferences) and diversification (i.e., less-than-perfect correlation opportunities) benefits, can decide whether to maintain the residual exposure on its balance sheet or transfer the residual exposure to another financial intermediary. That is, if they have adequate capital reserves, they can choose to absorb the price risk inherent in the 'warehousing' of derivatives by not offsetting the unmatched exposure with another party, or, alternatively, they could decide to 'run a balanced book' with matched assets and liabilities. However, it would appear that financial intermediaries, *or at least the prudent ones*, choose to run a balanced book by offsetting any residual exposures to outside parties (Culp 2004: 60; Haushalter 2000; Hull 2010: 72).

And although there may be systemic risks consequent of the potential of default by a major financial intermediary in the aforementioned inter-linked chain of risk management, this particular risk is reduced by the fact that a default by hedgers tends to be more idiosyncratic (i.e., a good candidate for diversification) than default on loans. In effect, the defaulted derivative contract will have to be characterised by both financial distress by the counterparty *and* a negative contract value.

With that, it may now be appropriate to broach the topic of fees charged by financial intermediaries, which is a topic that has been a point of contention in the Islamic finance discourse. To commence with, even though there are fees that accrue to the financial intermediary, they are not premiums to guarantee against a certain amount of loss as is done in the insurance industry, which is apparently negatively perceived by Islamic jurists.

Thus, as stated by Patterson in a manner that fits rather nicely with the *Alghonom Bialghorom* axiom: 'The hedger will not pay his "premium" in cash, he pays it by foregoing his gains on a rising market. This brings the "insurer" in as a participator in the enterprise, a situation which is incompatible with the analogy of insurance. To deduct a fixed premium from gross profit (as the insured does in shifting his fire risk) is quite a different matter from turning over to the risk-taker an unpredetermined portion of the possible profits of the enterprise. Hence hedging does not fit the Procrustean bed' (Patterson 1931: 882).

Notwithstanding the above, it is not self-evident from some of the Islamic finance literature on derivative contracts where the animosity towards fee generation by financial intermediaries resides and what is the rationale for its prohibition in a hedging context (Al-Shubaili 2012: 49–50). This is especially pertinent since, as has been argued by Kamali, the intermediaries, whether on a *Mudharib* (investment manager) or *Wakeel* (agent) basis, are allowed to earn remuneration for their efforts (Kamali 2000: 176). In effect, there is really no need for the fees, as advocated by Chapra and Khan, to be 'Islamised by resorting to Islamic instruments' (Chapra and Khan 2000: 81).

Apart from the ambiguity with regards to the religious permissibility for fee generation in some of the contemporary financial practices, it is difficult to economically rationalise an argument whereby the costs related to building an infrastructure to collect and analyse market intelligence (e.g., highly skilled personnel and expensive computational and statistical systems) in order to ascertain intrinsic values should be done without some form of compensation. The importance of these fees in building the necessary capital reserves that can respond to market shocks, as a counterparty to the hedging parties, is also not an insignificant consideration. In addition, the fees need to be contextualised in that they are in the form of a bid-ask spread that is quite competitive as a result of being determined by the supply-and-demand forces in the financial markets. Essentially, the hedging community has a wide array of financial intermediaries to choose from based on their contractual fees and reputation.

That said, there are merits to the argument that the for-profit nature of the financial intermediaries in the hedging sphere, especially when combined with pure speculative strategies, can result in aggressive behaviour that eventually goes beyond the positive role of financial intermediation into the unsustainable realm of gambling. This is perhaps what Al-Suwailem (2006) was referring to when he noted the classic problem of the willingness versus the ability to take risks in the financial markets. Although, in the case of market-risk management (i.e., not credit derivatives that are mostly priced on a mark-to-model basis), this has little to do with the professed distortions in pricing consequent of asymmetries of information between the hedging party and the financial intermediary (Al-Suwailem 2006: 37–8).

Interestingly, while recognising the aforementioned legitimate concern, it may be conjectured that the fee structure of financial intermediaries can be of value in the evolution from theoretical formulation of the normative scale of economic activities to practical application in that it can actually be a decent measure of the gambling inclinations by the non-hedging counterparties (i.e., financial intermediaries) in the derivatives markets.

In essence, it has been contended by some writers that distorted fee structures that are not backed by economic fundamentals and financial realities may actually encourage aggressive risk taking in a bid to generate excess profits (Murphy 2012; Whittaker 1987). Specifically, the willingness to take risks may not be commensurate with the ability to do so based on the size of the transaction, the characteristics of the warehoused inventory of derivatives, the capital base, the profile of the counterparty, investing and funding charges and any cost structures that should be factored explicitly into the willingness versus ability equation.

Accordingly, it becomes apparent. based on the above, that the social good offered by financial intermediaries in efficiently allocating the risks that exist in society as opposed to perhaps creating risk for its own sake depends in no small part on their fee structures. These fee structures are, in actual fact, observable to their own internal risk-management function and externally to the other counterparties, not least of which are the supervisory authorities.[6] In effect, the stability of the utility provided by the financial intermediary, as a speculator focusing on risk transfer, is contingent on their proper indication of willingness to take risks (i.e., competitive versus uncompetitive fees) in a manner that accurately corresponds to their ability to do so.[7] In short, it is not exclusively a weakness; it can also be an opportunity.

With that, one may conclude this section by stating that the discussion on the role of financial intermediaries in the hedging sphere and the expressed potential for improvement in the current modus operandi of the derivatives markets were elaborated with the objective of exploring the prospect of having Islamic financial institutions serve the role of financial intermediaries in the derivatives markets to facilitate the hedging activities of their clients, even if it is on a reverse-enquiry basis. This is something that does not currently exist; in fact, the conventional financial institutions have the Islamic finance industry as a 'captive market' in that regard.

Notably, this reality endures even for the Islamic swaps market. Effectively, even if the arguments for the permissibility of the derivative instruments were to be accepted by the Islamic finance scholarly community, the decision to preclude the speculative services of financial intermediaries in the hedging sphere would make the market-risk management endeavours by operators in the real economy a much more challenging task in terms of execution.

7.5 Conclusion

It has been contended throughout the book that the Islamic finance discourse should transcend the supreme emphasis on the legal sphere in the interpretation of the scripture and grant more credence to the economic theories that can explain human behaviour with resources. In this chapter, the discussion focused on one of the key topics that has been often repeated in the discussions on derivatives in Islamic finance, namely the linkages between these financial contracts and the prohibition of *Maysir*.

For this, it has been argued in this chapter that one ought to distinguish between the instrument, the framework and the act even if all of these centre on dealings that relate in one way or another to uncertainty about the future. More specifically, within the framework of *Shari'ah*, the act of *Maysir* should be the focus of the prohibition *not* the particular financial tools (i.e., derivatives) and frameworks (i.e., risk-transfer and financial intermediaries), which have been shown to provide positive economic effects. The significance of that argument becomes apparent in the paradoxical prohibitive stance with respect to derivatives that exist even in the face of appeals for allowing the use of these instruments only for market-risk management purposes.

In effect, it should be realised that the complete elimination of particular forms of financial instruments is not the answer to the *Maysir* problem since it eradicates positive benefits for no clear and attainable purpose (i.e., eliminating gambling behaviour). Essentially, as is markedly understood by the students of economic theory, one should be reminded that the formulation of any economic-related directive should be ambitious in that it should seek to maximise the benefits (human welfare) and reduce the costs (including negative externalities) associated with its implementation, but should not adopt an untenable objective of seeking to guarantee only the emergence of benefits.

In fact, what could be contended, instead, is that the aspiration for complete purity in financial transactions by way of the juristic rejection of the utilisation of derivatives as hedging instruments by real-sector operators, is that such a position can be a form of injustice. This is because it opens the door for increased uncertainty, and its effects, in the economic dealings in society (i.e., financial distress, reduced competitiveness, lower economic development, etc.).

Finally, it is appreciated that there is a concern among the majority, if not all, of the stakeholders in the Islamic finance industry regarding the possibility of the risk-and-return profile of derivative usage becoming so unbalanced that it overwhelms the beneficial economic functions of these instruments and results in financial crises with profound negative consequences. The answer to that concern, however, or any other for that matter, is not in the complete elimination of any financial tool that contains the prospect of instability, but, rather, it is in allowing an important instrument that assists in the mitigation of market risks under a regulatory framework that controls its usage. For this, the imposition of the IAS 39 Hedge Accounting rules, as outlined in the previous chapter, in addition to the prospect for increased disclosure with respect to inherent risk exposures of financial intermediaries along with their fee structures can be of great value.[8]

Notes

1. The discourse in the late nineteenth century and in the early twentieth and the discourse examined in the earlier chapters in contemporary Islamic finance is quite interesting in terms of similarity of arguments (underlying, delivery, set-off, etc.) (Kreitner 2007; Levy 2006; Patterson 1931; Raines and Leathers 1994).

2. The weapons of the courts in this process ranged from the nullification of the contract (i.e., rendering it not payable) on to even the prohibition of the existence of certain institutions (e.g., bucket shops).

3. The works of Al-Suwailem seem to suggest that *Gharar* (excessive uncertainty) and *Maysir* are more or less the same where both are 'a zero-sum exchange with uncertain payoffs' (Al-Suwailem 2000: 8; Al-Suwailem 2006: 69). This definition is disputable, but the argumentation is outside the scope of book; nonetheless, Al-Suwailem's linking between the two prohibitions will be used to articulate his argument.

4. This assumes no risk of default by the counterparty. However, even if this risk is included, it is likely to be viewed as being smaller than the full force of market risk; otherwise, hedging would not exist.

5. Al-Suwailem (1999: 74) references Binmore who clearly states that utility *can* be approximated as a monetary amount if games like '[two-player] poker and Backgammon' are being played by parties who are risk neutral, which is 'unlikely to be a good assumption about people's preferences in general' (Binmore 1992: 238). Interestingly, Binmore also contends that backgammon and two-player poker are not strictly competitive games if both players are risk averse (ibid.).

6. Of course, this would require an increased level of external disclosure than is currently present.

7. Some financial intermediaries are market makers and thus are expected, or required, to continuously quote spreads in their

designated markets. In other words, they may not be able to stop quoting fees for their services.

8. Notably, the financial intermediaries can be a Special Purpose Vehicle (an SPV) of a larger banking institution focusing on market risk management services for the Islamic finance industry. This would alleviate some of the fears associated with the sharing of proprietary information by these firms.

CHAPTER 8
CONCLUSION

The book has revealed what can arguably be described as an over-generalised discourse on the subject of derivatives and market-risk management in the Islamic finance literature and commentary. In particular, it was shown that the prohibitive stances on the market-risk-strategy and on derivative instruments as tools for the implementation of that strategy were adopted in a generous fashion without the needed level of extensiveness and depth in the understanding of what is essentially economic subject matter. This, of course, became apparent in that the standard-setting bodies in the Islamic finance industry have demonstrated a case of static rigidity consequent of the excessive reliance on the Islamic theory of *Qiyas* (analogical reasoning), untroubled not only by the potential for large and unmitigated market-risk exposures of a growing Islamic finance industry that is being increasingly interconnected to the international financial markets, but also in the probable negative implications of these open exposures on the real sector.

More specifically, the preceding chapters sought to contextualise the debate on the usage derivatives in the Islamic finance industry with a more thorough discussion on the economics, rationale and usage of derivative instruments in a *market-risk management* framework (i.e., not for gambling) that has numerous benefits for the hedging entities, in particular, and for sustainable growth of Islamic economies, in general.

The aforementioned approach, it is argued, surpasses the chosen path for the modus operandi of the Islamic finance industry with regards to facing up to the market-risk management challenges that appear to have been built on contentious juridical judgements based on incomplete analysis of contemporary contractual forms vis-à-vis their pre-modern 'Islamic' counterparts (with an ensuing circular-natured debate on technicalities). Accordingly, the hoped-for outcome here has been to transcend the modern 'Islamic' hedging instruments/frameworks that revolve around being either, one, transaction-level solutions that inherently disregard the difficulties of implementation along with an ostensible neglect of the benefits of a portfolio approach to risk management, or, two, a formulistic exercise of financial engineering with multiple Arabic-named contracts that generate the exact same risk-and-return profile as well as payoff structures of the prohibited conventional derivative instruments.

Notwithstanding the above, it is acknowledged that the contention that derivatives are effective instruments for the management of market risks in the most efficient manner will undoubtedly be met with hostility by some in the Islamic finance community who will continue to refuse to accept the presence of derivatives in the industry. In the course of the rebuttal, they may choose to continue to evoke a mixture of rationales (that have been disputed in many parts of the book) that seek to regenerate the attempts to superficially associate derivative usage for hedging purposes with the prohibitions of *Riba*, *Gharar* and *Maysir*.

This, almost certainly, will be undertaken by citing multiple opinions of some of the most respected jurists in Islam in an effort to gain juridical legitimacy for the proposed judgement without the necessary regard to the required contextualisation of these venerable opinions to whatever perspective they are applied to. Surprisingly, and for some paradoxical reason, it is not apparent that the indispensable Islamic theories of *Maslaha* and *Daroura* have had a role in this almost exclusive *Qiyas*-based framework of juridical determination.

To confront this conundrum, one should perhaps start with the recognition that the view of the *Shari'ah* on economic matters will inherently be an economic perspective, not a legal one that focuses on contractual technicalities. This realisation, in turn, leads to three essential theoretical foundations that underlie the substance of the whole book. First, economics is the scientific study of the behaviour of economic agents (individually, and as a society) with limited resources through time. Second, the behaviour of economic agents is indiscriminate in that a Muslim economic agent with resources will largely behave in the same way as a non-Muslim economic agent. That is, the Muslim brain is not wired any differently to a non-Muslim brain. To be certain, there may be religious and cultural factors that may affect behaviour; however, there has not been any evidence that would point to the fact that Muslims behave in a *fundamentally* different manner with resources than non-Muslims (although this may be a good candidate for future research). Finally, Islam as a religion that communicates the message of God to humankind (not just Muslims) shows a path for a better distribution of those limited resources among the economic agents.

The statement 'better distribution' in the last sentence, along with the acknowledgement that all economic agents behave in largely similar fashion, is fundamental to the proper understanding of economics in the Islamic finance industry and the formulation of an effective policy that focuses on the noble objectives in the *Shari'ah*. With that, one can proceed with the appeal to the Islamic finance industry to go beyond the emphasis of labelling contracts as being either Islamic or conventional along formulistic lines and proceed to grant greater credence to the all-too-important substance of the justice (or injustice) that surrounds the distribution of limited resources.

This should be undertaken in light of a better understanding of how the proscriptions of *Riba*, *Gharar* and *Maysir* (as divine clues cloaked in the garb of prohibitions) manifest themselves in contemporary commercial and financial environments. It is aspired that the present book on derivative hedging instruments and market-risk management in Islamic finance can be regarded as a step in that direction.

In terms of the implications arising from the elaboration of the book, one may start with the recommendation, based on the evidence presented earlier, that the *Shari'ah* scholarly community and the standard-setting bodies should adopt a position that grants permissibility, in theory and in practice, to the contemporary market-risk management framework. This should also entail the acceptance of derivative instruments as tools for the implementation for that purpose (i.e., not for gambling).

To be certain, it is recognised that the usage of the *option-based instruments* in the Islamic finance industry may be a contentious matter consequent of their asymmetric payoff structures wherein there is a potential for profit-making in a manner that exceeds the losses associated with original market-risk exposures. The above is an understandable position when the discussion, as in this book, focuses exclusively on market-risk management. That being said, the forward-based derivative instruments are not endowed with such payoff ambiguity if there is indeed an equal offsetting risk exposure to the hedging entity. Thus, given that the forward-based instruments, for the most part, neutralise the risk exposure then they should be allowed within the Islamic finance industry as an effective means of hedging market risks.

Moreover, it has been shown that there is no substantive evidence that backs the opinion that only commodity price risk can be hedged and that any other types of risk have to be dealt with exclusively through commodity *Murabaha* contracts combined with *Wa'ad* structures. Consequently, it is recommended that entities with legitimate hedging needs should be allowed to use derivative instruments (once more they can be limited to using the forward-based ones at this stage) to manage interest/profit rate and foreign exchange market-risk exposures in a manner that allows financial intermediaries to function as facilitators for the hedging activities of real-sector entities.

Finally, the standard-setting bodies should strive to ensure that the usage of these instruments is properly recognised on the financial statements of the entities that utilise them; for this, IAS 39 has been shown to offer confidence that the derivative instruments are properly accounted for in addition to an assurance that they are used in a hedging context. This IAS 39 framework can be conjoined with a derivative trading platform in the form of an exchange that is centred on market-risk management endeavours in a manner that incorporates the highest standards of transparency and good governance.

REFERENCES

Books

Abd Al-Qadir, A. (1982), *Ta'qib 'ala Ra'y Al-Tashri' fi Masa'il Al-Bursa*, Cairo: Al-Ittihad Al-Duwali li Al-Bunuk Al-Islamiyah.

Abu Sulayman, A. (2003), *Fiqh Al-Daroura wa Tatbikatou Al-Mo'asara*, Jeddah: Islamic Research and Training Institute.

Ahmad, Z. (1994), *Islamic Banking: State of the Art*, Jeddah: Islamic Research and Training Institute.

Al-Amarani, M. (2003), *Al-Manfa'a Fel Qard*, Dammam: Dar Ibn Al-Jauzi.

Al-Amine, M. (2008), *Risk Management in Islamic Finance: An Analysis of Derivatives Instruments in Commodity Markets*, Leiden and Boston: Brill.

Al-Baladhuri, A. (1983), *Futuh al-Buldan*, Beirut: Dar al-Kutub al-Ilmiyyah.

Al-Baz, A. (1999), *Ahkam Sarf Al-Nuqud wa Al-Omlat fi Al-Fiqh Al-Islami*, Amman: Dar Al-Nafa'is.

Al-Ghazali (1993a [n.d.]), *Al-Mustafa Min Ilm Al-Usul*, Jeddah: Sharikat Al-Madina Al-Munawwara.

Al-Ghazali (1993b [n.d.]), *Asas Al-Qiyas*, Riyadh: Maktabat Al-Abikan.

Al-Ghazali (n.d.), *Ihya Ulum al-Din* (vol. 4), Beirut: Dar Al-Nadwah.

Al-Ghazali and M. E. Marmura (1997 [n.d.]), *The Incoherence of the Philosophers: Tahafut Al-falasifah: A*

Parallel English–Arabic Text (1st edn), Provo: Brigham Young University Press.

Al-Ghazali and W. M. Watt (1953), *The Faith and Practice of Al-Ghazali*, London: G. Allen and Unwin.

Al-Masri, R. Y. (1991), *Al-Jami' fi Usul Al-Riba*, Damascus: Dar Al-Qalam.

Al-Masri, R. Y. (1993), *Al-Maysir wa Al-Qimar* (1st edn), Damascus and Beirut: Dar Al-Qalam and Al-Dar Al-Shamia.

Al-Qaradawi, Y. (1987), *Bay' Al-Murabahah li Al-Amir Bil-Shira'* (2nd edn), Cairo: Maktabah Wahbah.

Al-Razi, F. (1988 [n.d.]), *Al-Mahsul Fi Ilm Usul Al-Fiqh*, Beirut: Dar Al Kutub Al-Illmiyya.

Al-Rubaia, S. (1992), *Tahwil Al-Masraf Al-Ribawi ila Masraf Islami wa Muqtadayatuh*, Kuwait City: Markaz Al-Makhtutat wa Al-Turath.

Al-Shatibi, A. I. (2004 [n.d.]), *Al-Muwafaqat fi Usul Al-shari'ah*, Beirut: Darul Kutubul Ilmiyyah.

Al-Suwailem, S. (2006), *Hedging in Islamic Finance*, Jeddah: Islamic Research and Training Institute.

Al-Suwailem, S. (2007), *Al-Tahawuut fi Al-Tamweel Al-Islami*, Jeddah: Islamic Research and Training Institute.

Al-Zarqa, M. (1998a), *Al-Madkhal Al-Fiqhi Al-'Aam* (1st edn) (vol. 1), Damascus: Dar Al-Qalam.

Al-Zarqa, M. (1998b), *Al-Madkhal Al-Fiqhi Al-'Aam* (1st edn) (vol. 2), Damascus: Dar Al-Qalam.

Al-Zuhayli, W. (1998), *Nazariyah Al-Dhaman*, Beirut: Dar Al-Fikr Al-Mou'asser.

Al-Zuhayli, W. and M. A. El-Gamal (2003), *Islamic Jurisprudence and its Proofs: Financial Transactions in Islamic Jurisprudence*, Beirut: Dar Al-Fikr.

Amanat, A. and F. Griffel (2007), *Shari'a: Islamic Law in the Contemporary Context*, Stanford: Stanford University Press.

Arrow, K. J. (1971), *Essays in the Theory of Risk-bearing*, Chicago: Markham Publishing Co.

Askari, H., Z. Iqbal, N. Krichene and A. Mirakhor (2012), *Risk Sharing in Finance: The Islamic Finance Alternative*, Singapore: John Wiley & Sons.

Azzam, M. (1985), *Al-Fatawa Al-Shar'iyyah fi Masail Al-Iqtisadiyyah* (2nd edn), Kuwait: Bayt Al-Tamwil Al-Kuwaiti.

Bernstein, P. (1996), *Against the Gods: The Remarkable Story of Risk*, New York: John Wiley & Sons.

Binmore, K. (1992), *Fun and Games: A Text on Game Theory*, Lexington: D. C. Heath.

Blumer, H. (1969), *Symbolic Interactionism: Perspective and Method*, Englewood Cliffs: Prentice-Hall.

Brenner, R. and G. A. Brenner (1990), *Gambling and Speculation: A Theory, A History, and A Future of Some Human Decisions*, Cambridge and New York: Cambridge University Press.

Brown, K. and D. Smith (1995), *Interest Rate and Currency Swaps: A Tutorial*, Charlottesville: Research Foundation of the Institute of Chartered Financial Analysts.

Catania, P. J. and P. Alonzi (1997), *Commodity Trading Manual*, Chicago: Chicago Board of Trade.

Chambers, R. J. (1966), *Accounting, Evaluation, and Economic Behavior*, Englewood Cliffs: Prentice-Hall.

Chance, D. and R. Brooks (2010), *An Introduction to Derivatives and Risk Management*, Mason: South-Western Cengage Learning.

Chancellor, E. (1999), *Devil Take The Hindmost: A History of Financial Speculation* (1st edn), New York: Farrar, Straus, Giroux.

Chapra, M. U. and T. Khan (2000), *Regulation and Supervision of Islamic Banks* (vol. 3), Jeddah: Islamic

Development Bank and Islamic Research and Training Institute.

Crump, A. (1875), *The Theory of Stock Exchange Speculation* (4th edn), London: Longmans, Green, and Co.

Culp, C. (2004), *Risk Transfer: Derivatives in Theory and Practice*, Hoboken J. Wiley.

Debreu, G. (1959), *Theory of Value: An Axiomatic Analysis of Economic Equilibrium*, New York: Wiley.

Devlin, K. (2008), *The Unfinished Game: Pascal, Fermat, and the Seventeenth-century Letter That Made the World Modern*, New York: Basic Books.

Dilthey, W. (1989), *Introduction to the Human Sciences*, Princeton: Princeton University Press.

Dowd, K. (1998), *Beyond Value at Risk: The New Science of Risk Management*, Chichester and New York: John Wiley & Sons.

Dowd, K. (2005), *Measuring Market Risk* (2nd edn), Hoboken: John Wiley & Sons.

Droysen, J. and R. Hübner (1937), *Historik; Vorlesungen über Enzyklopädie und Methodologie der Geschichte*, München and Berlin: R. Oldenbourg.

El-Gamal, M. (2006), *Islamic Finance: Law, Economics and Practice*, New York: Cambridge University Press.

Emery, H. C. (1896), *Speculation on the Stock and Produce Exchanges of the United States*, New York: Columbia University Press.

Finch, G. (1896), *A Selection of Cases on the English Law of Contract* (2nd edn), Cambridge: Cambridge University Press.

Fisher, I. (1906), *The Nature of Capital and Income*, New York and London: Macmillan & Co.

Gadamer, H. (1989), *Truth and Method* (2nd edn), New York: Crossroad.

Gärdenfors, P. and N. Sahlin (1988), *Decision, Probability, and Utility: Selected Readings,* Cambridge and New York: Cambridge University Press.

Gastineau, G., D. Smith, and R. Todd (2001), *Risk Management, Derivatives, and Financial Analysis under SFAS,* Charlottesville: The Research Foundation of AIMR.

Gintis, H. (2009), *Game Theory Evolving: A Problem-centered Introduction to Modeling Strategic Interaction* (2nd edn), Princeton: Princeton University Press.

Graham, B. and D. Dodd (1934), *Security Analysis,* New York: McGraw-Hill.

Greuning, H. van and Z. Iqbal (2008), *Risk Analysis for Islamic Banks,* Washington, DC: World Bank.

Halliday, J. and P. Fuller (1975), *The Psychology of Gambling,* New York: Harper & Row.

Hammad, N. (1986), *Bay' Al-Kali Bil-Kali fi Al-Fiqh Al-Islami,* Jeddah: Jami'at Al-Malik 'Abd Al-Aziz.

Hardy, C. (1999 [1923]), *Risk and Risk-bearing,* Chicago: University of Chicago Press.

Haroun, A. (1953), *Al-Maysir wa Al-Azlam* (1st edn), Cairo: Dar Al-Fikr Al-Arabi.

Harrington, J. (2009), *Games, Strategies and Decision Making,* New York: Worth Publishers.

Hassan, H. (1994), *Jurisprudence of Maslaha and its Contemporary Applications* (1st edn), Jeddah: Islamic Research and Training Institute.

Hassan, K. and M. Mahlknecht (2011), *Islamic Capital Markets: Products and Strategies,* Chichester: Wiley.

Heffernan, S. (1996), *Modern Banking in Theory and Practice,* Chichester: Wiley.

Herak, A. (1988), *Al-Bonouk Al-Islamiya Malaha wa Ma'alayha,* Cairo: Dar Al-Sahwa.

Hicks, J. (1971), *The Social Framework: An Introduction to Economics* (4th edn), Oxford: Clarendon Press.

Hopkin, P. (2012), *Fundamentals of Risk Management:*

Understanding Evaluating and Implementing Effective Risk Management (2nd edn), London and Philadelphia: Kogan Page.

Horcher, K. (2005), *Essentials of Financial Risk Management*, Hoboken: Wiley.

Hull, J. (2009), *Options, Futures and other Derivatives* (7th edn), Upper Saddle River: Prentice Hall.

Ibn Al-Qayyim (1955 [n.d.]), *I'lam Al-Muwaqqin 'an Rabb Al-Alamein* (vol. 2), Cairo: Maktabah al-Sa'adah.

Ibn Al-Qayyim (1991 [n.d.]), *I'lam Al-Muwaqqin 'an Rabb Al-Alamein* (vol. 3), Beirut: Dar Al-Kutub Al-Ilmiyah.

Ibn Khaldun, F. Rosenthal and N. J. Dawood (1969 [1377]), *The Muqaddimah: An Introduction to History*, Princeton: Princeton University Press.

Ibn Rushd (1998 [n.d.]), *Bidayat al-Mujtahid wa Nihayet al-Muqtasid* (vol. 2), Beirut: Dar al-Ma'rifah.

Ibn Taymiyyah, T. (1899), *Nazariyyah Al-'Aqd*, Beirut: Dar Al-Ma'arifah.

Ibn Taymiyyah, T. (1963), *Majmua'ah Fatawa Shiekh Al-Islam Ibn Taymiyyah* (vol. 29), Riyadh: Matabi' Al-Riyadh.

Ibn Taymiyyah, T. and A. R. Al-Qasim (1978), *Majmua'ah Fatawa Shiekh Al-Islam Ibn Taymiyyah*, Beirut: Mu'assah Al-Risalah.

Iqbal, Z. and A. Mirakhor (2007), *An Introduction to Islamic Finance: Theory and Practice*. Singapore: John Wiley & Sons.

IRTI (2000), *Resolutions and Recommendations of the Council of the Islamic Fiqh Academy 1985–2000*, Jeddah: Islamic Research and Training Institute

Islahi, A. A. (2005), *Contributions of Muslim Scholars to Economic Thought and Analysis: (11–905 A.H.–632–1500 A.D.)*, Jeddah: Scientific Publishing Centre, King Abdulaziz University.

Jorion, P. and S. Khoury (1996), *Financial Risk Management:*

Domestic and International Dimensions, Cambridge, MA: Blackwell Publishers.

Al-Jundi, M. (1988), *Mu'amalat Al-Bursa fi Al-Shariah Al-Islamiyah*, Cairo: Dar Al-Nahda Al-Arabiya.

Kamali, M. (2000), *Islamic Commercial Law: An Analysis of Futures and Options*, Cambridge: Islamic Texts Society.

Kamali, M. (2003), *Principles of Islamic Jurisprudence*, Cambridge: Islamic Texts Society.

Khan, M. (1997), *Islamic Futures and Their Markets: With Special Reference to Their Role in Developing Rural Financial Market* (1st edn), Jeddah: Islamic Research and Training Institute.

Khan, T. and H. Ahmed (2001), *Risk Management: An Analysis of Issues in Islamic Financial Industry*, Jeddah: Islamic Research and Training Institute.

Kindleberger, C. and R. Z. Aliber (2005), *Manias, Panics, and Crashes: A History of Financial Crises* (5th edn), Hoboken: John Wiley & Sons.

Knight, F. (1921), *Risk, Uncertainty and Profit*, New York: Harper.

Kreitner, R. (2007), *Calculating Promises: The Emergence of Modern American Contract Doctrine*, Stanford: Stanford University Press.

Lamberton, D. M. (1965), *The Theory of Profit*, Oxford: Blackwell.

Langlois, C., C. Seignobos and G. Berry (1898), *Introduction to the Study of History*, London: Duckworth & Co.

Lavington, F. (1968), *The English Capital Market* (1st edn), London: Cass.

Littleton, A. C. and V. Zimmerman (1962), *Accounting Theory: Continuity and Change*, Englewood Cliffs: Prentice-Hall.

Markowitz, H. (1959), *Portfolio Selection: Efficient Diversification of Investments*, New York: Wiley.

Marshall, A. (1910), *Principles of Economics: An Introductory Volume* (6th edn), London: Macmillan & Co.

Marshall, A. (1923), *Money, Credit, and Commerce*, London: Macmillan.

Marshall, J. F. and K. Kapner (1993), *Understanding Swaps*, New York: Wiley.

Newman, J. R. (1956), *The World of Mathematics I* (vol. 1). New York: Simon and Schuster.

Obaidullah, M. (2005), *Islamic Financial Services*, Jeddah: Scientific Publishing Centre, King Abdulaziz University.

OIC (1992), *Majallah Majma' Al-Fiqh Al-Islami* (vol. 7, part 1), Jeddah: OIC Islamic Fiqh Academy.

Popper, K. (1959), *The Logic of Scientific Discovery*, New York: Basic Books.

Popper, K. (1969), *Conjectures and Refutations: The Growth of Scientific Knowledge* (3rd edn), London: Routledge and K. Paul.

Robbins, L. R. (2007 [1932]), *An Essay on the Nature and Significance of Economic Science*, London: Macmillan & Co.

Rosenthal, F. (1975), *Gambling in Islam*, Leiden: Brill.

Samuelson, P. (1976), *Economics* (10th edn), New York: McGraw Hill.

Samuelson, P. (1998), *Economics: An Introductory Analysis*, New York: McGraw-Hill.

Savage, L. J. (1954), *The Foundations of Statistics*, New York: John Wiley & Sons.

Schacht, J. (1964), *An Introduction to Islamic Law*, Oxford: Clarendon Press.

Schumpeter, J. (1939), *Business Cycles: A Theoretical, Historical, and Statistical Analysis of the Capitalist Process* (1st edn), New York and London: McGraw-Hill.

Schumpeter, J. (1950), *Capitalism, Socialism, and Democracy* (3rd edn), New York: Harper.

Simmel, G. and D. Frisby (2004), *The Philosophy of Money* (3rd edn), London and New York: Routledge.

Smith, A. (1778), *An Inquiry into the Nature and Causes of the Wealth of Nations* (2nd edn), London: W. Strahan and T. Cadell.

Sombart, W. and M. Epstein (1967 [1913]), *The Quintessence of Capitalism: A Study of the History and Psychology of the Modern Business Man*, New York: H. Fertig.

Teweles, R., F. Jones and B. Warwick (1999), *The Futures Game: Who Wins? Who Loses? And Why?* (3rd edn), New York: McGraw-Hill.

Usmani, M. T. (2002), *An Introduction to Islamic Finance*, Hague and New York: Kluwer Law International.

Vogel, F. and S. Hayes (1998), *Islamic Law and Finance: Religion, Risk, and Return*, Boston: Kluwer Law International.

von Neumann, J. and O. Morgenstern (1953), *Theory of Games and Economic Behavior* (3rd edn), Princeton: Princeton University Press.

Weber, M. (1981 [1923]), *General Economic History*, New Brunswick, NJ: Transaction Books.

Weber, M., G. Roth and C. Wittich (1978 [1922]), *Economy and Society: An Outline of Interpretive Sociology*, Berkeley: University of California Press.

Articles

Abu Saud, M. (2002), 'Money, interest and *Qirad*', *IIUM Journal of Economics and Management*, 10(1), 67–97.

Al-Masri, R. Y. (2003), 'The binding unilateral promise (*wa'd*) in Islamic banking operations: is it permissible for a unilateral promise (*wa'd*) to be binding as an alternative to a proscribed contract?', *Journal of King Abdulaziz University: Islamic Economics*, 15(1), 29–33.

Al-Saati, A. R. (2007), 'Speculation and gambling in financial markets: economic and legal analysis', *Journal of King Abdulaziz University: Islamic Economics*, 20(1), 3–34.

Al-Suwailem, S. (1999), 'Towards an objective measure of *Gharar* in exchange', *Islamic Economic Studies*, 7(1–2), 61–102.

Allayannis, G. and J. P. Weston (2001), 'The use of foreign currency derivatives and firm market value', *Review of Financial Studies*, 14(1), 243–76.

Archer, S. and R. Abdel Karim (2006), 'On capital structure, risk sharing and capital adequacy in Islamic banks', *International Journal of Theoretical and Applied Finance*, 9(3), 269–80.

Arrow, K. J. (1951), 'Alternative approaches to the theory of choice in risk-taking situations', *Econometrica*, 19(4), 404–37.

Arrow, K. J. (1964), 'The role of securities in the optimal allocation of risk-bearing', *The Review of Economic Studies*, 31(2), 91–6.

Ayoub, S. (2012a), 'The global financial crisis, securitization and Islamic finance: an opportunity for inward and outward reform', *ISRA International Journal of Islamic Finance*, 4(2), 53–87.

Bacha, O. (1999), 'Derivative instruments and Islamic finance: some thoughts for reconsideration', *International Journal of Islamic Financial Services*, 1(1), 9–25.

Bacha, O. (2004a), 'Dual banking systems and interest rate risk for Islamic banks', *The Journal of Accounting, Commerce & Finance – Islamic Perspective*, 8(1), 1–42.

Bacha, O. (2004b), 'Value preservation through risk management: a Shariah compliant proposal for equity risk management', *The European Journal of Management and Public Policy*, 3(1), 65–83.

Basak, S. and A. Shapiro (2001), 'Value-at-risk-based risk management: optimal policies and asset prices', *Review of Financial Studies*, 14(2), 371–405.

Bernoulli, D. (1954 [1738]), 'Exposition of a new theory on the measurement of risk', *Econometrica*, 22(1), 23–36.

Bessembinder, H. (1991), 'Forward contracts and firm value: investment incentive and contracting effects', *The Journal of Financial and Quantitative Analysis*, 26(4), 519–32.

Bessembinder, H. and P. J. Seguin (1993), 'Price volatility, trading volume, and market depth: evidence from futures markets', *The Journal of Financial and Quantitative Analysis*, 28(1), 21–39.

Bicksler, J. and A. H. Chen (1986), 'An economic analysis of interest rate swaps', *The Journal of Finance*, 41(3), 645–55.

Black, F. (1976), 'The pricing of commodity contracts', *Journal of Financial Economics*, 3(1–2), 167–79.

Black, F. and S. Myron (1973), 'The pricing of options and corporate liabilities', *Journal of Political Economy*, 81(3), 637–54.

Bloom, R. and W. J. Cenker (2008), 'Derivatives and hedging: accounting vs. taxation', *Journal of Accountancy*, 206(4), 54–8.

Borna, S. and J. Lowry (1987), 'Gambling and speculation', *Journal of Business Ethics*, 6(3), 219–24.

Brown, G. (2001), 'Managing foreign exchange risk with derivatives', *Journal of Financial Economics*, 60, 401–48.

Brunner, K. and A. H. Meltzer (1971), 'The uses of money: money in the theory of an exchange economy', *American Economic Review*, 61(5), 784–805.

Carruthers, B. and W. Espeland (1991), 'Accounting for rationality: double-entry bookkeeping and the rhetoric of economic rationality', *American Journal of Sociology*, 97(1), 31–69.

Chang, E., R. Chou and E. Nelling (2000), 'Market

volatility and the demand for hedging in stock index futures', *Journal of Futures Markets*, 20(2), 105–25.

Chapra, M. U. (1996), 'Monetary management in an Islamic economy', *Islamic Economic Studies*, 4(1), 1–34.

Cooper, I. and A. Mello (1991), 'The default risk of swaps', *The Journal of Finance*, 46(2), 597–620.

Cornell, B. and M. Reinganum (1981), 'Forward and futures prices: evidence from the foreign exchange markets', *The Journal of Finance*, 36(5), 1,035–45.

Cox, J. C., J. Ingersoll, Jr. and S. Ross (1980), 'An analysis of variable rate loan contracts', *The Journal of Finance*, 35(2), 389–403.

Cox, J. C., J. Ingersoll, Jr. and S. Ross (1981), 'The relation between forward prices and futures prices', *Journal of Financial Economics*, 9(4), 321–46.

de Roon, F., T. Nijman and C. Veld (2000), 'Hedging pressure effects in futures markets', *Journal of Finance*, 55(3), 1,437–56.

DeMarzo, P. M. and D. Duffie (1995), 'Corporate incentives for hedging and hedge accounting', *The Review of Financial Studies*, 8(3), 743–71.

Duffie, D. and J. Pan (1997), 'An overview of value at risk', *Journal of Derivatives*, 4(3), 7–49.

Ederington, L. (1979), 'The hedging performance of the new futures markets', *The Journal of Finance*, 34(1), 157–70.

El-Ashkar, A. (1995), 'Towards an Islamic stock exchange in a transitional stage', *Islamic Economic Studies*, 3(1), 79–112.

El-Gamal, M. (2001), 'An economic explication of the prohibition of *Gharar* in classical Islamic jurisprudence', *Islamic Economic Studies*, 8(2), 29–58.

El-Gamal, M. (2008), 'Incoherence of contract-based Islamic financial jurisprudence in the age of financial engineering', *Wisconsin International Law Journal*, 25, 605–23.

El-Gari, M. (1993), 'Towards an Islamic stock market', *Islamic Economic Studies*, 1(1), 1–20.

Emery, H. C. (1900), 'The place of the speculator in the theory of distribution', *Publications of the American Economic Association*, 1(1), 103–22.

Emm, E., G. Gay and L. Chen-Miao (2007), 'Choices and best practice in corporate risk management disclosure', *Journal of Applied Corporate Finance*, 19(4), 82–93.

Freeman, F. N. (1907), 'The ethics of gambling', *International Journal of Ethics*, 18(1), 76–91.

Fridson, M. S. (1993), 'Exactly what do you mean by speculation?', *Journal of Portfolio Management*, 20(1), 29–39.

Friedman, M. and L. Savage (1948), 'The utility analysis of choices involving risk', *Journal of Political Economy*, 56(4), 279–304.

Froot, K., D. Scharfstein and J. Stein (1993), 'Risk management: coordinating corporate investment and financing policies', *The Journal of Finance*, 48(5), 1,629–58.

Geczy, C., B. Minton and C. Schrand (1997), 'Why firms use currency derivatives', *The Journal of Finance*, 52(4), 1,323–54.

Glaser, M. and M. Weber (2009), 'Which past returns affect trading volume?', *Journal of Financial Markets*, 12(1), 1–31.

Graham, J. R. and C. W. Smith, Jr. (1999), 'Tax incentives to hedge', *Journal of Finance*, 54(6), 2,241–62.

Haque, N. and A. Mirakhor (1999), 'The design of instruments for government finance in an Islamic economy', *Islamic Economic Studies*, 6(2), 27–43.

Haushalter, G. (2000), 'Financing policy, basis risk, and corporate hedging: evidence from oil and gas producers', *The Journal of Finance*, 55(1), 107–52.

Hicks, J. R. (1931), 'The theory of uncertainty and profit', *Economica*, 32, 170–89.

Hilliard, J. and J. Reis (1998), 'Valuation of commodity futures and options under stochastic convenience yields, interest rates, and jump diffusions in the spot', *The Journal of Financial and Quantitative Analysis*, 33(1), 61–86.

Hobson, J. A. (1905), 'The ethics of gambling', *International Journal of Ethics*, 15(2), 135–48.

How, J., M. Karim and P. Verhoeven (2005), 'Islamic financing and bank risks: the case of Malaysia', *Thunderbird International Business Review*, 47(1), 75–94.

Hull, J. (2010), 'OTC derivatives and central clearing: can all transactions be cleared?', *Financial Stability Review*, 14, 71–78.

Hussain, K. and F. Mehboob (2008), 'Hedging market risk in Islamic finance', *World Commerce Review*, 2(3), 20–5.

Iqbal, Z. (1999), 'Financial engineering in Islamic finance', *Thunderbird International Business Review*, 41(4/5), 541–59.

Jacque, L. (1981), 'Management of foreign exchange risk: a review article', *Journal of International Business Studies*, 12(1), 81–101.

Jarrow, R. and G. Oldfield (1981), 'Forward contracts and futures contracts', *Journal of Financial Economics*, 9(4), 373–82.

Kamali, M. (2007), 'Commodity futures: an Islamic legal analysis', *Thunderbird International Business Review*, 49(3), 309–39.

Kane, E. (1980), 'Market incompleteness and divergences between forward and futures interest rates', *The Journal of Finance*, 35(2), 221–34.

Kasri, R. and S. Kassim (2009), 'Empirical determinants of saving in the Islamic banks: evidence from Indonesia', *Journal of King Abdulaziz University: Islamic Economics*, 22(2), 181–201.

Keynes, J. M. (1937), 'The general theory of employment', *The Quarterly Journal of Economics*, 51(2), 209–23.

Khan, M. (1988), 'Commodity exchange and stock exchange in an Islamic economy', *Journal of Islamic Economics*, 1(2), 31–55.

Khan, M. (1991), 'Time value of money and discounting in Islamic perspective', *Review of Islamic Economics*, 1(2), 35–45.

Khan, M. and A. Mirakhor (1994), 'Monetary management in an Islamic economy', *Journal of King Abdulaziz University: Islamic Economics*, 6(1), 3–21.

Kreitner, R. (2000), 'Speculations of contract, or how contract law stopped worrying and learned to love risk', *Columbia Law Review*, 100(4), 1,096–138.

Kunhibava, S. (2011), 'Reasons on the similarity of objections with regards to gambling and speculation in Islamic finance and conventional finance', *Journal of Gambling Studies*, 27, 1–13.

Kuprianov, A. (1994), 'The role of interest rate swaps in corporate finance', *Federal Reserve Bank of Richmond Economic Quarterly*, 80(3), 49–68.

Lessard, D. (1991), 'Global competition and corporate finance in the 1990s', *Journal of Applied Corporate Finance*, 3(4), 59–72.

Levy, J. (2006), 'Contemplating delivery: futures trading and the problem of commodity exchange in the United States, 1875–1905', *American Historical Review*, 111(2), 307–35.

LiPuma, E. and B. Lee (2005), 'Financial derivatives and the rise of circulation', *Economy and Society*, 34(3), 404–27.

Litzenberger, R. (1992), 'Swaps: plain and fanciful', *The Journal of Finance*, 47(3), 831–50.

MacNeil, I. (1974), 'The many futures of contracts', *Southern California Law Review*, 47(3), 691–816.

Markowitz, H. (1952), 'Portfolio selection', *The Journal of Finance*, 7(1), 77–91.

Mello, A. and J. Parsons (2000), 'Hedging and liquidity', *Review of Financial Studies*, 13(1), 127–53.

Merton, R. C. (1973), 'Theory of rational option pricing', *The Bell Journal of Economics and Management Science*, 4(1), 141–83.

Minton, B. (1997), 'An empirical examination of basic valuation models for plain vanilla U.S. interest rate swaps', *Journal of Financial Economics*, 44(2), 251–77.

Murphy, D. (2012), 'The systemic risks of OTC derivatives central clearing', *Journal of Risk Management in Financial Institutions*, 5(3), 319–34.

Obaidullah, M. (1998), 'Financial engineering with Islamic options', *Islamic Economic Studies*, 6(1), 73–103.

Obaidullah, M. (2002), 'Islamic risk management: towards greater ethics and efficiency', *International Journal of Islamic Financial Services*, 3(4), 1–18.

Patterson, E. W. (1918), 'Insurable interest in life', *Columbia Law Review*, 18(5), 381–421.

Patterson, E. W. (1931), 'Hedging and wagering on produce exchanges', *The Yale Law Journal*, 40(6), 843–84.

Pratt, J. W. (1964), 'Risk aversion in the small and in the large', *Econometrica: Journal of the Econometric Society*, 32(1), 122–36.

Raines, J. and C. Leathers (1994), 'Financial derivative instruments and social ethics', *Journal of Business Ethics*, 13(3), 197–204.

Ramaswamy, K. and S. Sundaresan (1986), 'The valuation of floating-rate instruments: theory and evidence', *Journal of Financial Economics*, 17(2), 251–72.

Richard, S. and M. Sundaresan (1981), 'A continuous time equilibrium model of forward prices and futures prices in a multigood economy', *Journal of Financial Economics*, 9(4), 347–71.

Ricoeur, P. (1973), 'The model of the text: meaningful action considered as a text', *New Literary History*, 5(1), 91–117.

Rosly, S. (1999), 'Al-Bay' Bithaman Ajil financing: impacts on Islamic banking performance', *Thunderbird International Business Review*, 41(4/5), 461–80.

Salamon, H. (2000), 'Speculation in the stock market from an Islamic perspective', *Review of Islamic Economics*, 9(1), 103–26.

Shapiro, A. and S. Titman (1985), 'An integrated approach to corporate risk management', *Midland Corporate Finance Journal*, 3, 215–29.

Simonson, D (1972), 'The speculative behavior of mutual funds', *Journal of Finance*, 27(2), 381–91.

Smith, C. W. and R. Stulz (1985), 'The determinants of firms' hedging policies', *The Journal of Financial and Quantitative Analysis*, 20(4), 391–405.

Smith, C. W., C. Smithson and L. Wakeman (1988), 'The market for interest rate swaps', *Financial Management*, 17(4), 34–44.

Stevens, A. C. (1887), '"Futures" in the wheat market', *The Quarterly Journal of Economics*, 2(1), 37–63.

Stout, L. (1999), 'Why the law hates speculators: regulation and private ordering in the market for OTC derivatives', *Duke Law Journal*, 48(4), 701–86.

Sun, T., S. Sundaresan and C. Wang (1993), 'Interest rate swaps: an empirical investigation', *Journal of Financial Economics*, 34(1), 77–99.

Thornton, D. (2000), 'Money in a theory of exchange', *Federal Reserve Bank of St. Louis Review*, 82(1), 35–60.

Tobin, J. (1956), 'The interest-elasticity of transactions demand For cash', *The Review of Economics and Statistics*, 38(3), 241–7.

Tobin, J. (1965), 'Money and economic growth', *Econometrica*, 33(4), 671–84.

Turnbull, S. (1987), 'Swaps: a zero-sum game?', *Financial Management*, 16(1), 15–21.

Tversky, A. and D. Kahneman (1986), 'Rational choice and the framing of decisions', *The Journal of Business*, 59(4), 251–78.

Usmani, M. T. (1999), 'What Shariah experts say: futures, options, and swaps', *International Journal of Islamic Financial Services*, 1(1), 34–6.

Visvanathan, G. and C. Schrand (1998), 'Who uses interest rate swaps? A cross-sectional analysis', *Journal of Accounting, Auditing and Finance*, 13(3), 173–205.

Wang, C. (2003), 'The behavior and performance of major types of futures traders', *Journal of Futures Markets*, 23(1), 1–31.

Whittaker, J. (1987), 'Interest rate swaps: risk and regulation', *Economic Review*, 72(3), 3–13.

Working, H. (1953), 'Futures trading and hedging', *American Economic Review*, 43(3), 314–43.

Chapters in books

Archer, S. and R. Abdel Karim (2007), 'Measuring risk for capital adequacy: the issue of profit sharing investment accounts', in S. Archer and R. Abdel Karim (eds), *Islamic Finance: The Regulatory Challenge*, Singapore: John Wiley & Sons, pp. 223–36.

Azhar, R. A. (1992), 'A theory of optimal investment decisions in an Islamic economy', in A. Ahmad and K. R. Awan (eds), *Lectures on Islamic Economics* (1st edn), Jeddah: Islamic Research and Training Institute, pp. 214–44.

Brennan, M. J. (1991), 'The price of convenience and the valuation of commodity contingent claims', in D.

Lund and B. K. Øksendal (eds), *Stochastic Models and Option Values: Applications to Resources, Environment, and Investment Problems*, Bingley: Emerald Group, pp. 33 72.

Cooke, M. (1984), 'Khaldun and language: from linguistic habit to philological craft', in B. B. Lawrence (ed.), *Ibn Khaldun and Islamic Ideology*, Leiden: E. J. Brill, pp. 27–34.

Harsany, J. C. (1977), 'On the rationale of the Bayesian approach: comments on Professor Watkin's paper', in R. E. Butts and J. Hintikka (eds), *Foundational Problems in the Special Sciences*, Dordrecht and Boston: D. Reidel, pp. 381–92.

Laylor, R. E. (1956), 'Luca Pacioli', in A. C. Littleton and B. S. Yamey (eds), *Studies in the History of Accounting*, Homewood: R. D. Irwin, pp. 175–84.

Opwis, F. (2007), 'Islamic law and legal change: the concept of Maslaha in classical and contemporary Islamic legal theory', in A. Amanat and F. Griffel (eds), *Shari'a: Islamic Law in the Contemporary Context*, Stanford: Stanford University Press, pp. 62–82.

Siddiqi, M. N. (1982), 'Islamic approach to money, banking and monetary policy – a review', in M. Ariff (ed.), *Money and Fiscal Economics in Islam*, Jeddah: International Centre for Research in Islamic Economics, King Abdul Aziz University, pp. 28–48.

Yamey, B. S. (1956), 'Introduction', in A. C. Littleton and B. S. Yamey (eds), *Studies in the History of Accounting*, Homewood: R. D. Irwin, pp. 1–13.

Zarqa, M. A. (1983), 'An Islamic perspective on the economics of discounting in project evaluation', in Z. Ahmed, M. Iqbal and M. Fahim Khan (eds), *Fiscal Policy and Resource Allocation in Islam*, Islamabad and Jeddah: Institute of Policy Studies and International Centre for Research in Islamic Economics, King Abdul Aziz University, pp. 203–51.

Official/Professional guidelines or standards

AAOIFI (2010), *Accounting, Auditing, and Governance Standards for Islamic Financial Institutions*, Bahrain: Accounting and Auditing Organisation for Islamic Financial Institutions.

IFSB (2005), *Guiding Principles of Risk Management for Institutions (Other Than Insurance Institutions) Offering Only Islamic Financial Services*, Kuala Lumpur: Islaic Financial Services Board.

IIFM (2010), *Introduction to ISDA/IIFM Tahawwut Master Agreement and its Significance as a Framework Document*, Bahrain: International Islamic Financial Management.

KFH (2012), *Al-Fatawa Al-Shari'iyya Fi Al-Masa'il Al-Iqtisadiya. Fatwa Number 18*, Kuwait: Bayt Al-Tamwil Al-Kuwaiti.

Research papers

Al-Suwailem, S. (2000), *Decision under Uncertainty: An Islamic Perspective*, Riyadh: Al-Rajhi Banking and Investment Corporation.

Al-Suwailem, S. (2001), *Aqd Al-Kali' Bil-Kali'*, Riyadh: Sharikat Al-Rajhi Al-Masrifiya wa Al-Istithmar.

Boudoukh, J., M. Richardson and R. F. Whitelaw (1997), *The Best of Both Worlds: A Hybrid Approach to Calculating Value At Risk*, NYU Working Paper Series No. 31.

Jobst, A. and J. Sole (2012), *Operative Principles of Islamic Derivatives: Towards a Coherent Theory*, IMF Working Papers: 12/63.

Conference papers

Al-Shubaili, Y. (2012), *'Tatbiqat Al-Himaya Al Badila 'an Uqud Al-Tuhawwut wa Al-Daman'*, paper presented at the The AAOIFI Annual Shari'ah Conference, Manama, 7–8 May 2012.

Al-Suwailem, S. (2012), *'Mou'alaga Makhatir As'aar Al-Sarf fi Al-Ta'amoulat Al-Maliya Al-Islamiya'*, paper presented at the The 33rd Al-Baraka Symposium on Islamic Economics, Jeddah, 25–6 July 2012.

Dusuki, A. (2009), 'Shariah parameters on Islamic foreign exchange swap as hedging mechanism in Islamic finance', paper presented at the International Conference on Islamic Perspectives on Management and Finance, University of Leicester, 29 April–1 May 2009.

El-Gari, M. (2010), 'Ethical dimensions of Islamic finance: lessons from the financial crisis', paper presented at the 5th IDB Forum on Islamic Finance, Baku, 21 June 2010.

Hassan, H. (2012), *'Mou'alaga Makhatir As'aar Al-Sarf wa Al-Ta'amul Khilal Al-Mouhla Al-Masrafiya'*, paper presented at The 33rd Al-Baraka Symposium on Islamic Economics, Jeddah, 25–6 July 2012.

Jobst, A. (2007), 'Derivatives in Islamic Finance', paper presented at the International Conference on Islamic Capital Markets, Jakarta, 27–9 August 2007.

Kahf, M. (2006), 'Innovation and Risk Management in Islamic Finance', paper presented at the Seventh Harvard International Forum on Islamic Finance, Cambridge, MA, 22–3 April 2006.

Newspaper/Magazine articles

Ayoub, S. (2012b), 'Islamic finance: a look into the past, present, and future', *Islamic Finance News*, 9, 23–4.

Usmani, M. T. (2010), 'Post crisis reforms: some points to ponder', *Islamic Finance News*, 30 January.

Reports

BIS (2004), *Principles for the Management and Supervision of Interest Rate Risk*, Basel: Bank for International Settlements.

BMB (2010), *Global Islamic Finance Report*, London: BMB Islamic UK Limited.

Deloitte (2010), *The Deloitte Islamic Finance Leaders Survey in the Middle East: Benchmarking Practices*, Deloitte.

E&Y (2011), *The World Islamic Banking Competitiveness Report 2011–2012*, Dubai: Ernst & Young.

G30 (1993), *Derivatives: Practices and Principles*, Washington, DC: G30.

Moody's Global Corporate Finance (2010), *Derivatives in Islamic Finance: Examining the Role of Innovation in the Industry*, Paris: Moody's Global Corporate Finance.

PricewaterhouseCoopers (2005), *International Financial Reporting Standards IAS 39 – Achieving Hedge Accounting in Practice*, PricewaterhouseCoopers.

Promisel (1992), *Recent Developments in International Interbank Relations*, Report Prepared by a Working Group Established by the Central Banks of the Group of Ten Countries, Basel: Bank for International Settlements.

Tredgett, R. and P. Uberoi (2008), *Islamic Derivatives Case Study*, London: Allen & Overy.

Tredgett, R., P. Uberoi and N. Evans (2008), *Cross Currency Swap*, London: Allen & Overy.

Uberoi, P. and N. Evans (2008), *Islamic Finance: Profit Rate Swap*, London: Allen and Overy.

INDEX

EU Authorised Representative: Easy Access System Europe Mustamäe tee 5
0, 10621 Tallinn, Estonia gpsr.requests@easproject.com

Printed and bound by CPI Group (UK) Ltd, Croydon, CR0 4YY
16/04/2025
01846989-0002